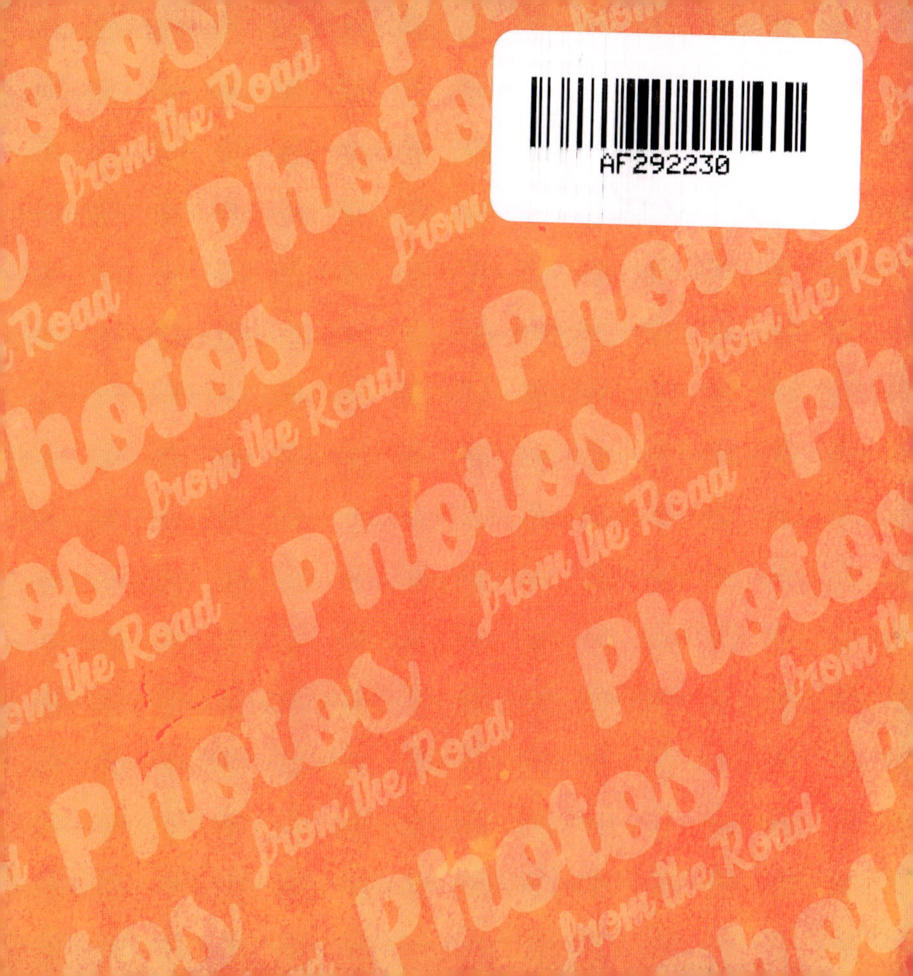
AF292230

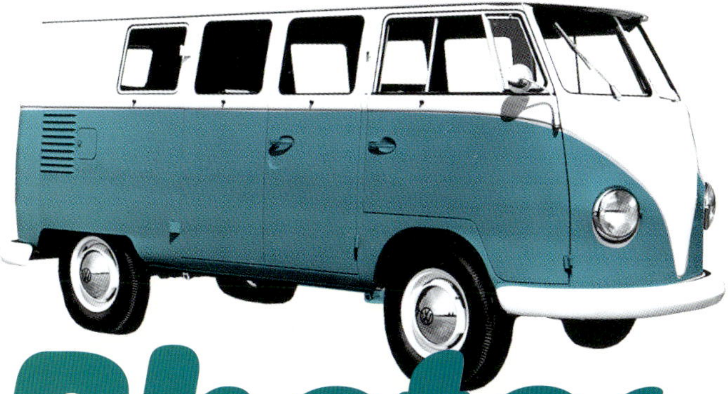

Photos
from the Road

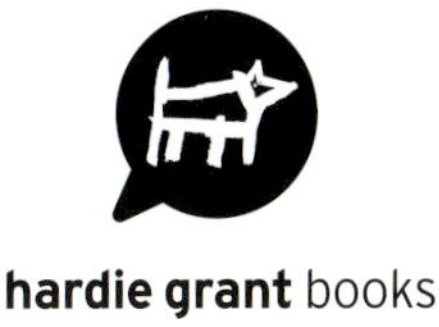

hardie grant books

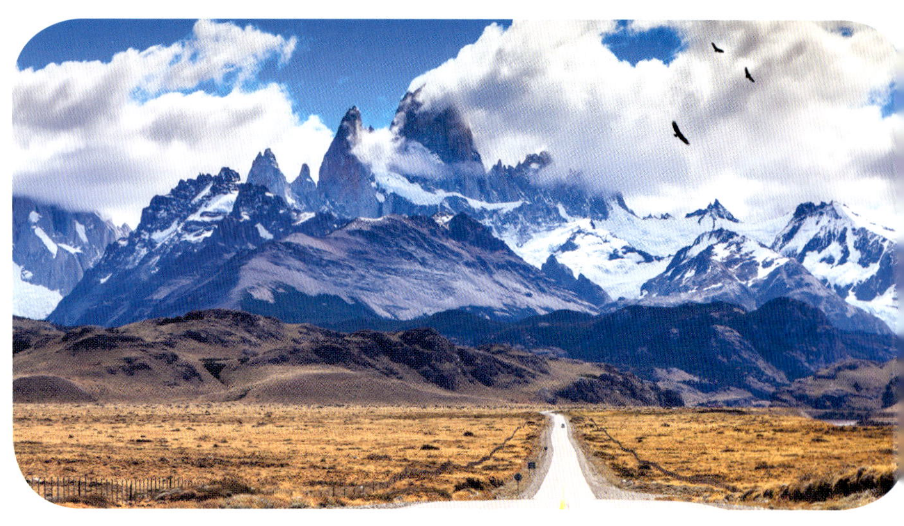

Travel isn't always about the destination – it's also about the beautiful and surprising sights you catch along the way. Some of the most memorable vistas are just beside the road, glimpsed out of the car window as you move from one place to another. This book will take you on a rambling around-the-world road trip down city streets, country lanes, coastal drives and mountain passes, showcasing sights that are worth pulling over for.

Get ready for a journey along the world's most spectacular roads!

Contents

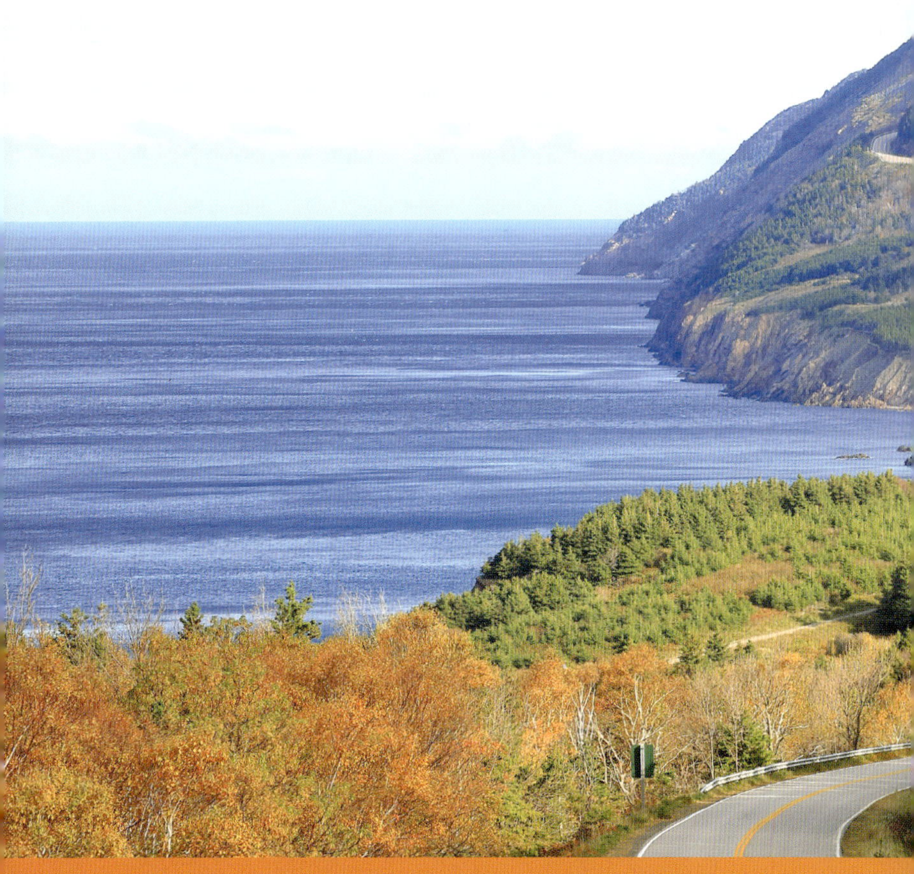

Driving down the Cabot Trail in Cape Breton, Nova Scotia, Canada

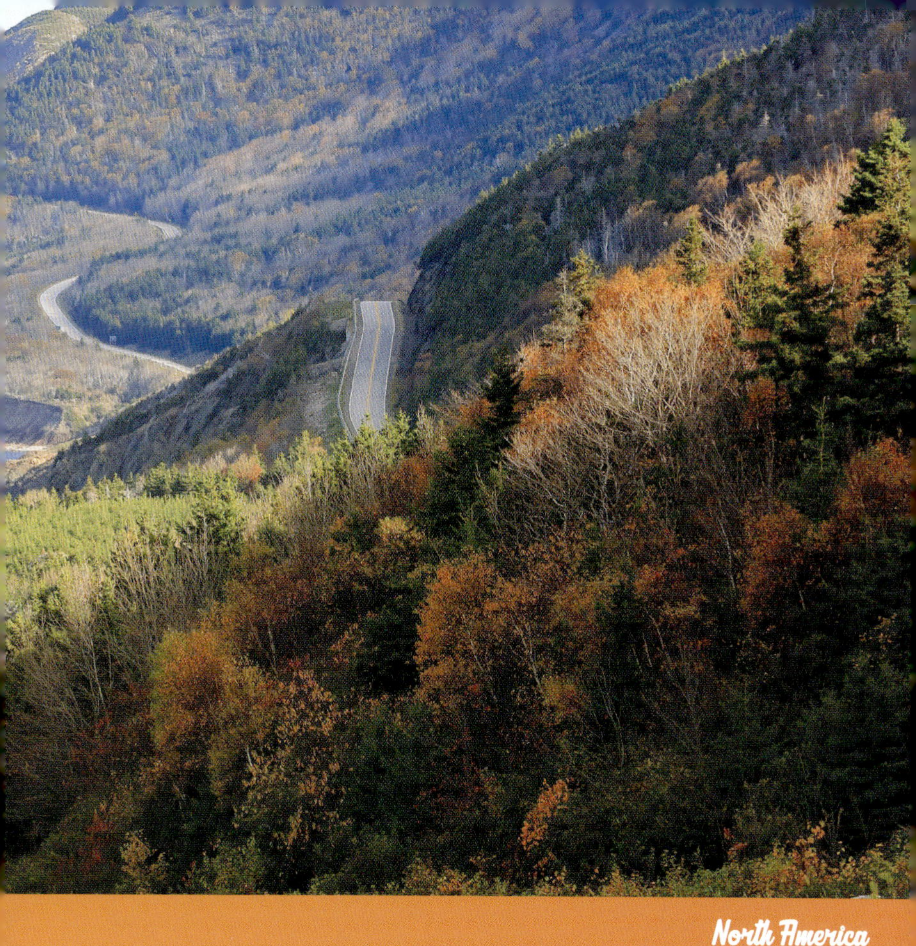
North America

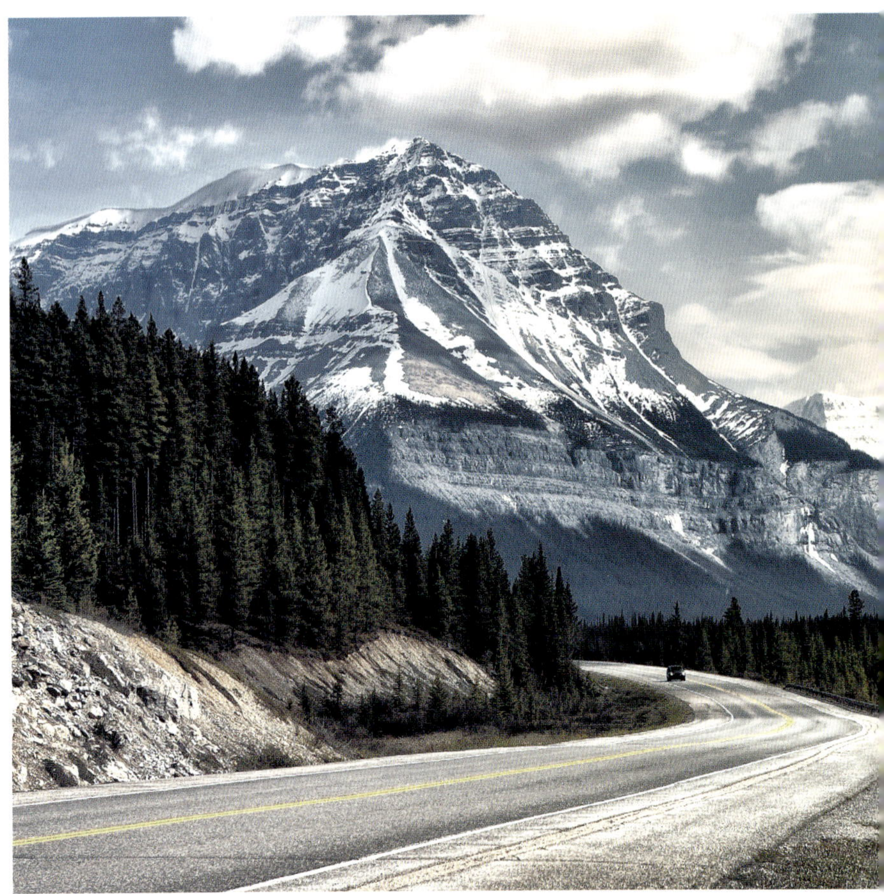

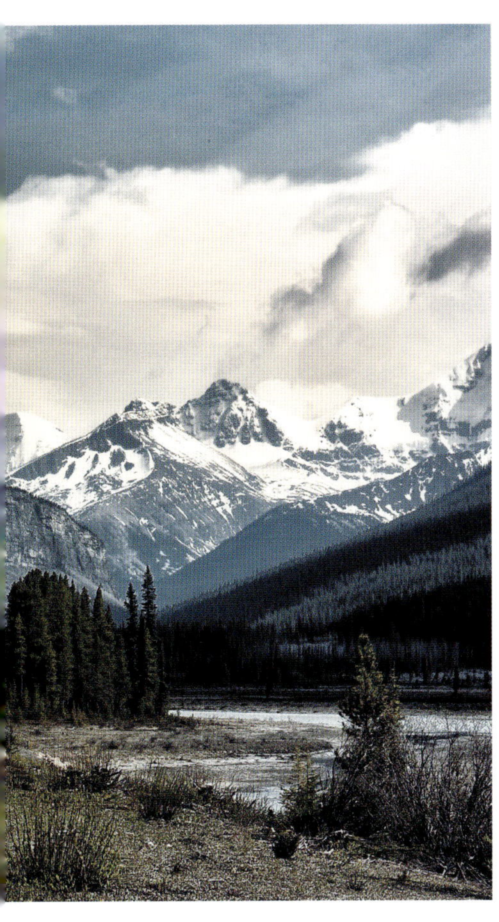

Winding between mountains along Icefields Parkway in Alberta/British Columbia, Canada

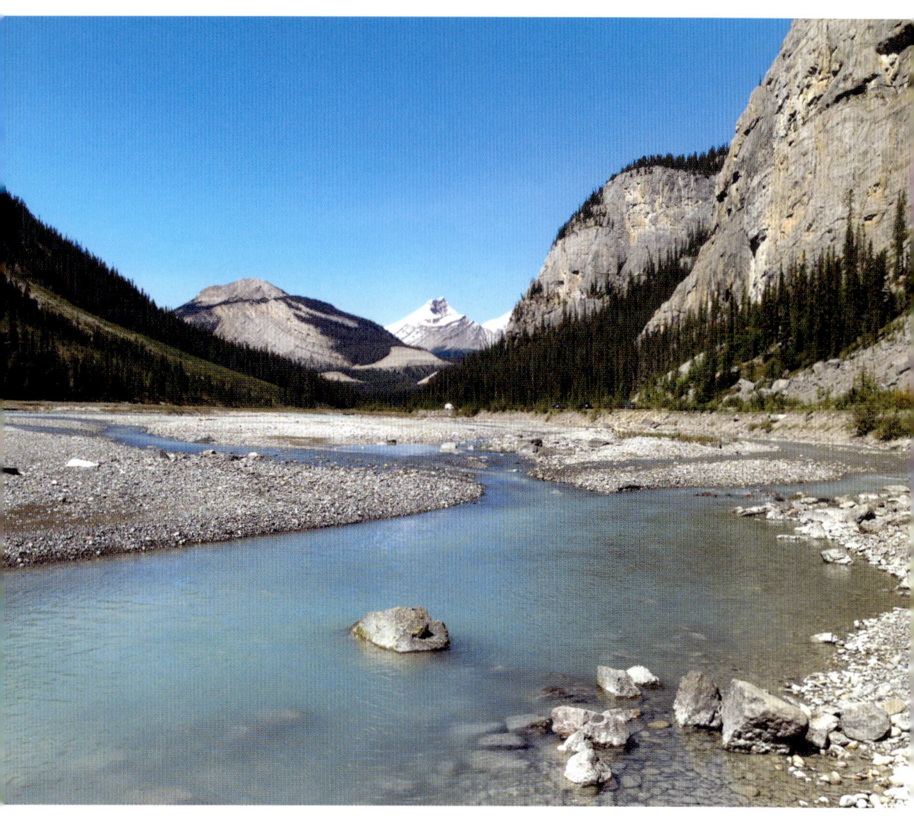

The Bow River winds alongside Icefields Parkway between Jasper and Banff in Alberta/British Columbia, Canada

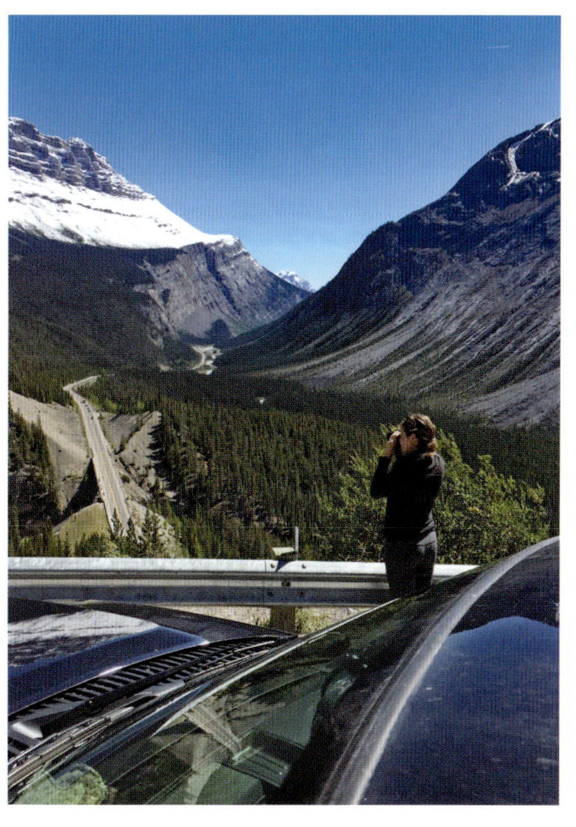

A roadside view of Icefields Parkway in Jasper National Park, Alberta, Canada

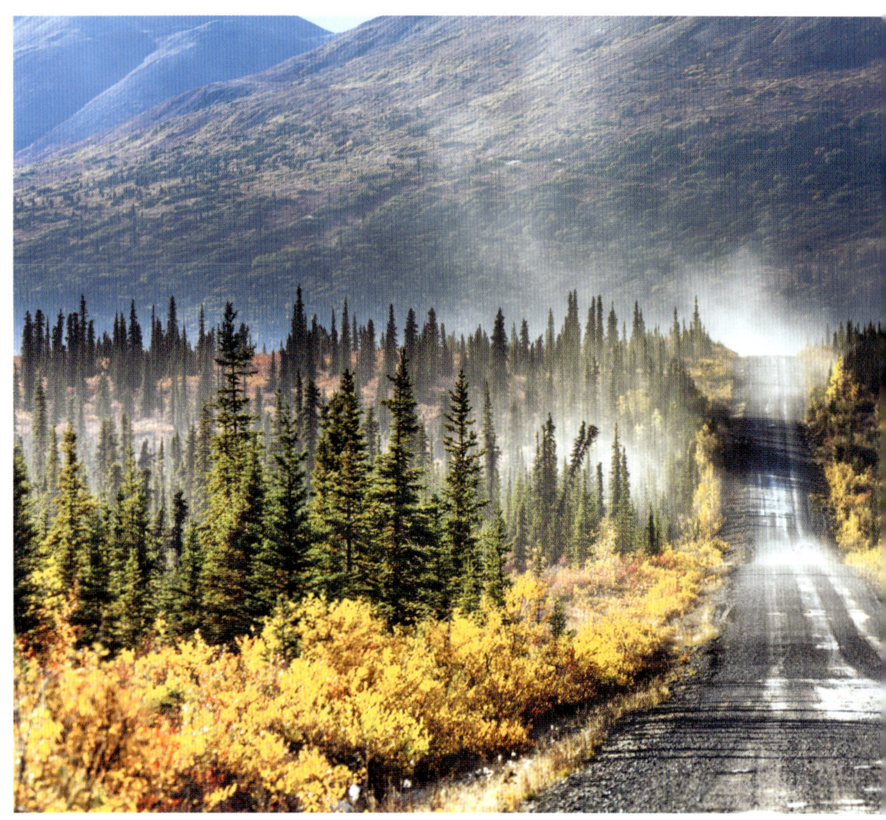

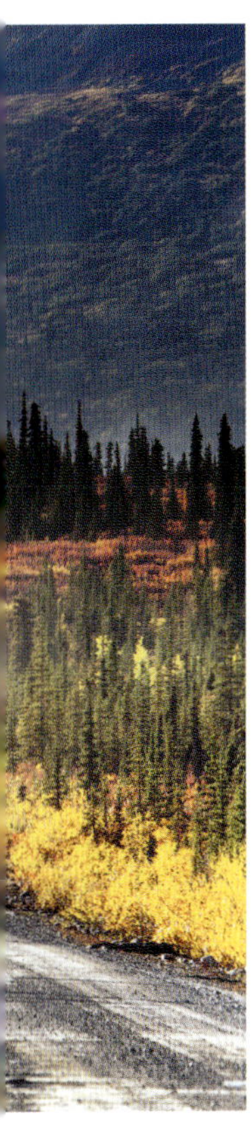

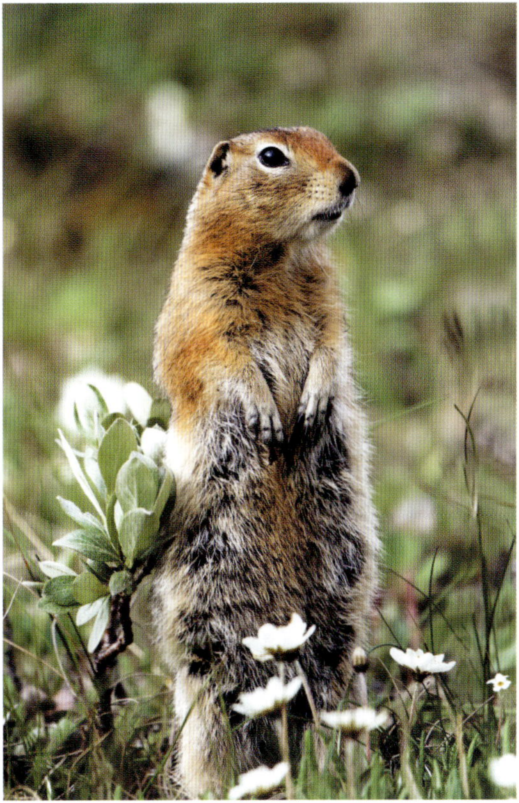

LEFT Driving down Denali Highway in Alaska, USA
ABOVE An arctic ground squirrel stands alert near Denali Park Road in Denali National Park, Alaska, USA

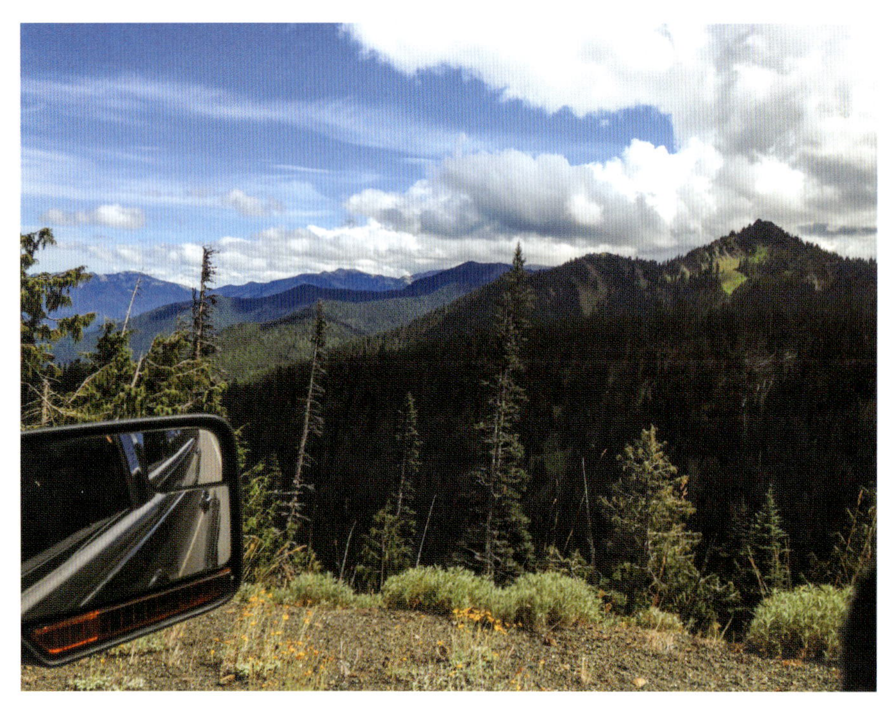

Winding along Hurricane Ridge in Washington state's Olympic National Park, USA

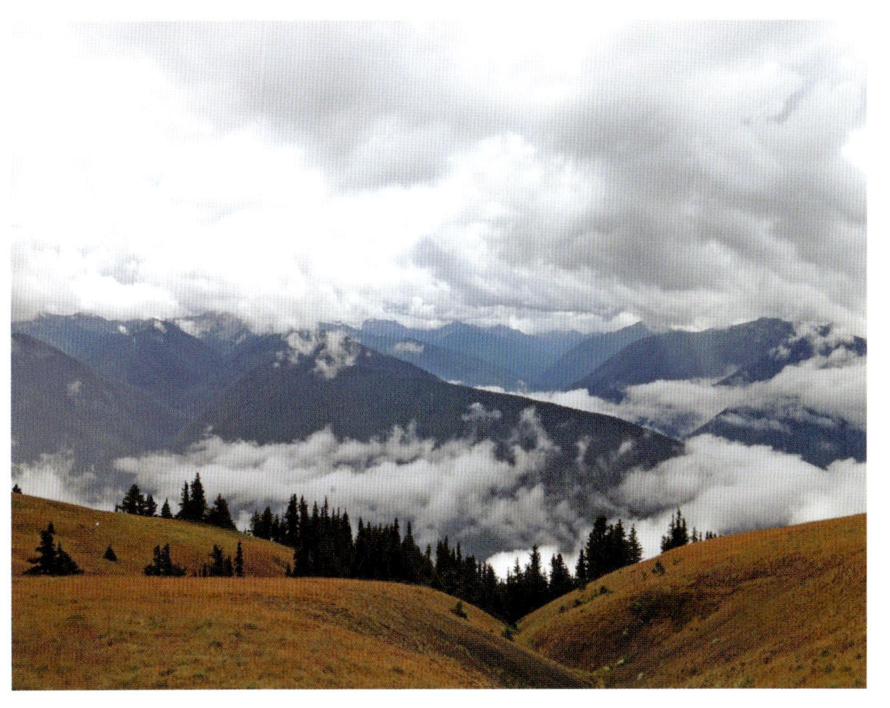

View of Olympic Range from the end of Hurricane Ridge Road in Olympic National Park, USA

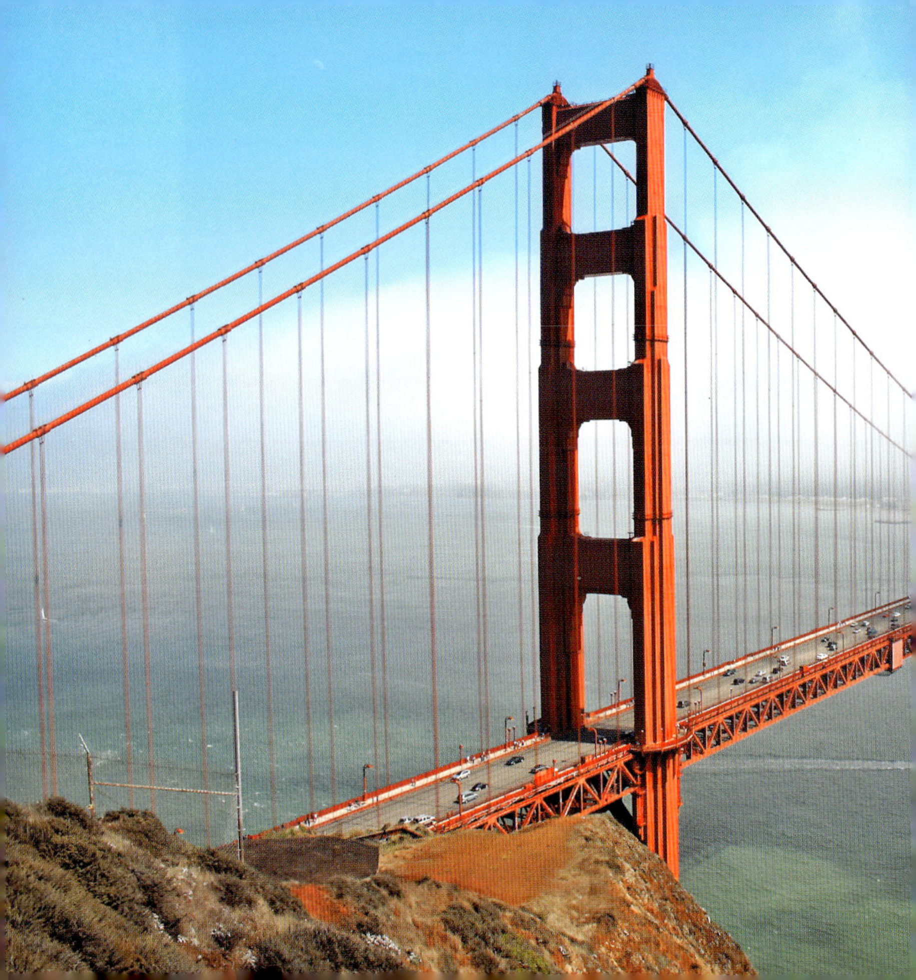

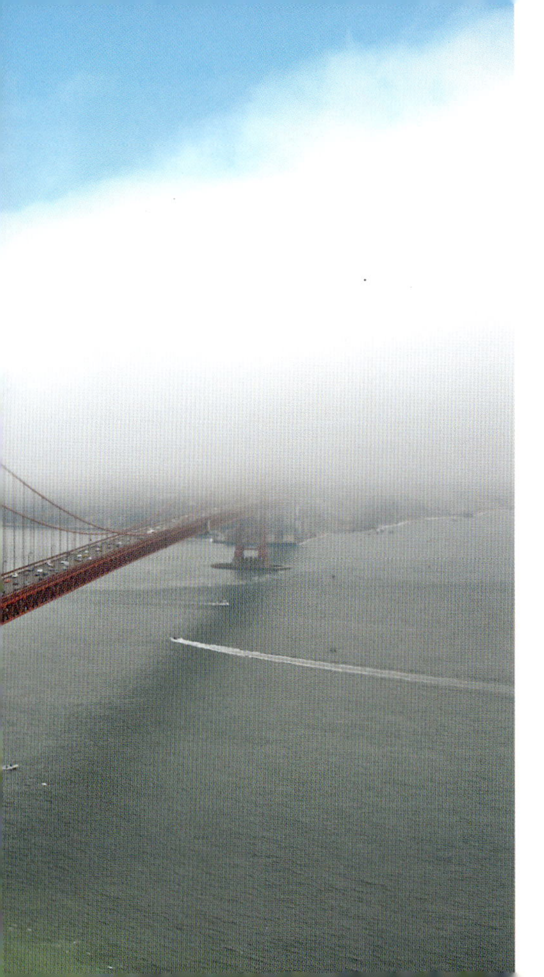

The view of Golden Gate Bridge in
San Francisco from Battery Spencer,
California, USA

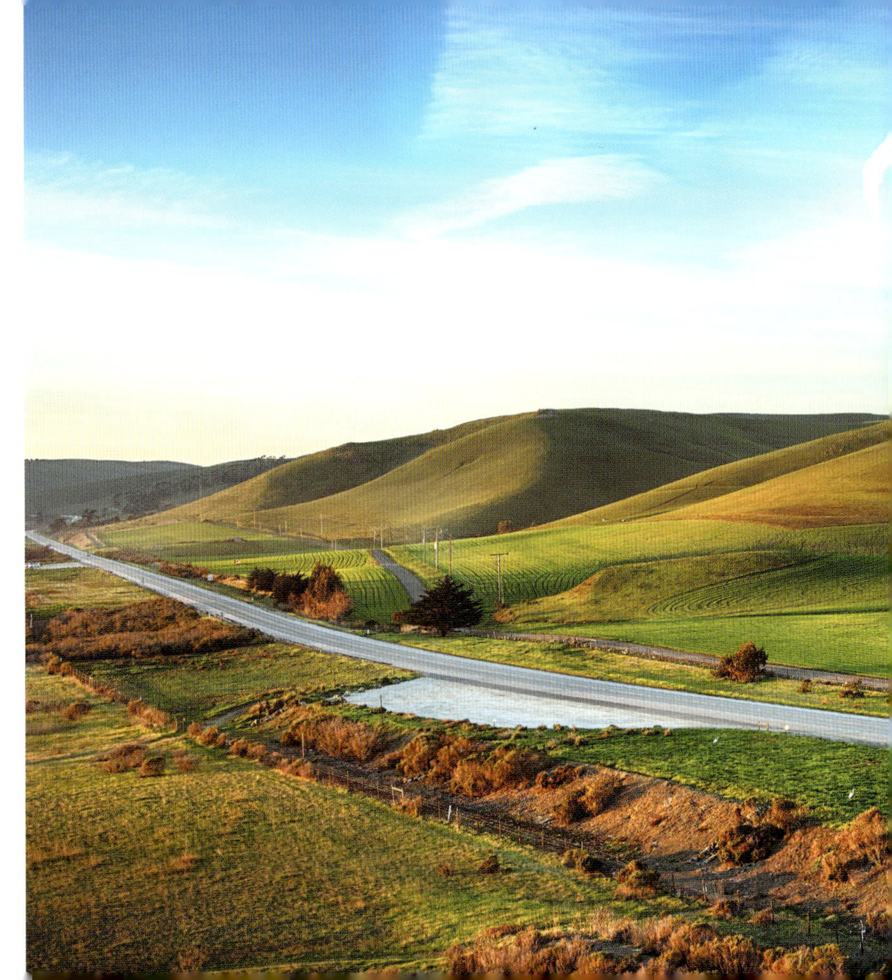

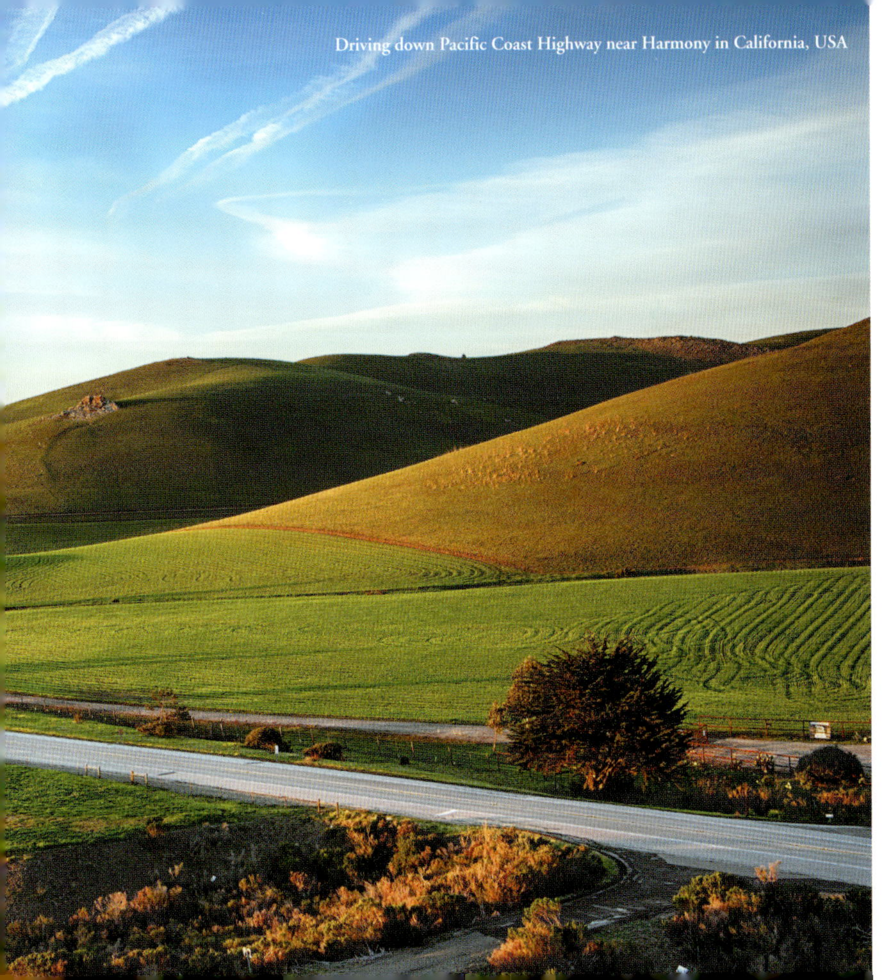

Driving down Pacific Coast Highway near Harmony in California, USA

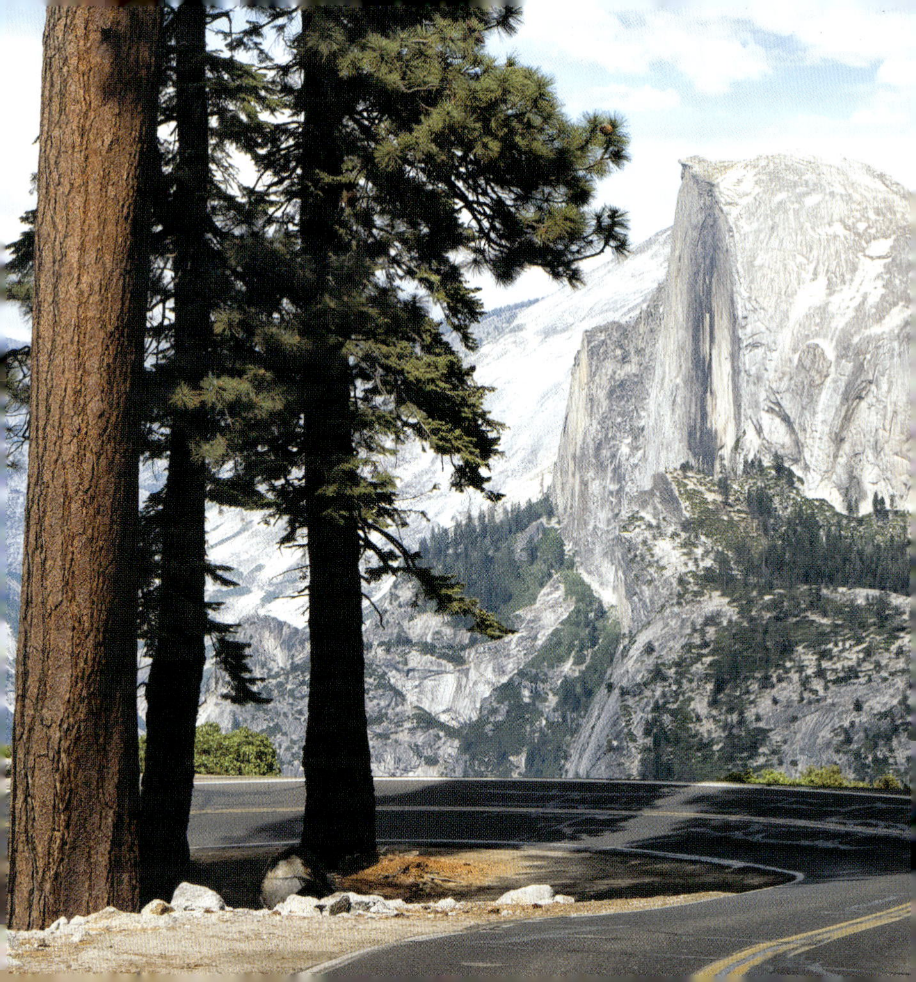

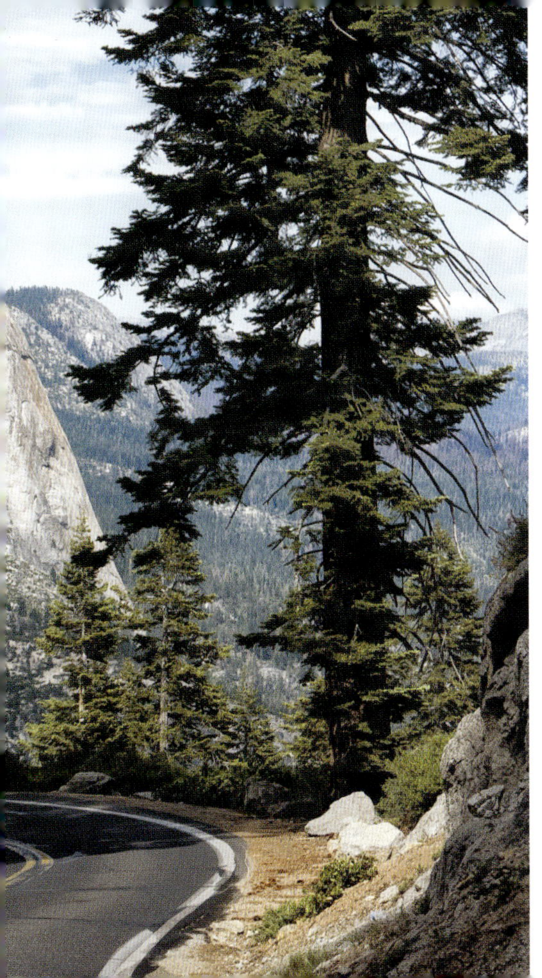

Half Dome glimpsed from the road to
Glacier Point in Yosemite National Park,
California, USA

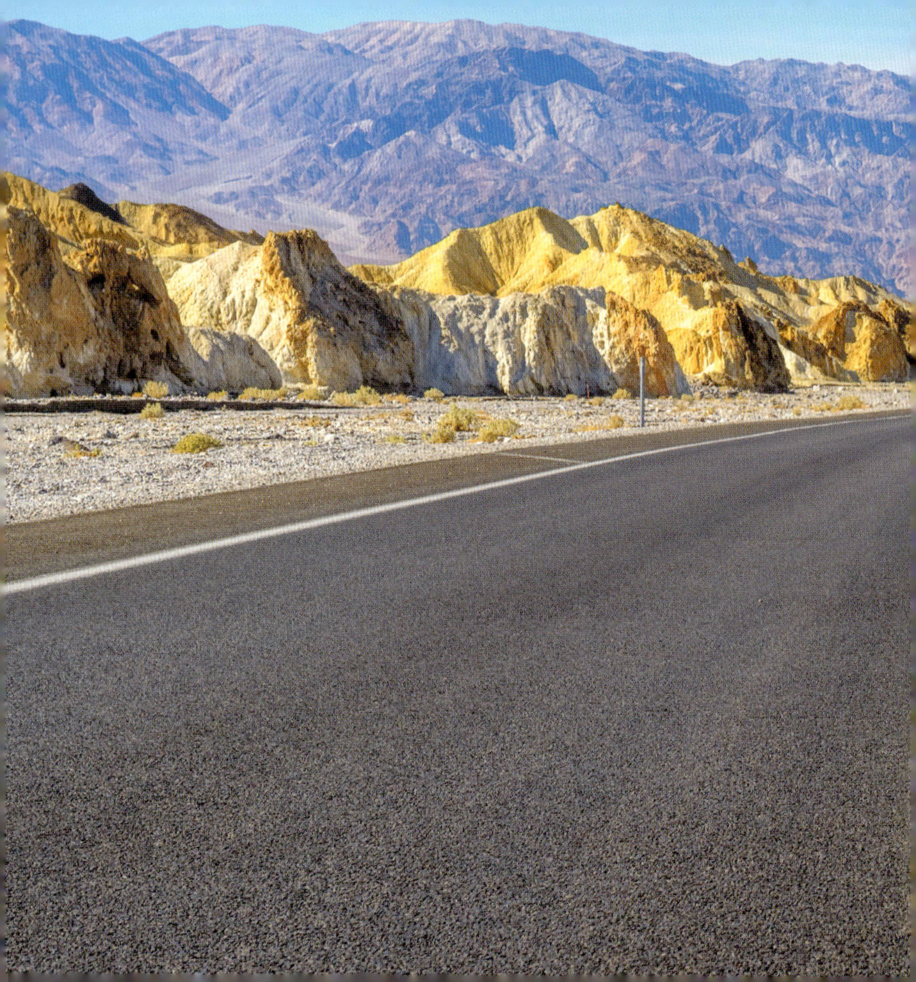

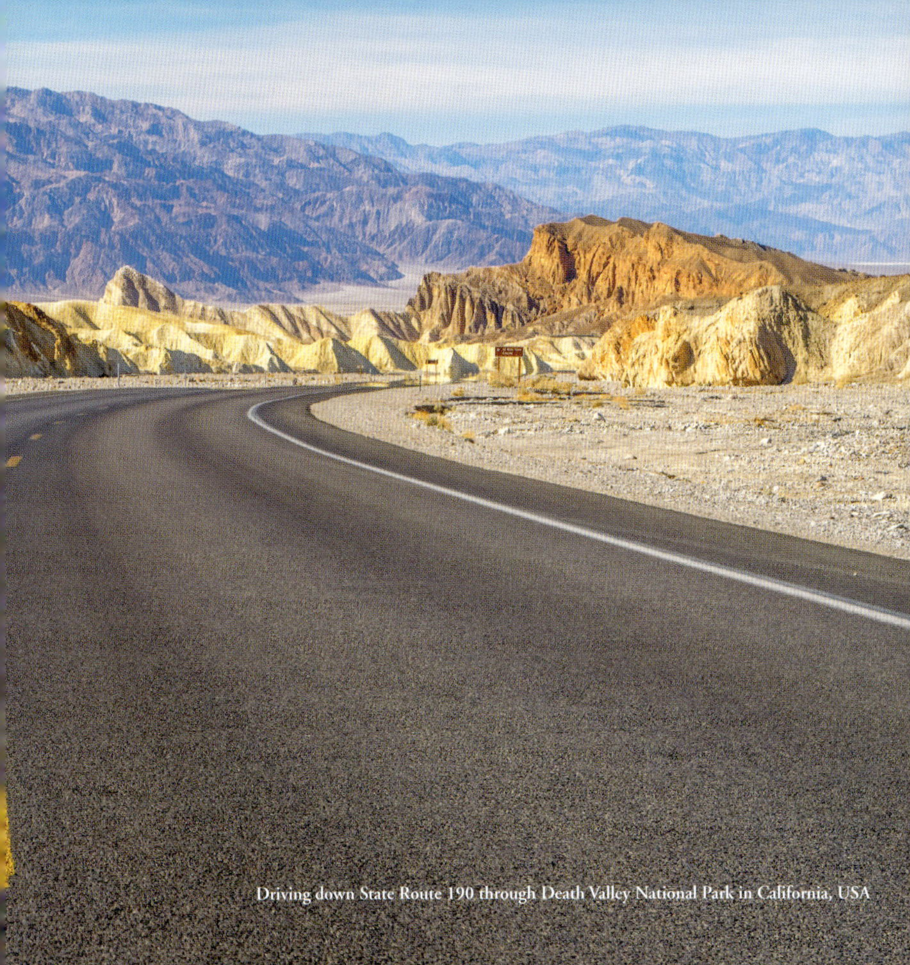

Driving down State Route 190 through Death Valley National Park in California, USA

The Las Vegas strip in Nevada, USA

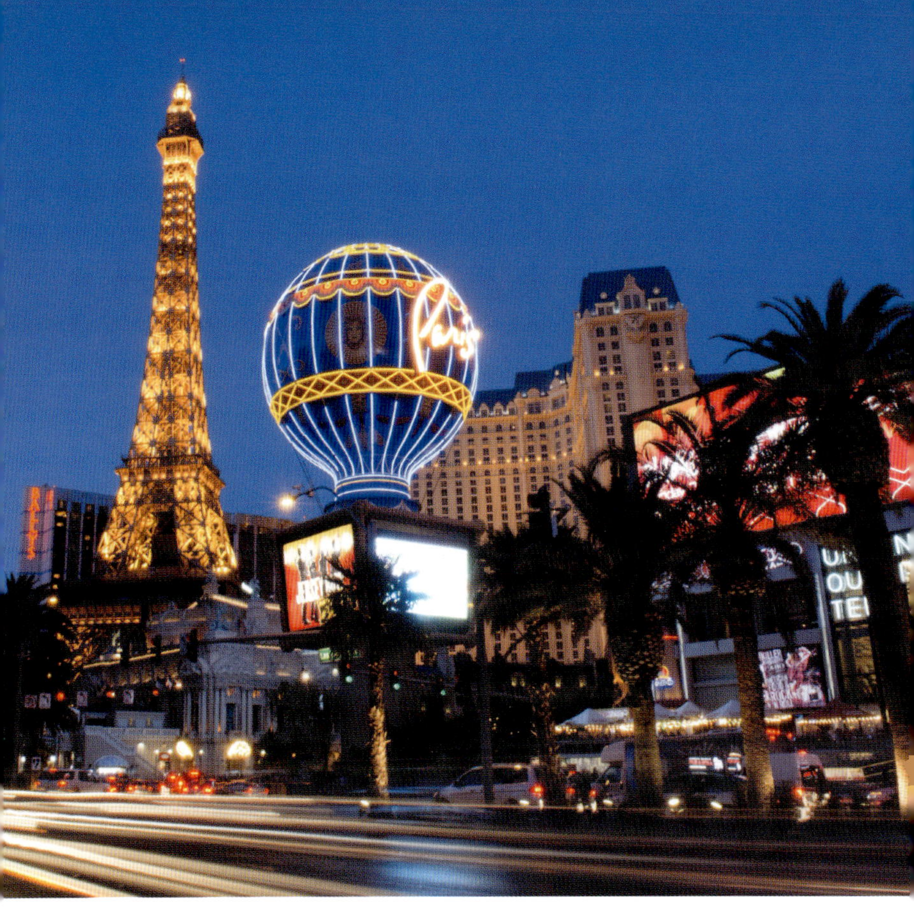

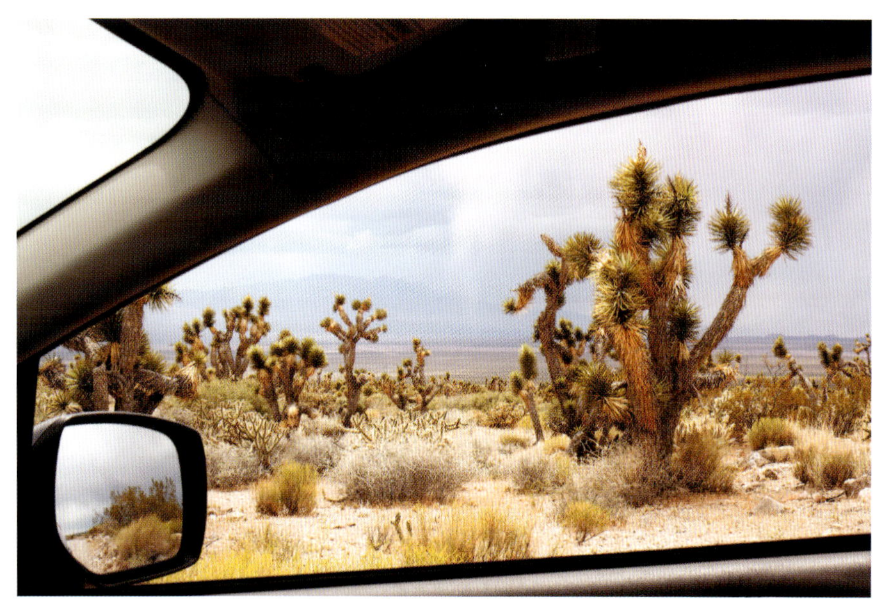

Driving past Joshua trees in Snow Canyon State Park, Utah, USA

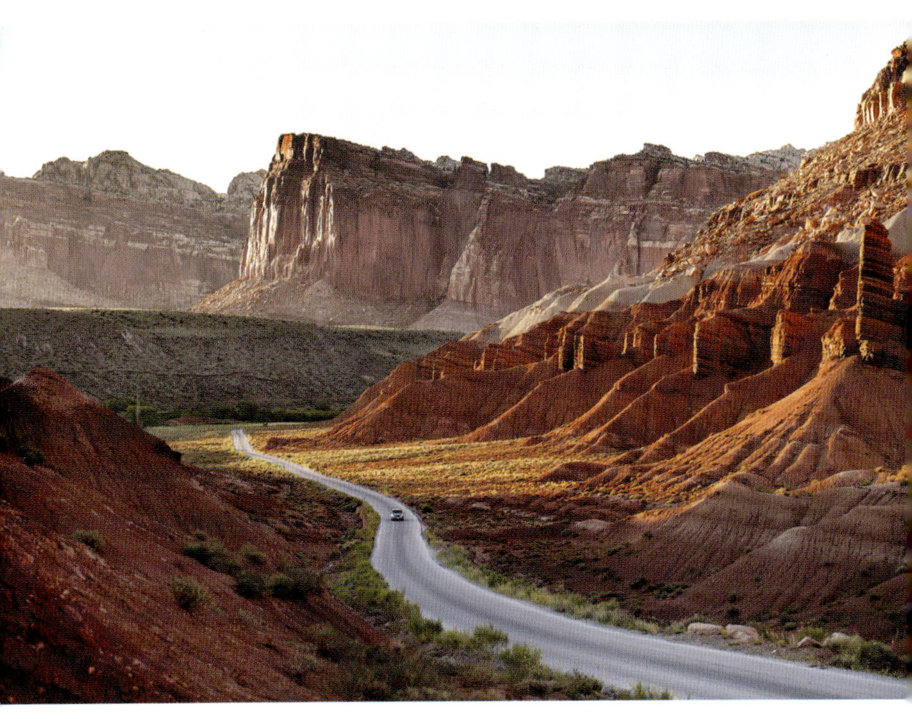

The red rocks of Capitol Reef National Park in Utah, USA

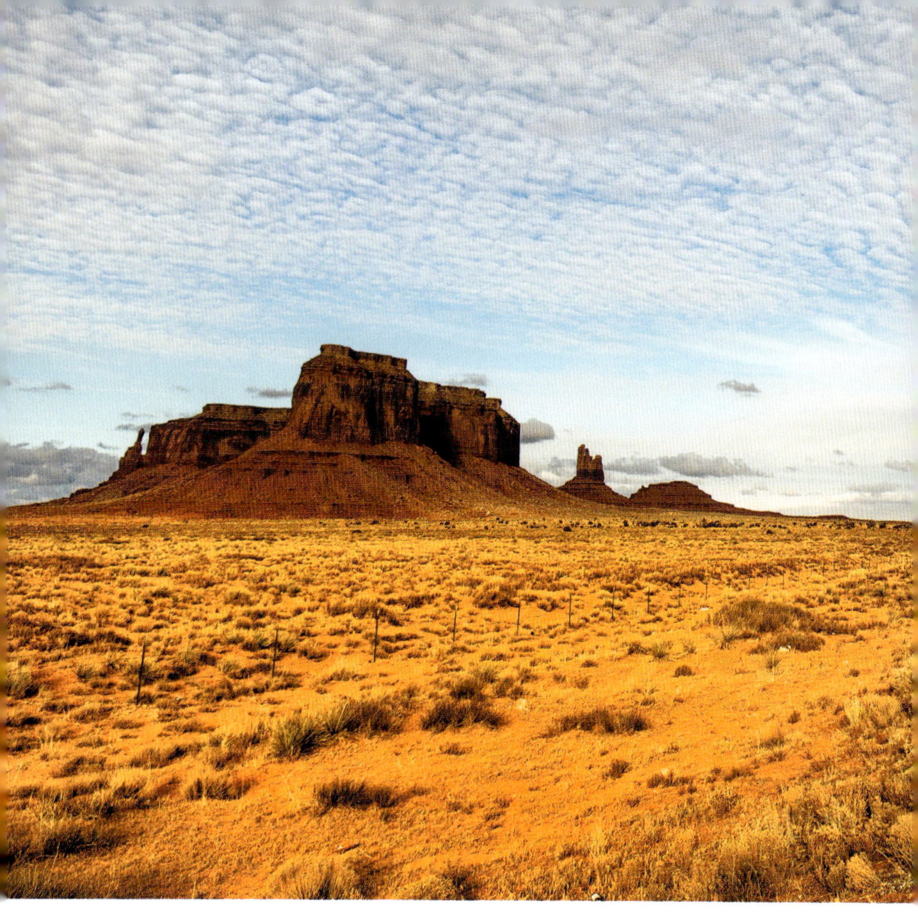

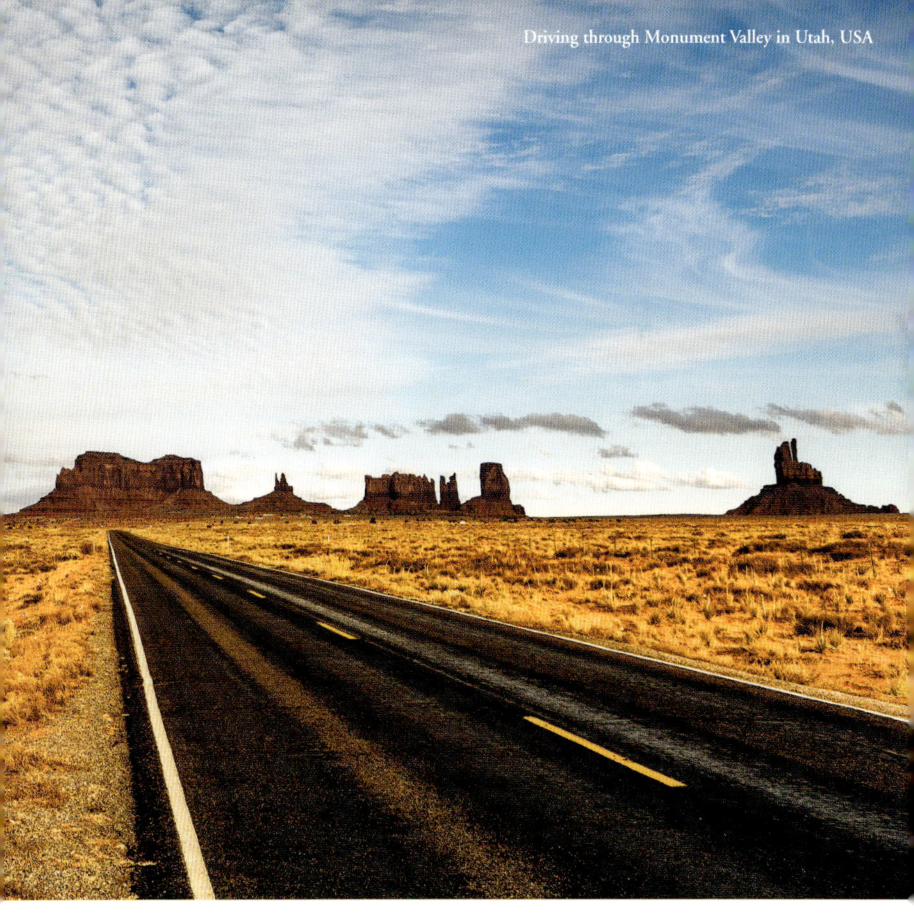
Driving through Monument Valley in Utah, USA

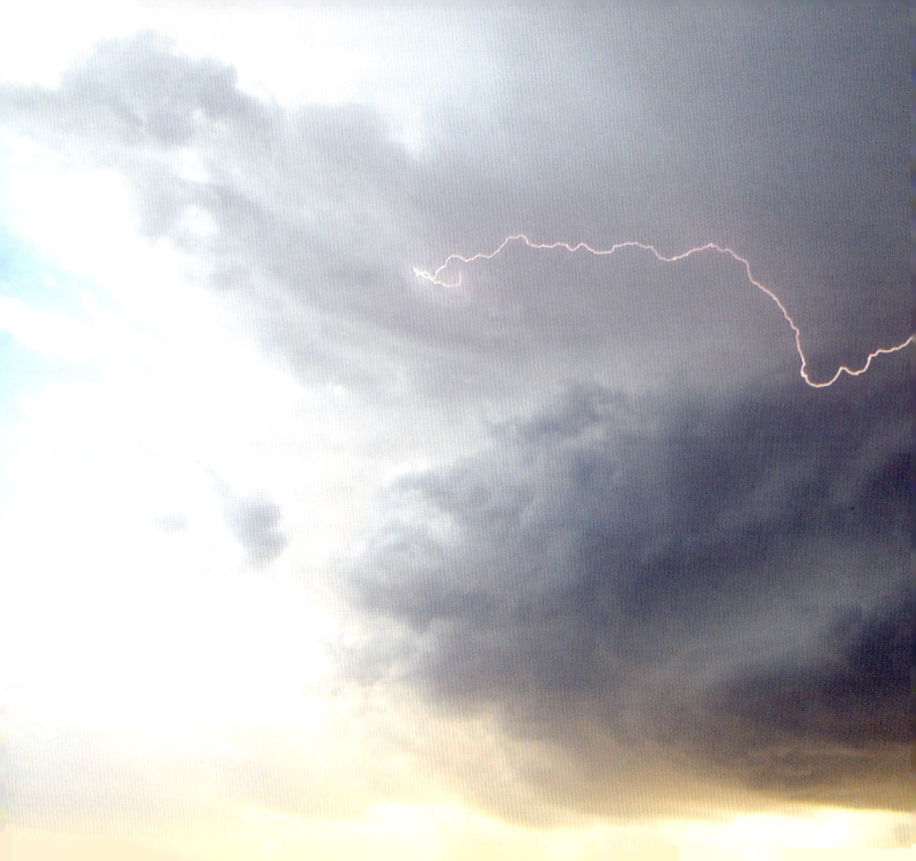

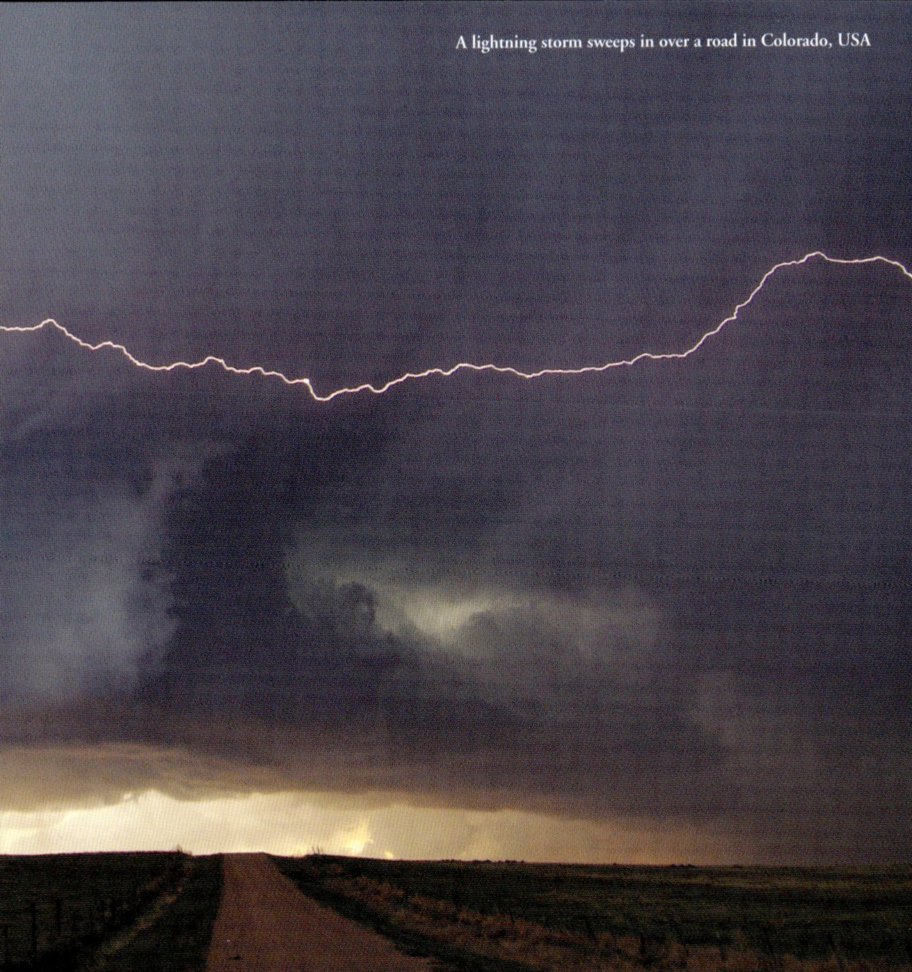
A lightning storm sweeps in over a road in Colorado, USA

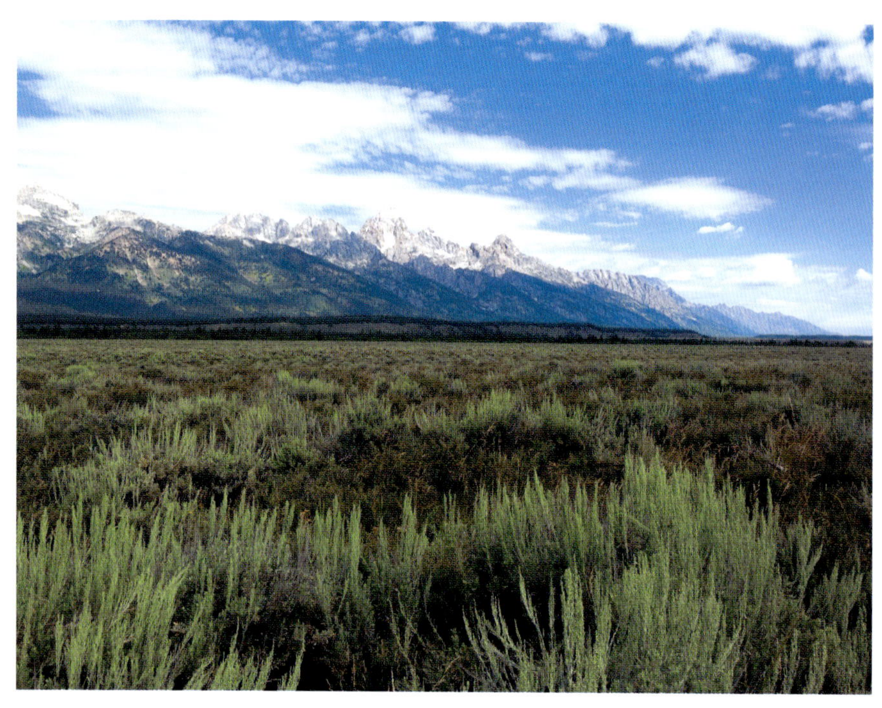

ABOVE Mountains run alongside Route 191 in Grand Teton National Park, Wyoming, USA
RIGHT The Tetons rise up to meet you at every turn through Grand Teton National Park, Wyoming, USA

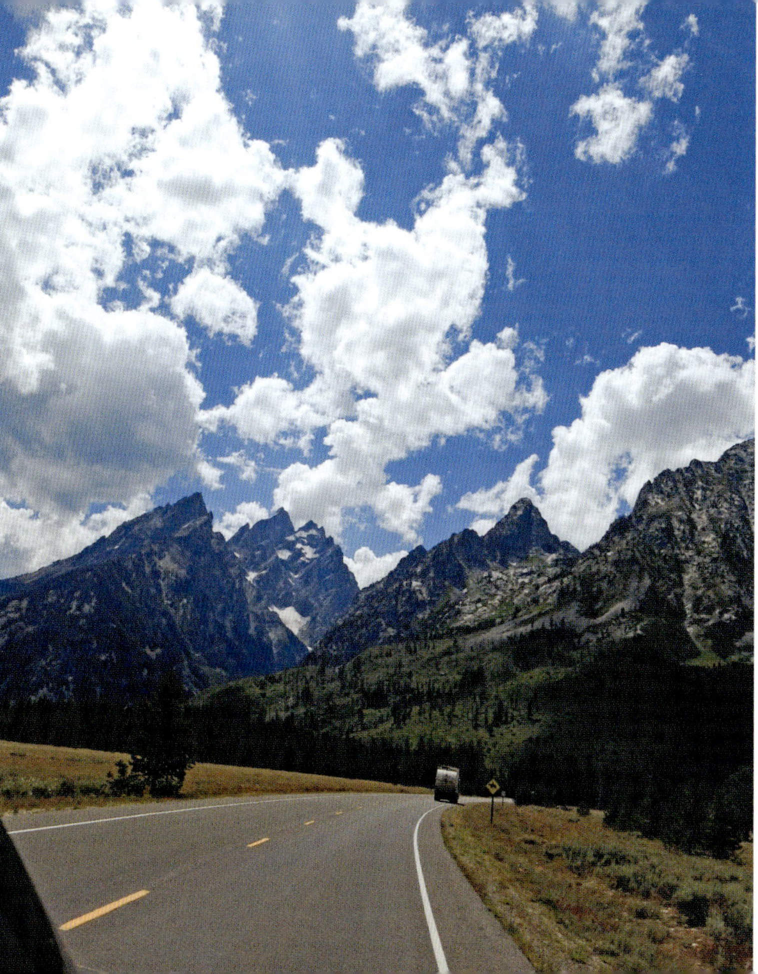

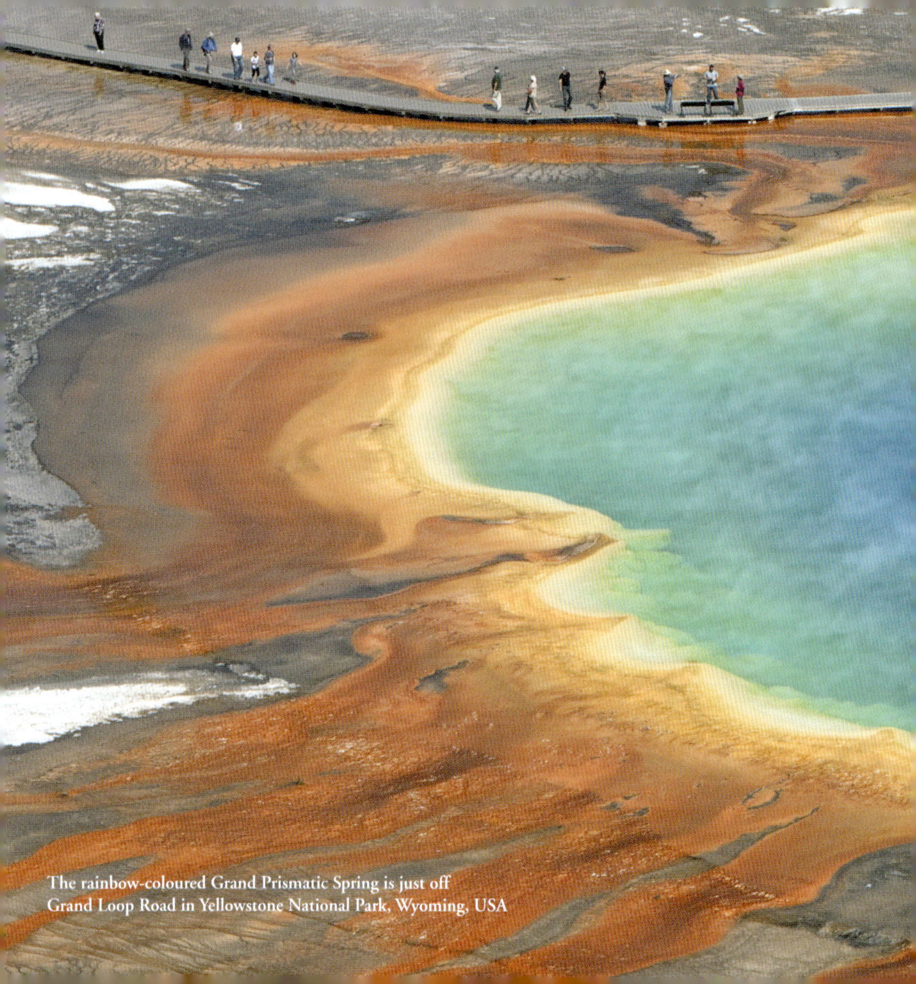

The rainbow-coloured Grand Prismatic Spring is just off
Grand Loop Road in Yellowstone National Park, Wyoming, USA

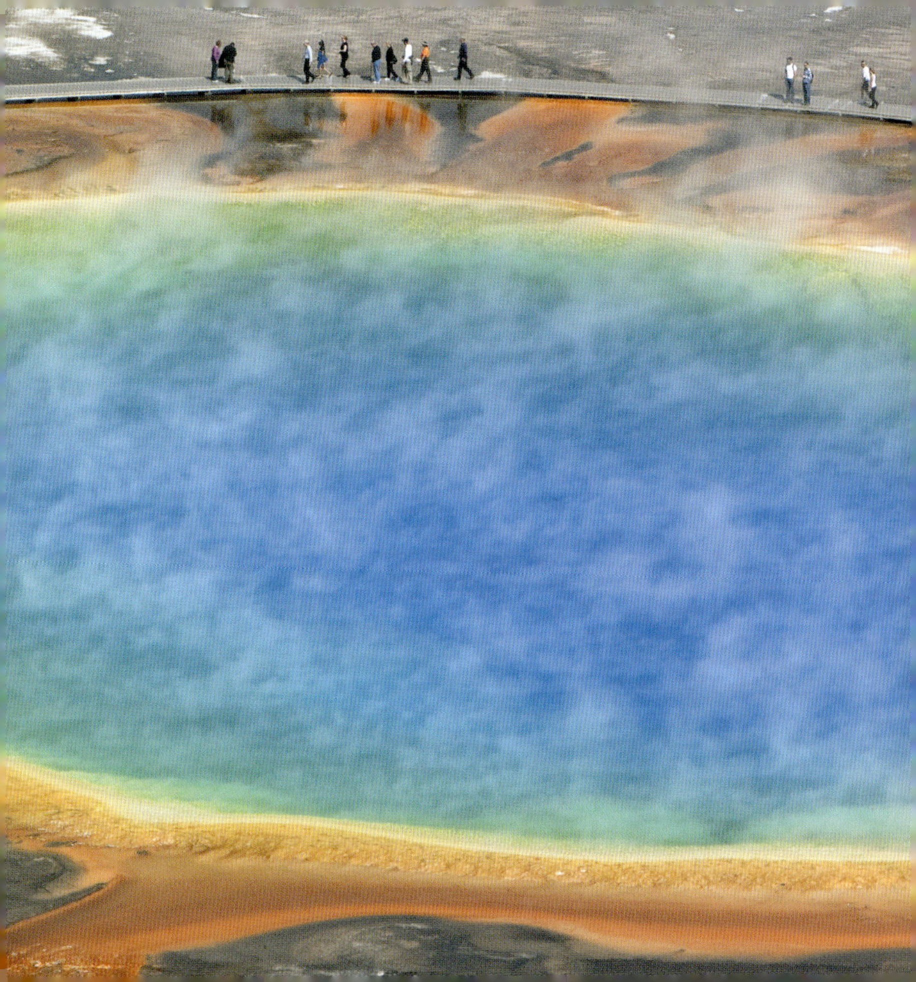

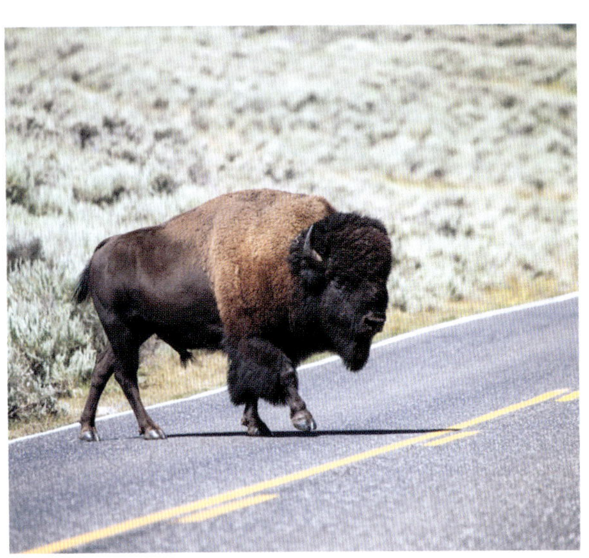

A buffalo crosses Route 212 in Yellowstone National Park, Wyoming, USA

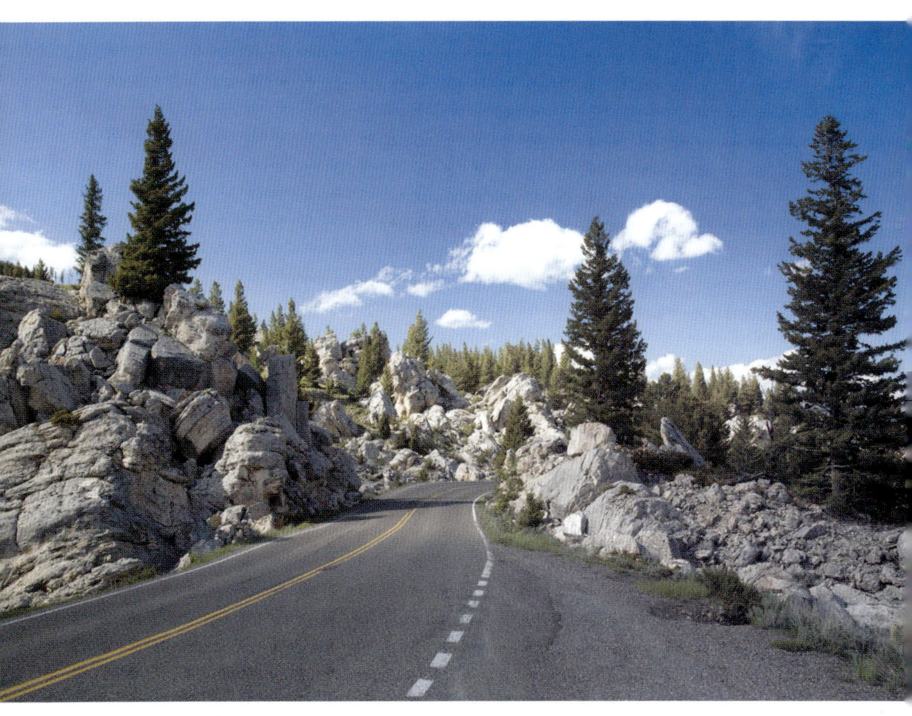

A road near Mammoth Hot Springs in Yellowstone National Park, Wyoming, USA

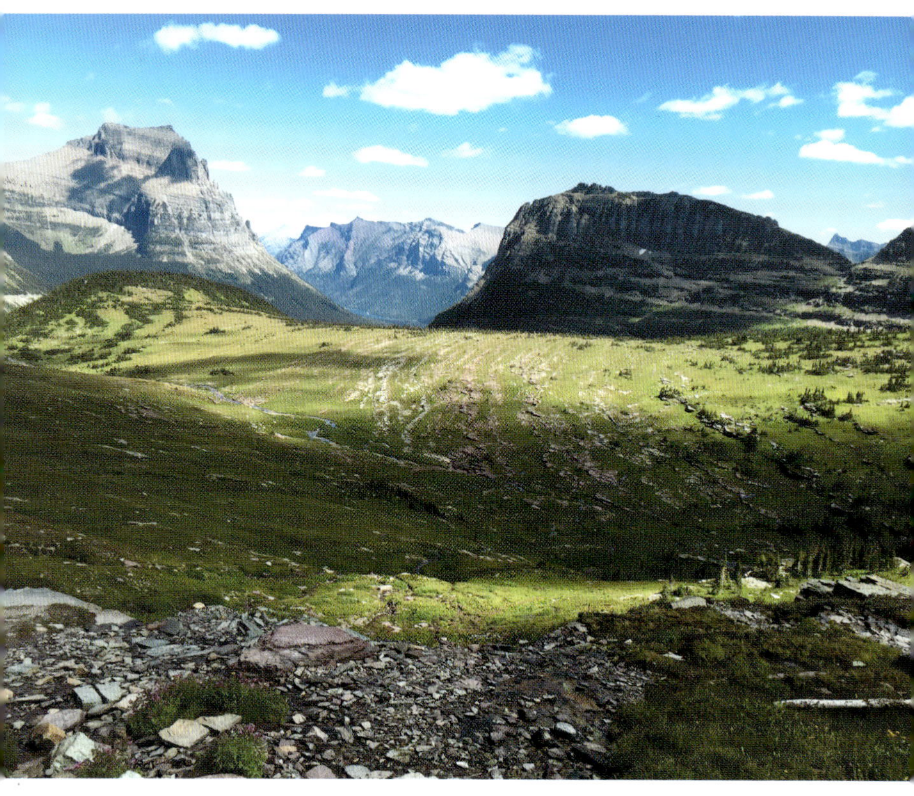

Shadows pass over the fields behind Logan Pass Visitor Center in Glacier National Park, Montana, USA

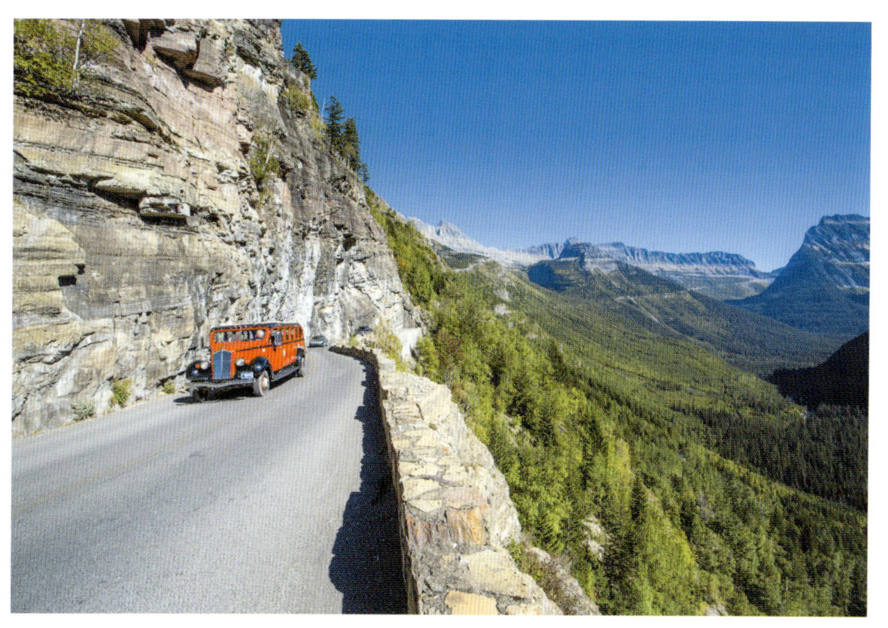

A tour bus winds along Going-to-the-Sun Road, which cuts through Glacier National Park in Montana, USA

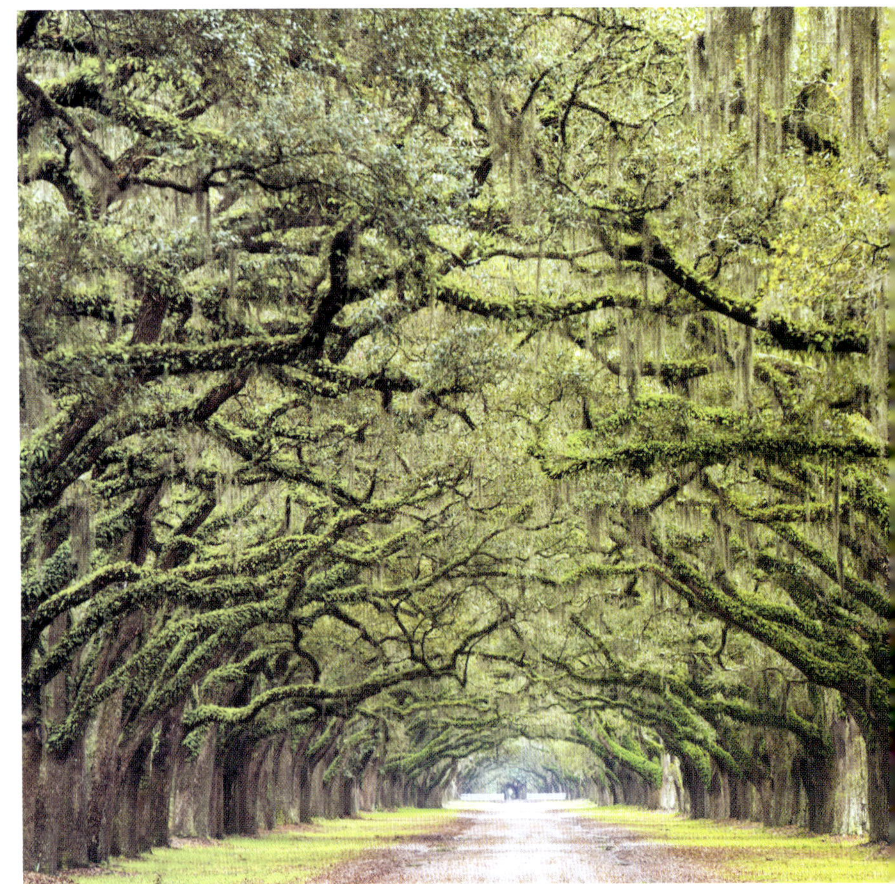

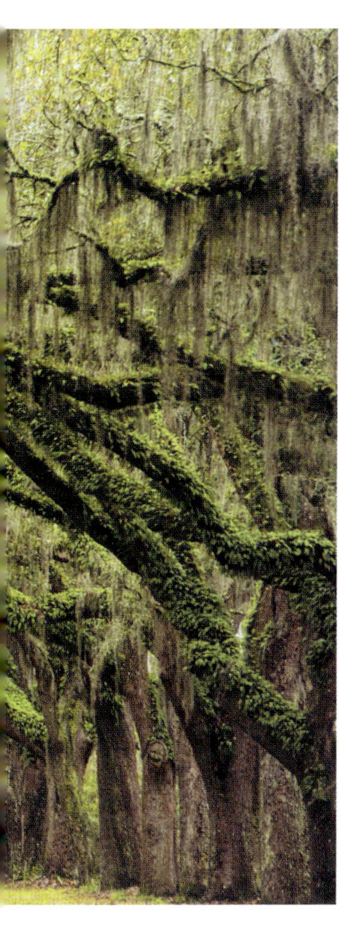

The Spanish moss–draped entrance to Wormsloe Historic Site near
Savannah in Georgia, USA

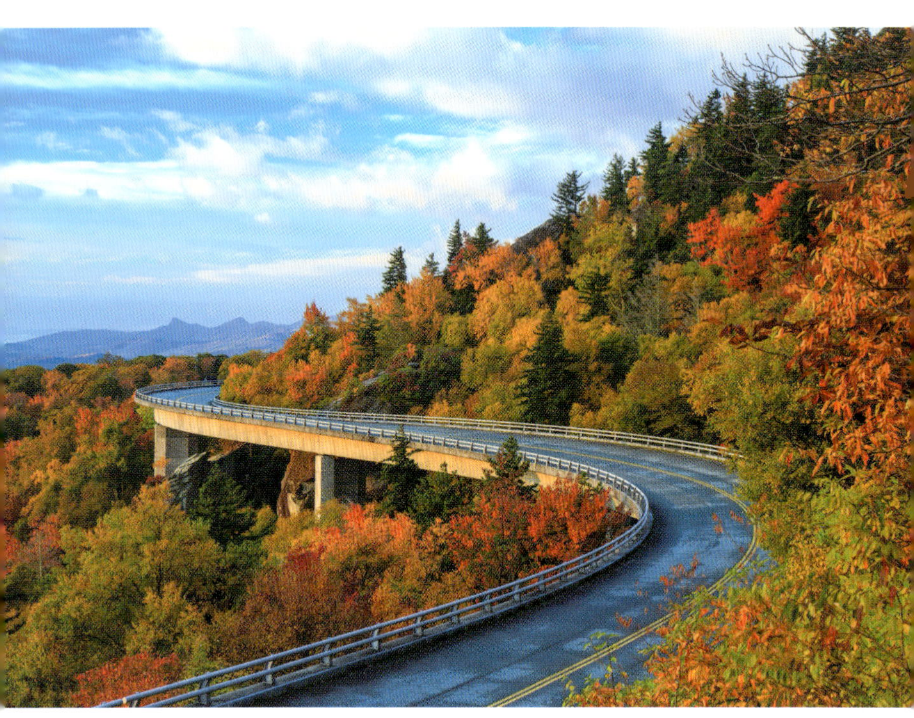

ABOVE The curving Linn Cove Viaduct on Blue Ridge Parkway in North Carolina, USA
RIGHT View from Stony Man Mountain, a short hike from Blue Ridge Parkway in Virginia, USA

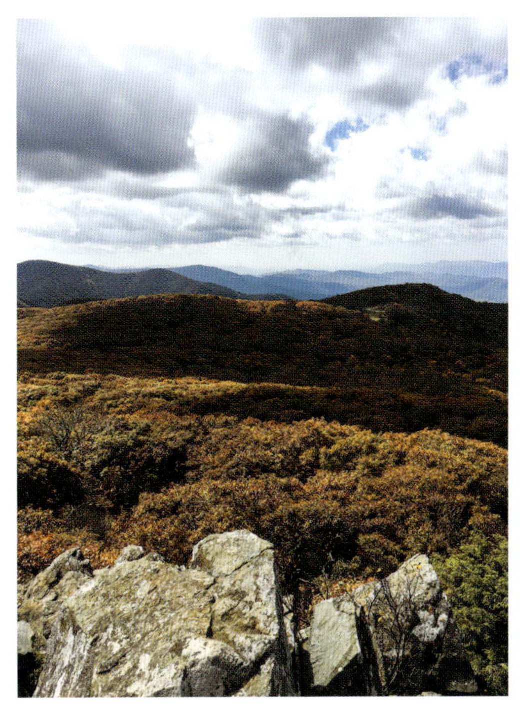

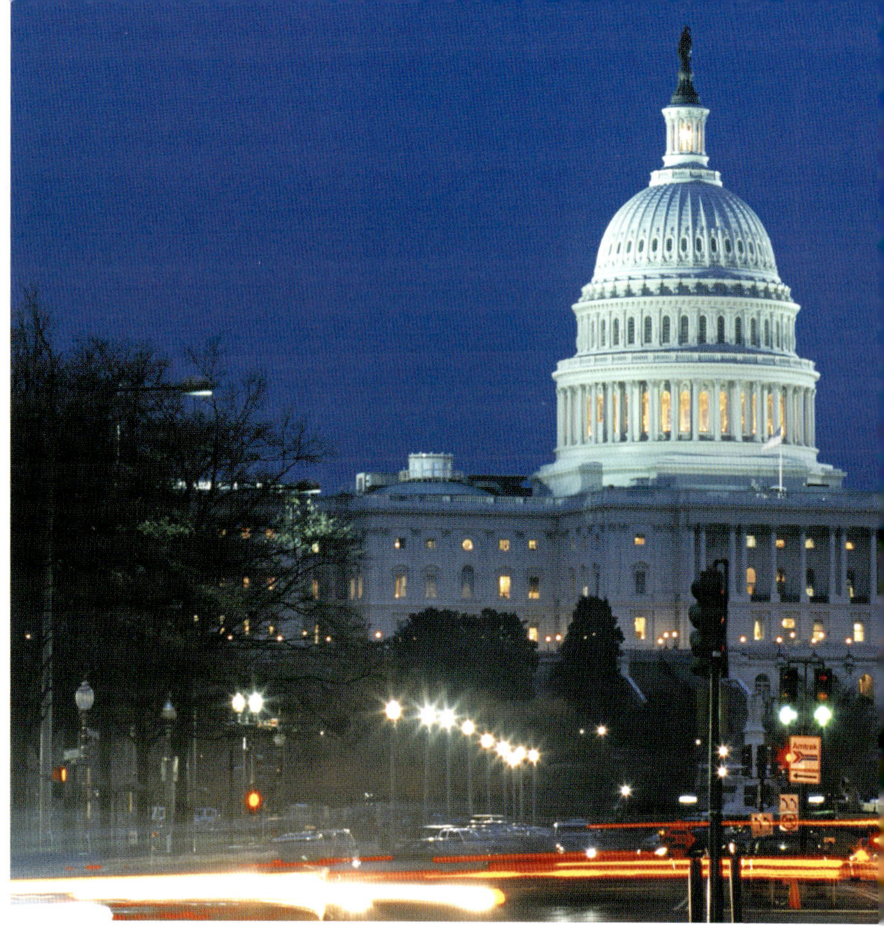

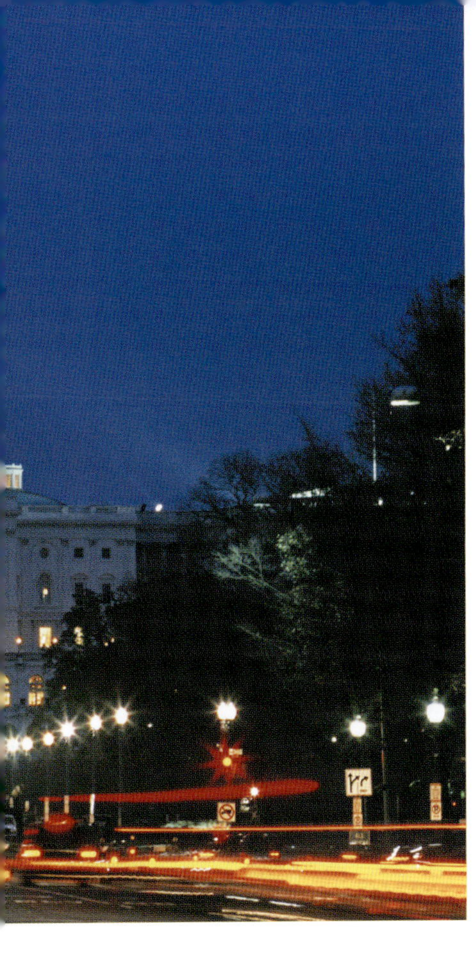

View of the Capitol Building from Pennsylvania Avenue
in Washington, D.C., USA

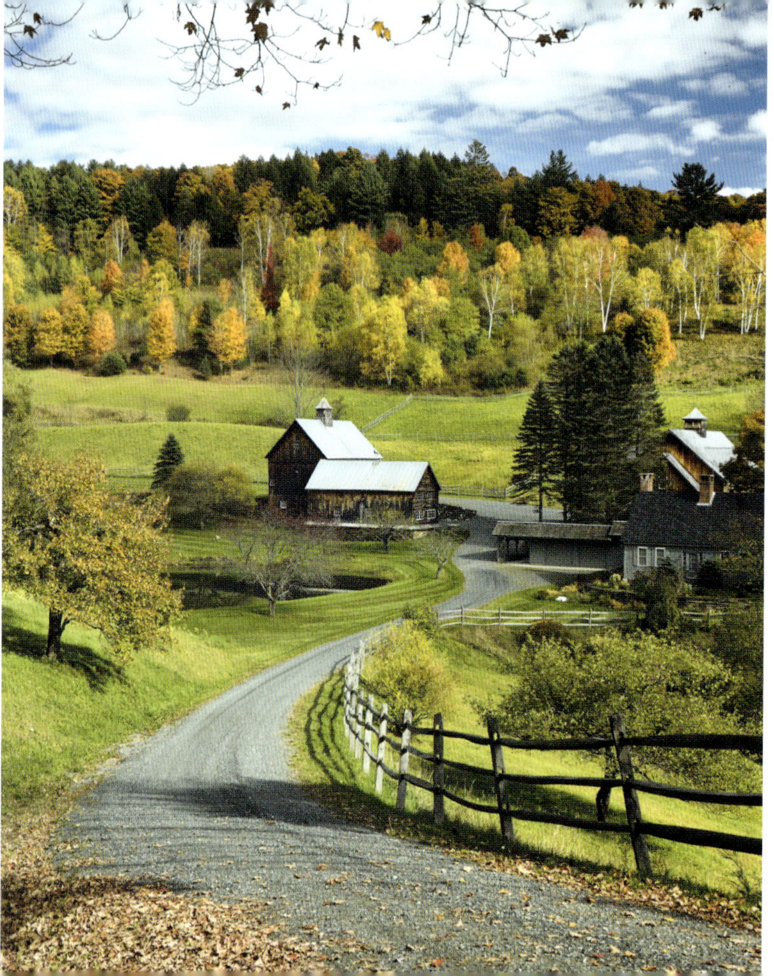

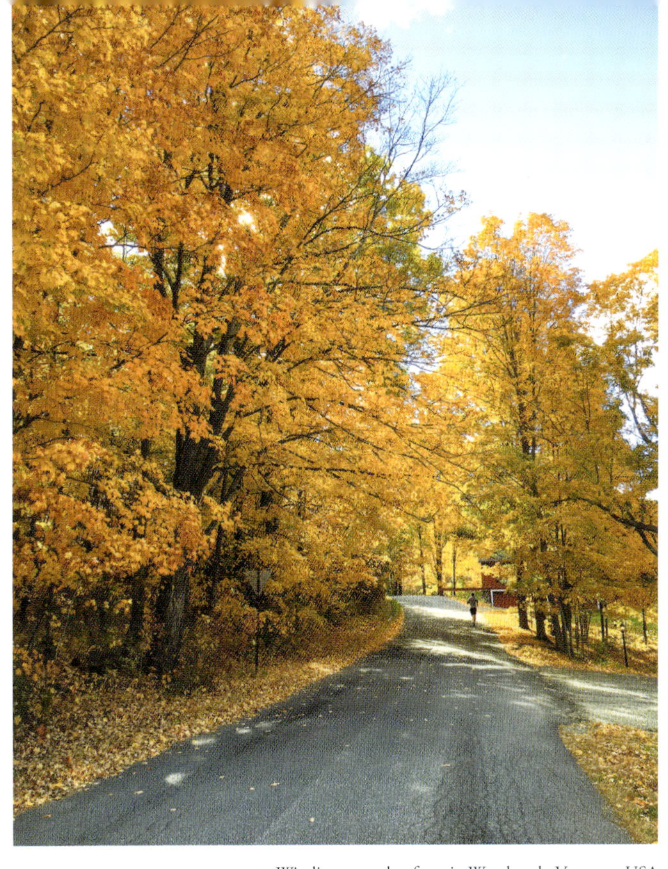

LEFT Winding towards a farm in Woodstock, Vermont, USA
ABOVE An autumn-fringed road in New York state, USA

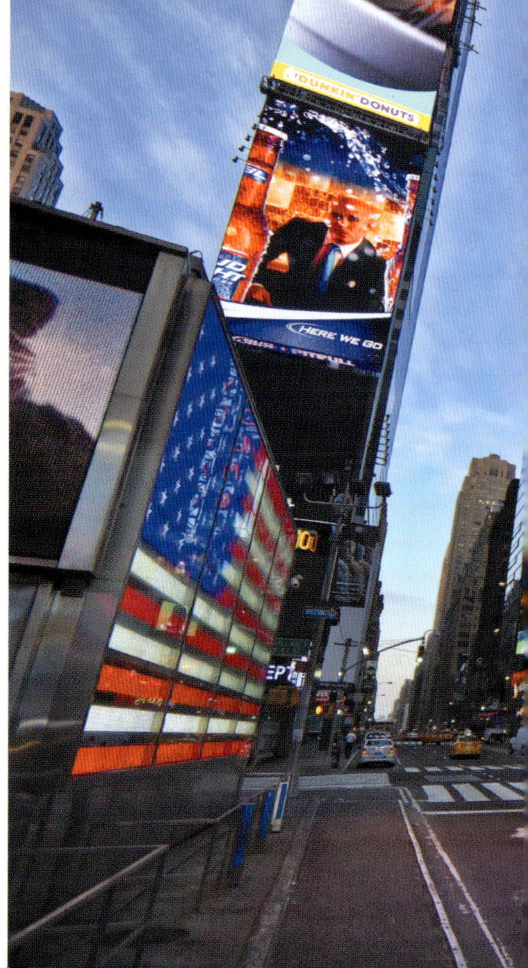

The shining lights of Times Square in
New York City, USA

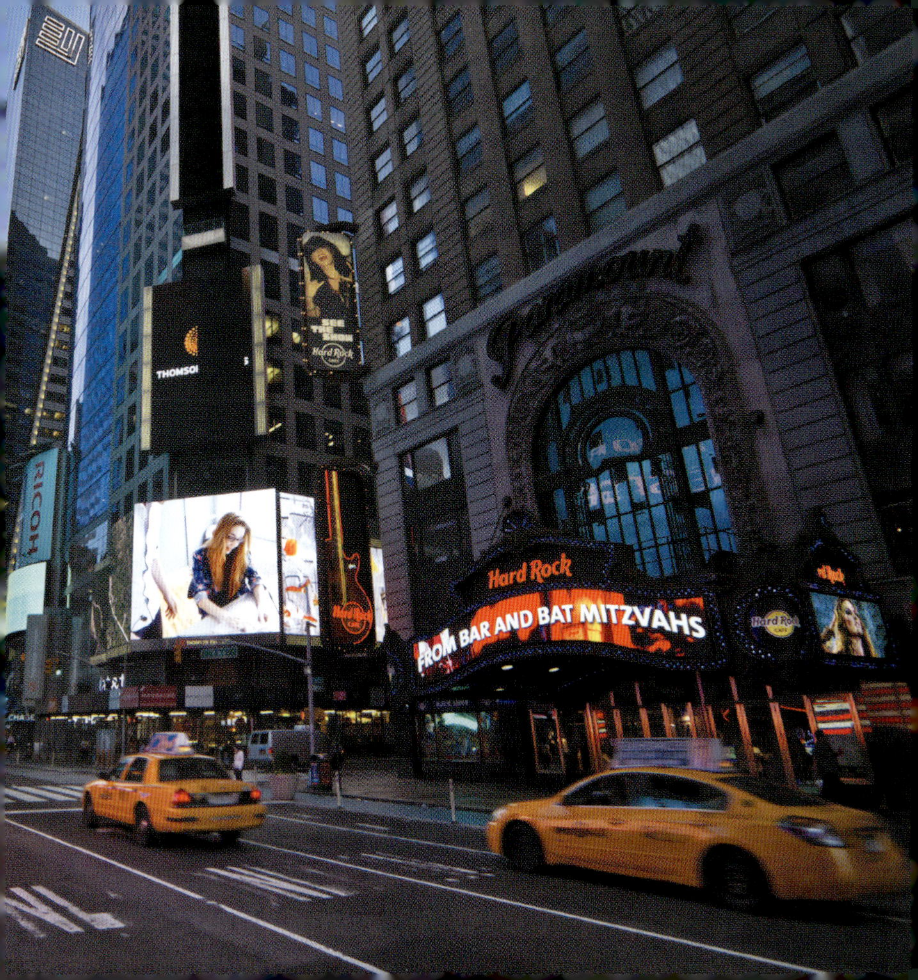

RICOH
THOMSOI
SEE THE SHOW
Hard Rock CAFE
Paramount
Hard Rock
FROM BAR AND BAT MITZVAHS
Hard Rock CAFE
CHASE

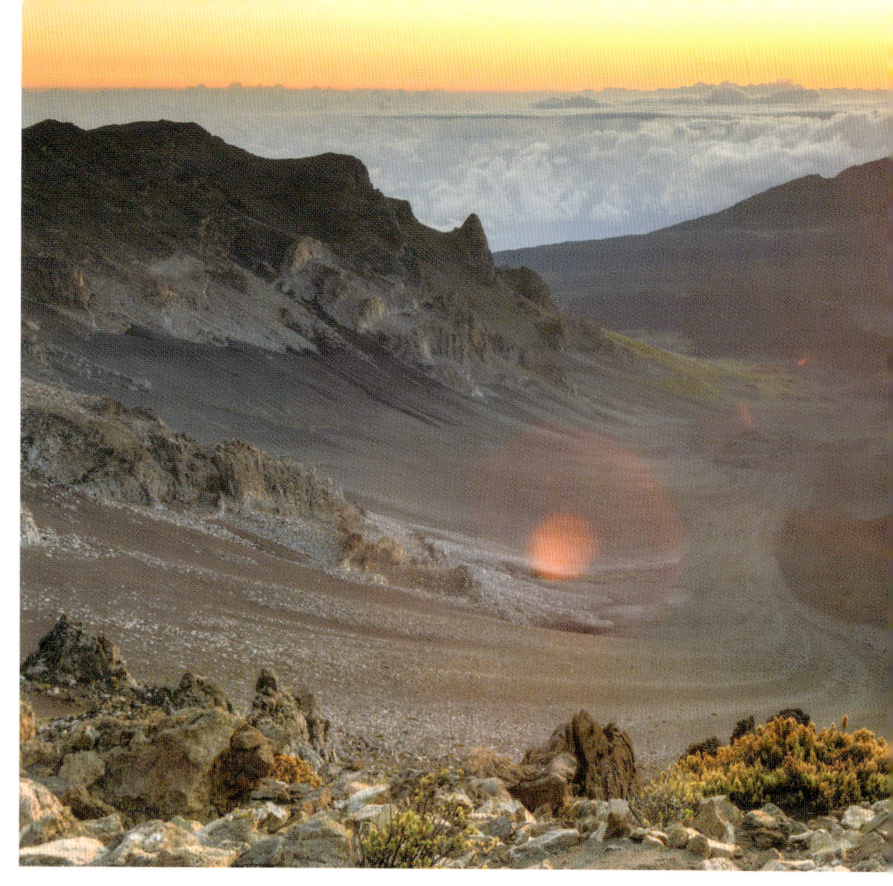

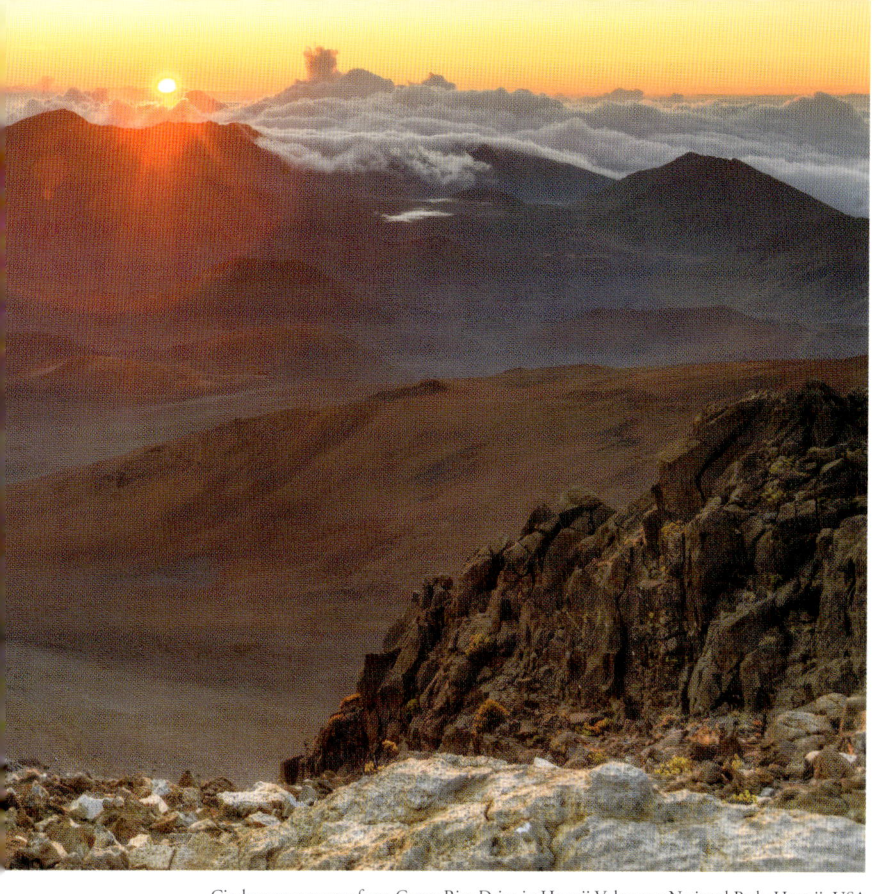

Cinder cones as seen from Crater Rim Drive in Hawaii Volcanoes National Park, Hawaii, USA

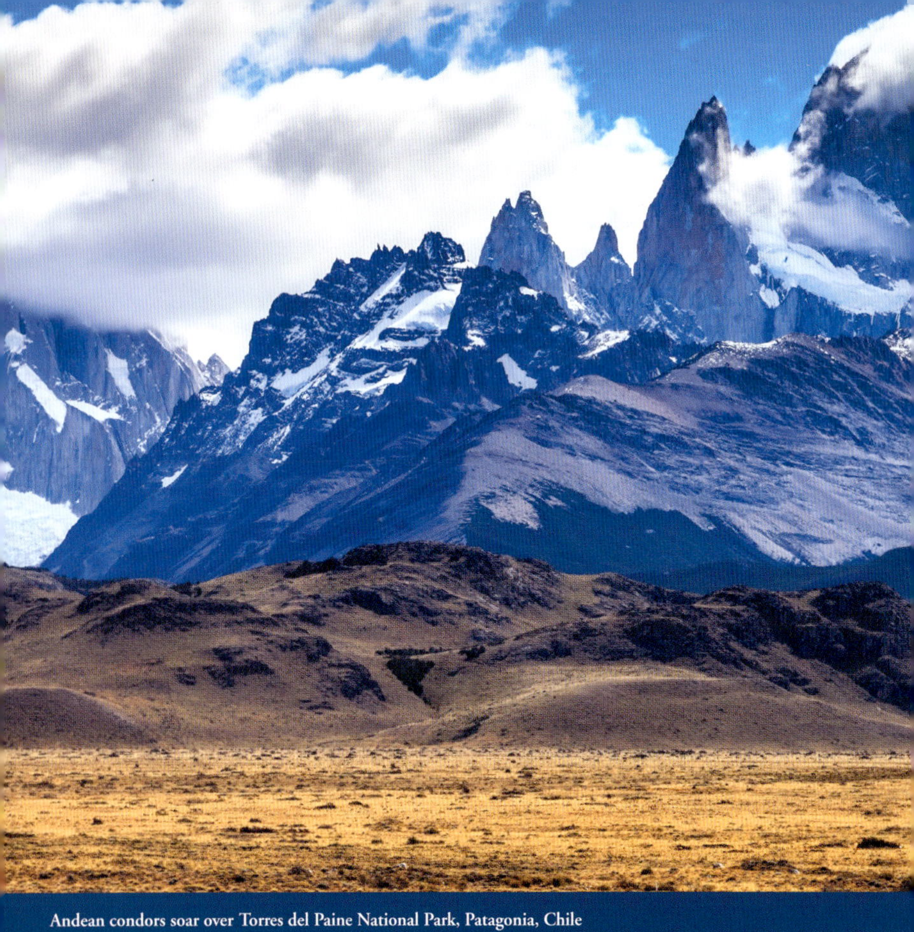

Andean condors soar over Torres del Paine National Park, Patagonia, Chile

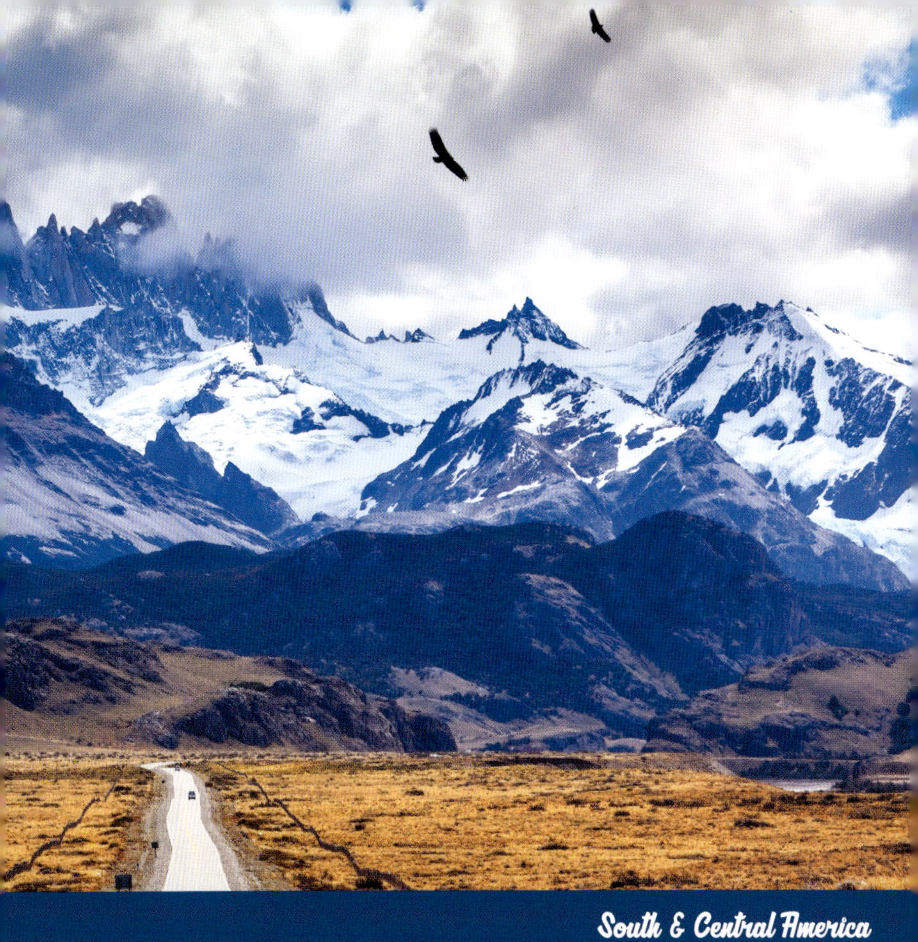

South & Central America

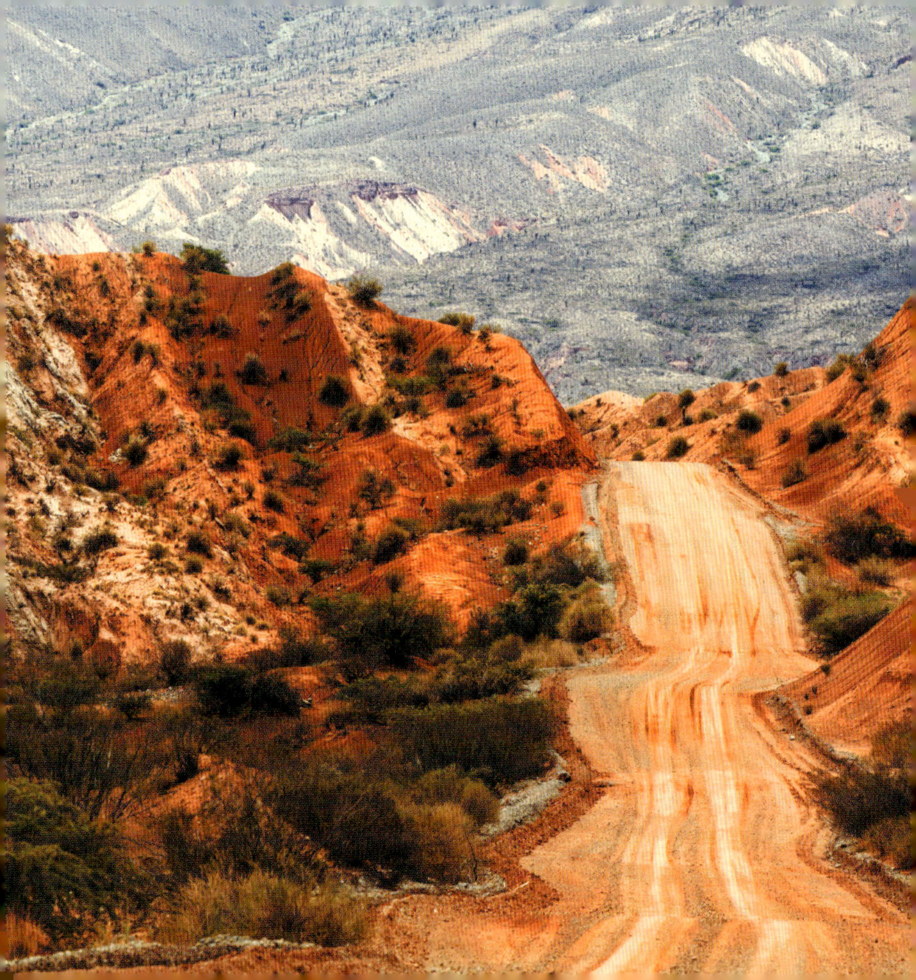

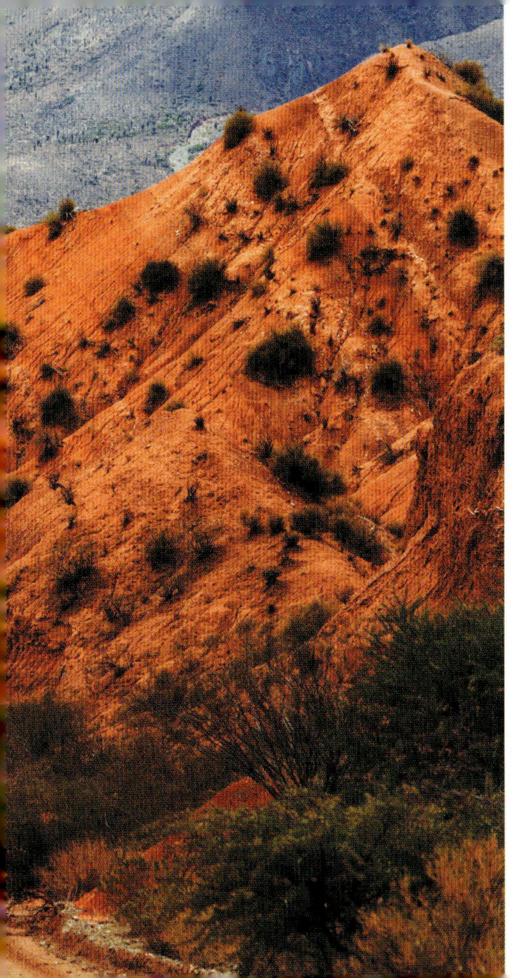

A red-tinged dirt road winds through the hills
of northern Argentina

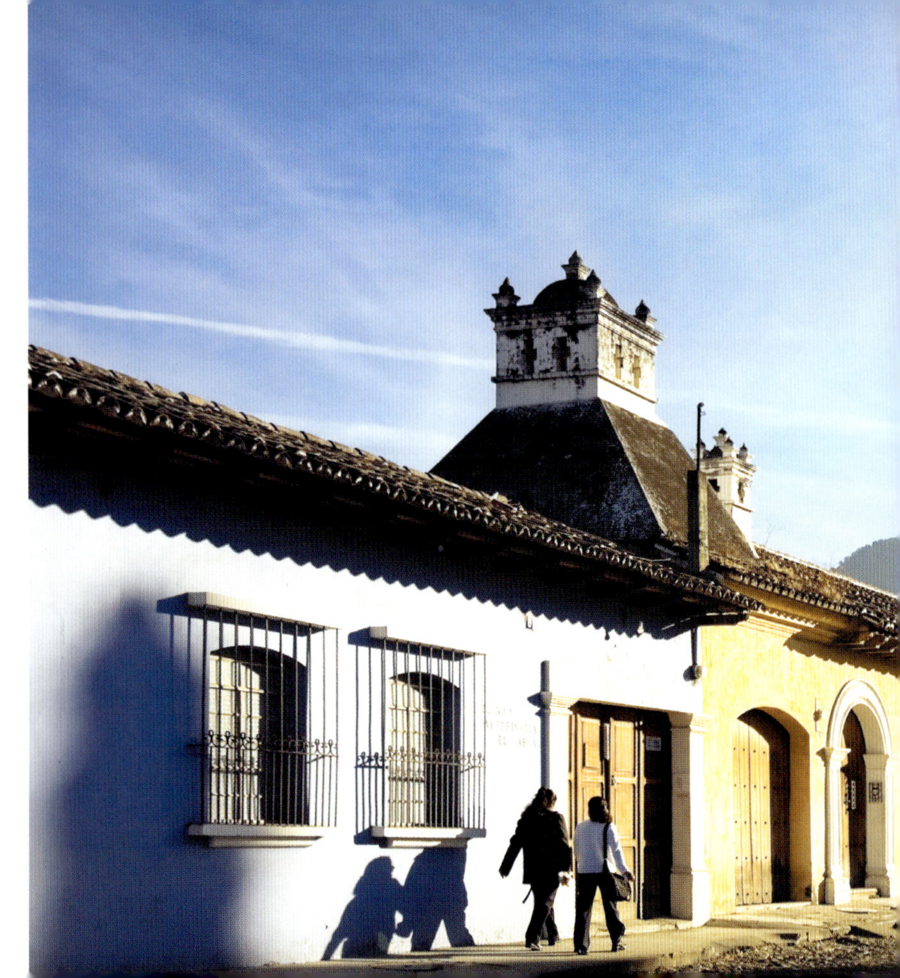

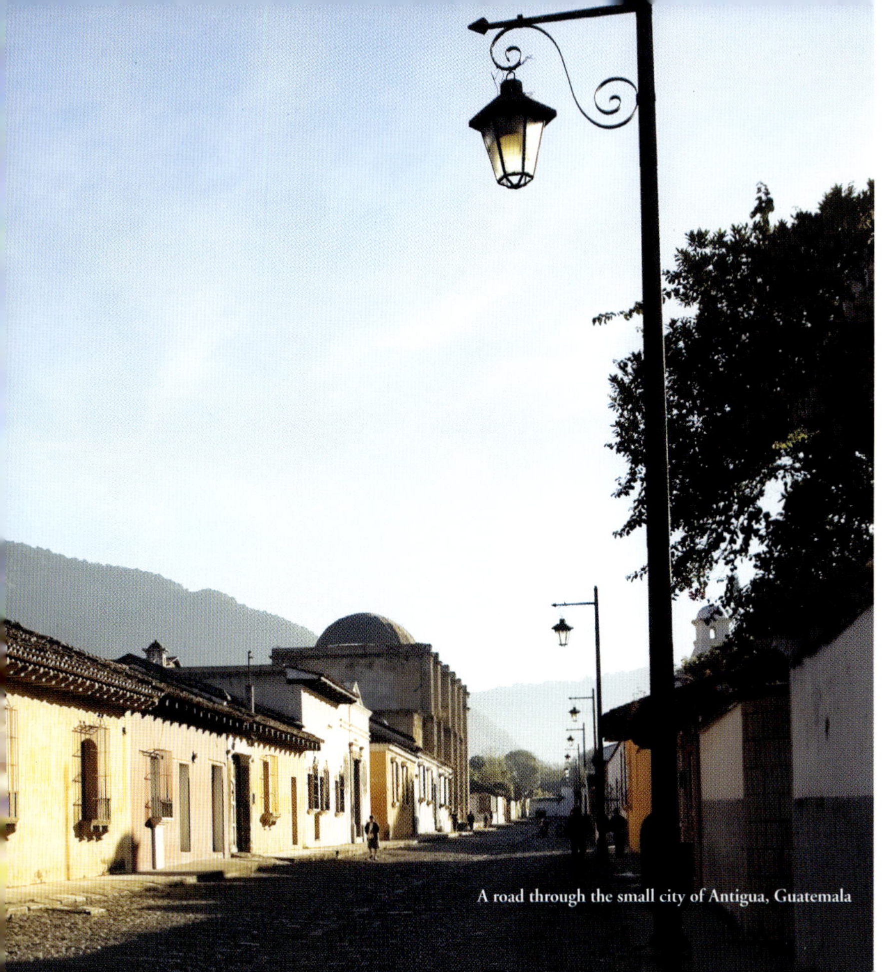

A road through the small city of Antigua, Guatemala

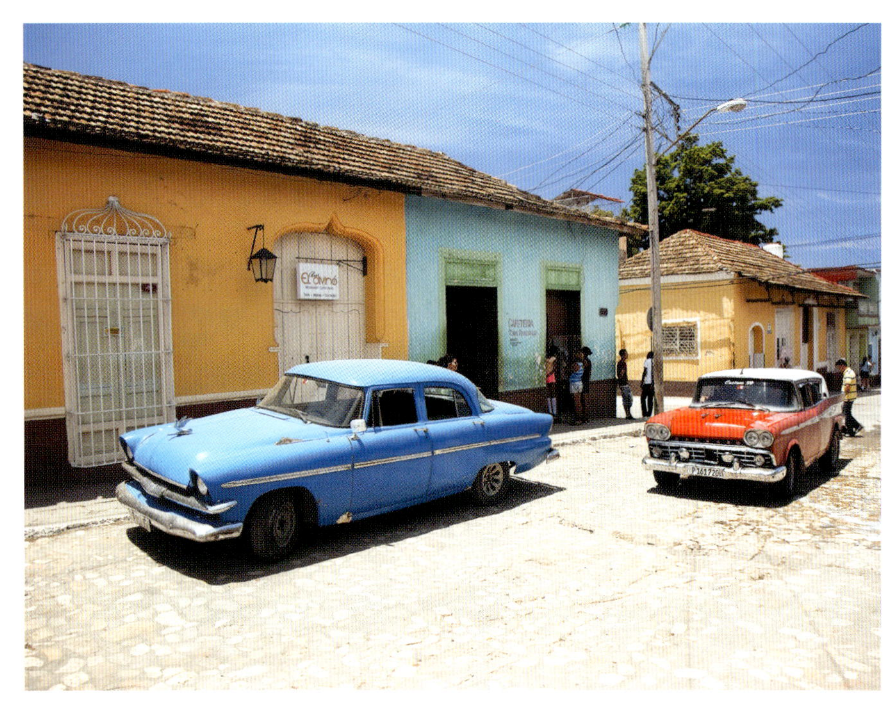

Vintage American cars pass through a street in Trinidad, Cuba

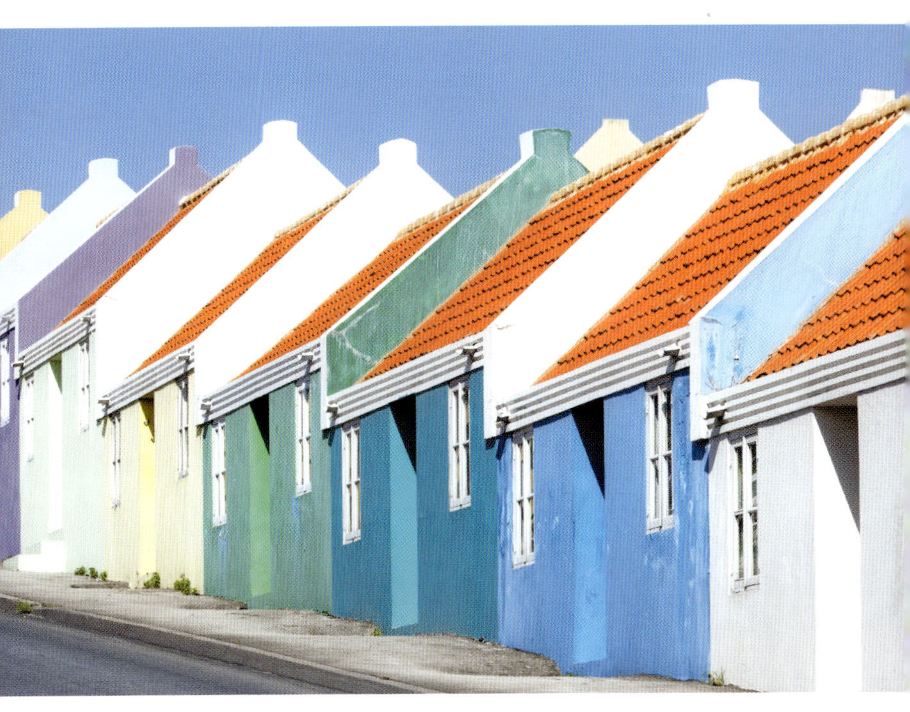

Driving past colourful houses on Berg Altena Road on the Caribbean island of Curacao

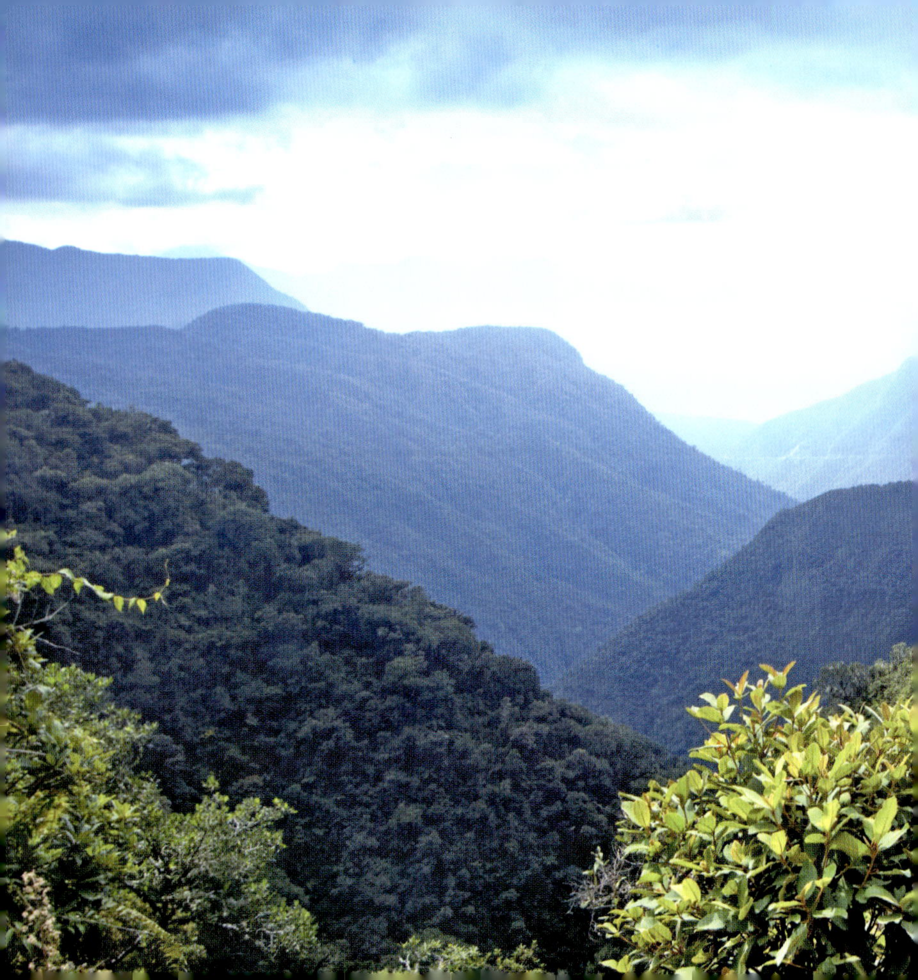

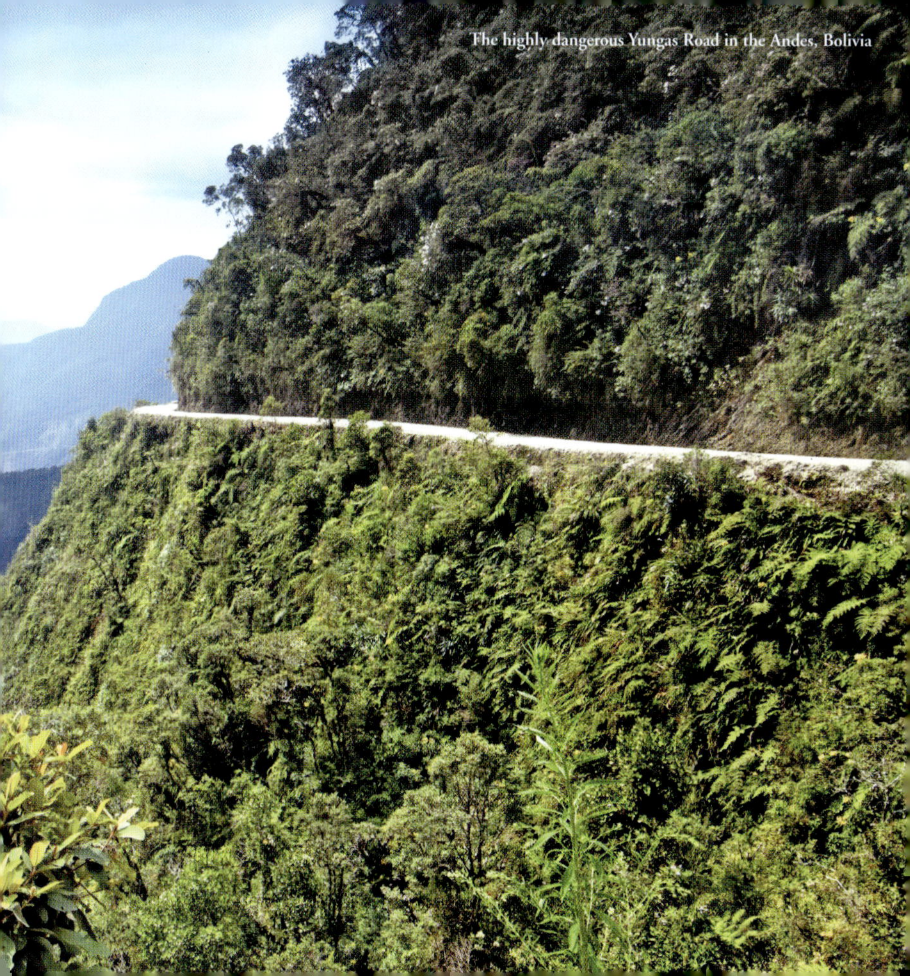

The highly dangerous Yungas Road in the Andes, Bolivia

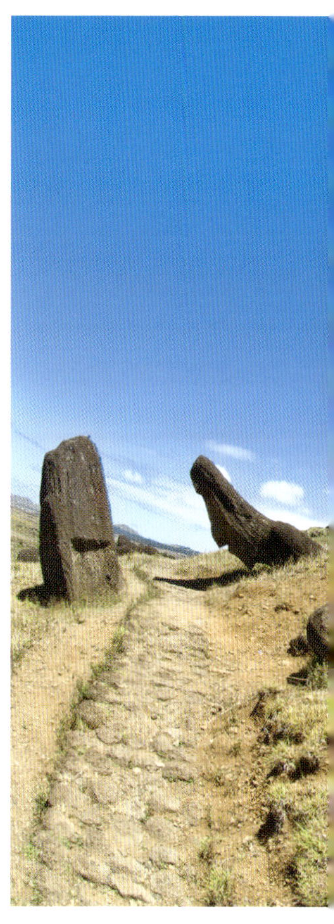

Abandoned Moai (also called the 'Easter Island heads')
along a road, Easter Island

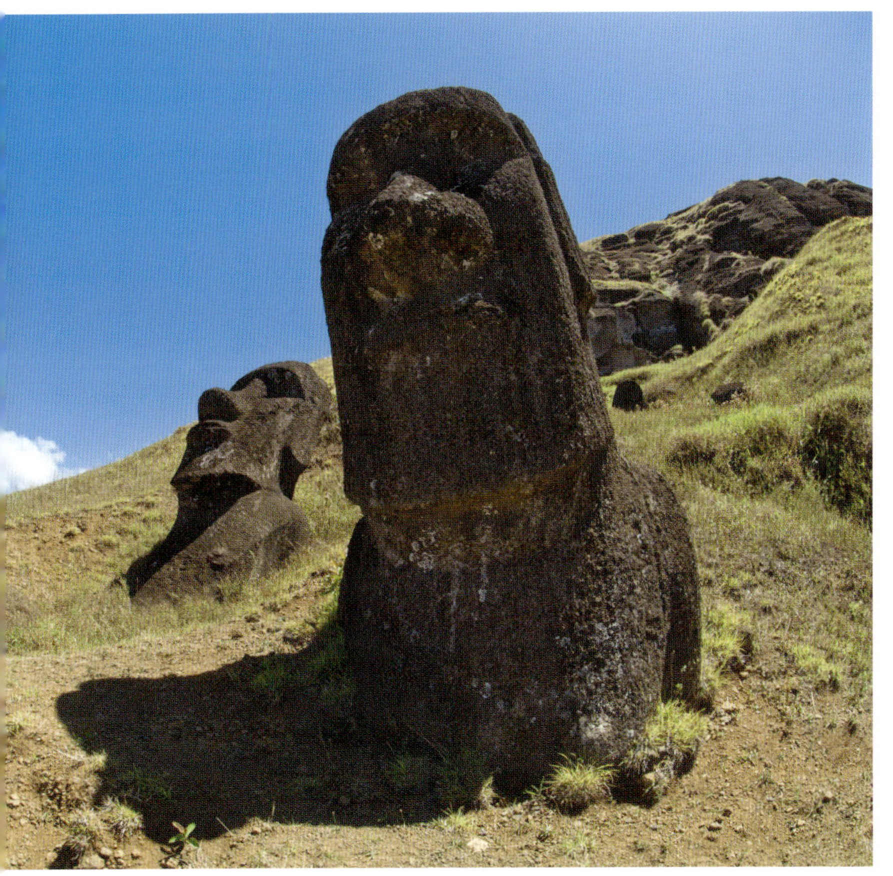

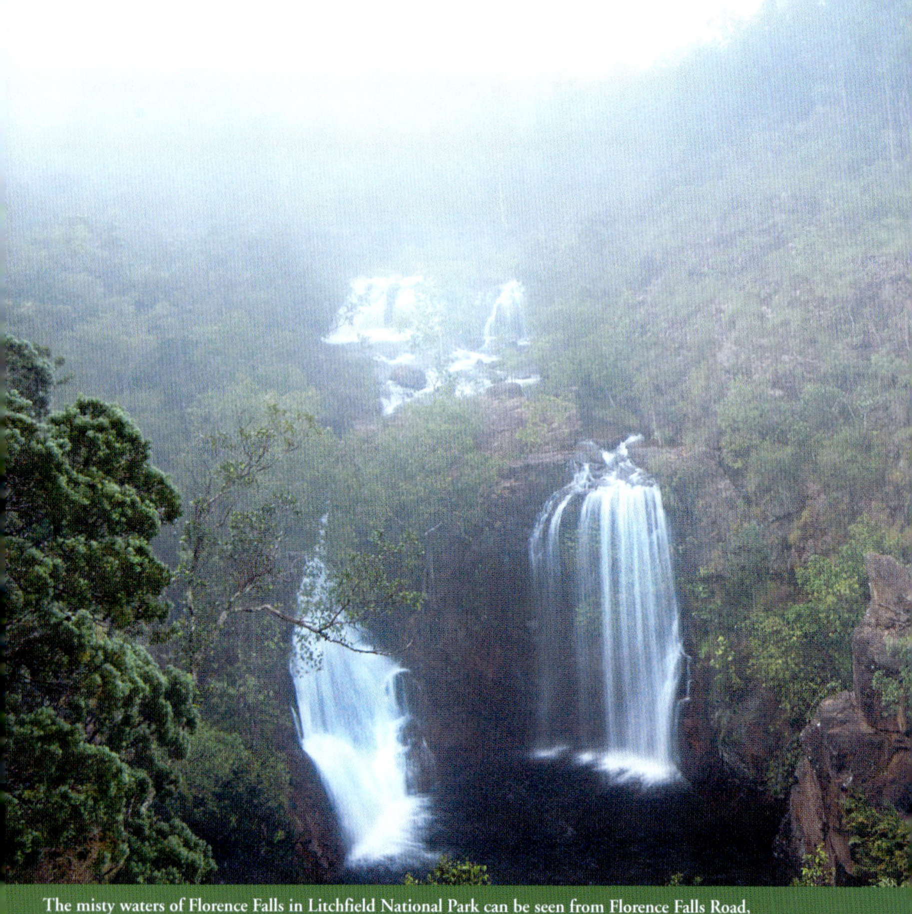

The misty waters of Florence Falls in Litchfield National Park can be seen from Florence Falls Road, Northern Territory, Australia

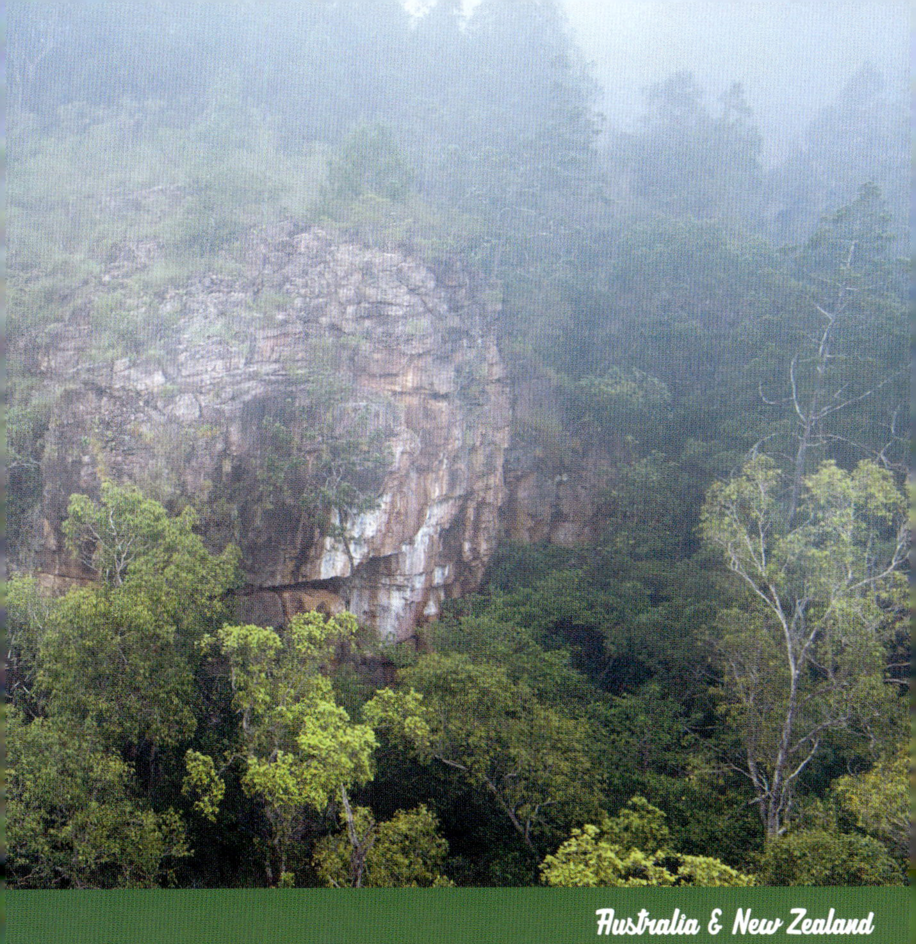

Australia & New Zealand

Sunset along Barkly Highway in the Northern Territory, Australia

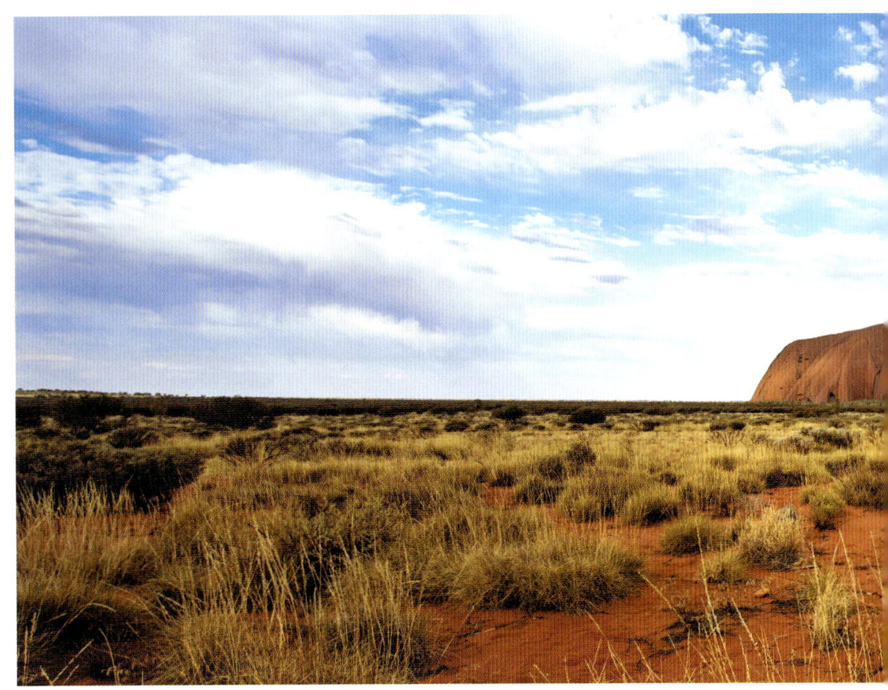

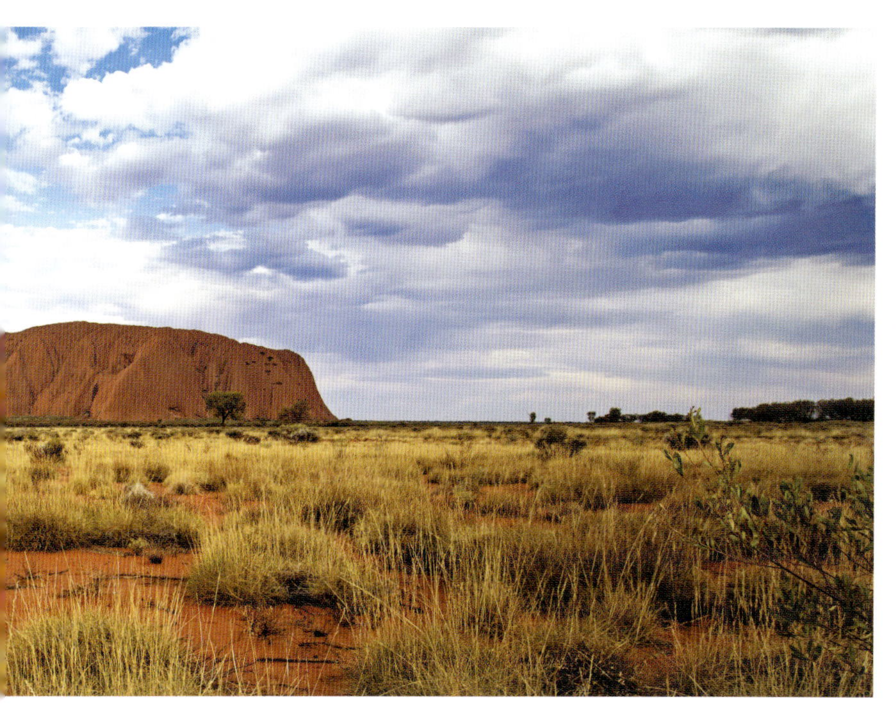

The view of Uluṟu from Sunset carpark in the Northern Territory, Australia

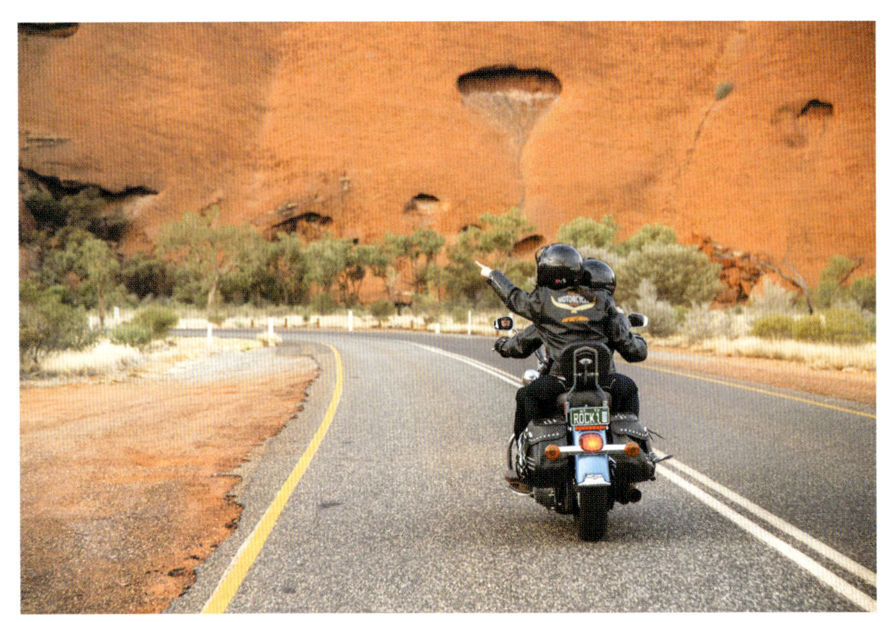

Motorcyclists pass Kata Tjuṯa in the Northern Territory, Australia

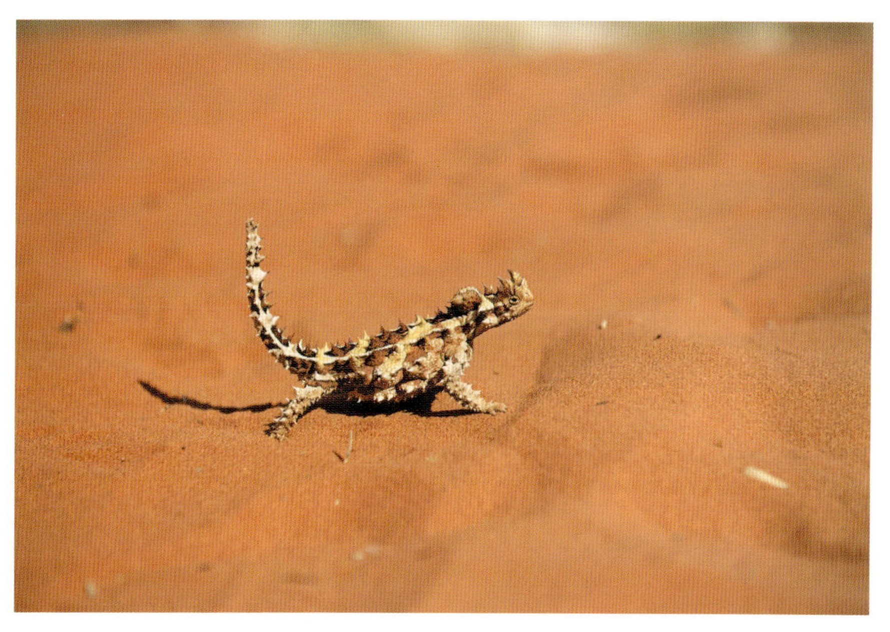

Thorny devil near Gosses Bluff Conservation Reserve in the Northern Territory, Australia

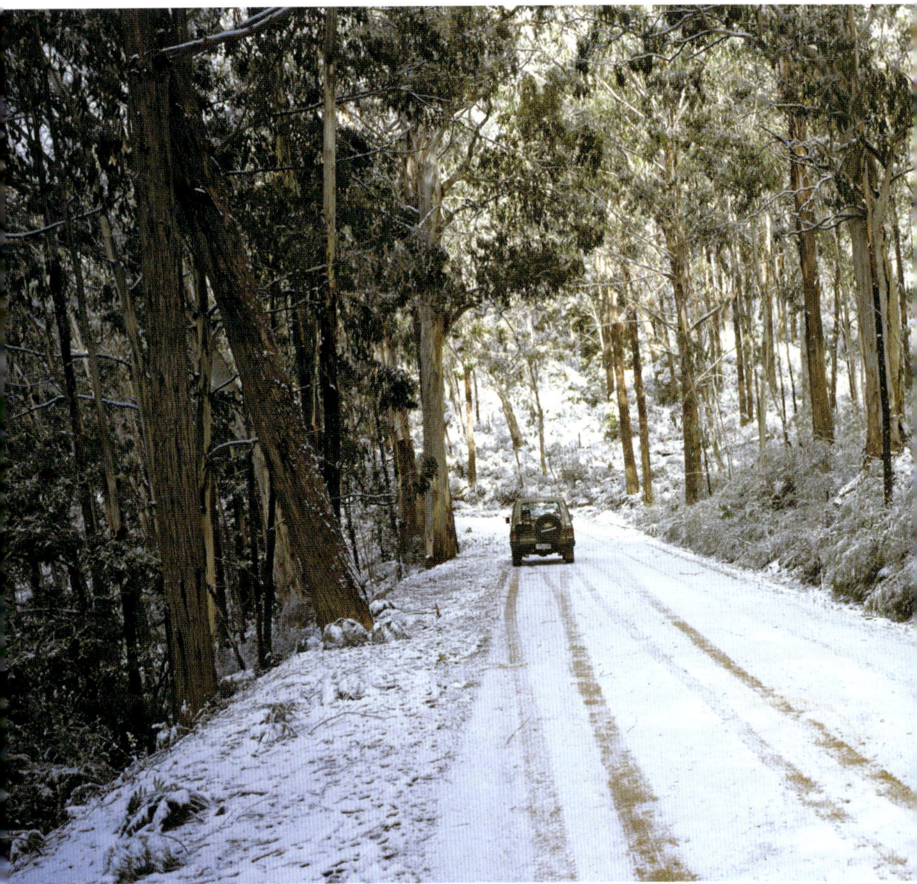

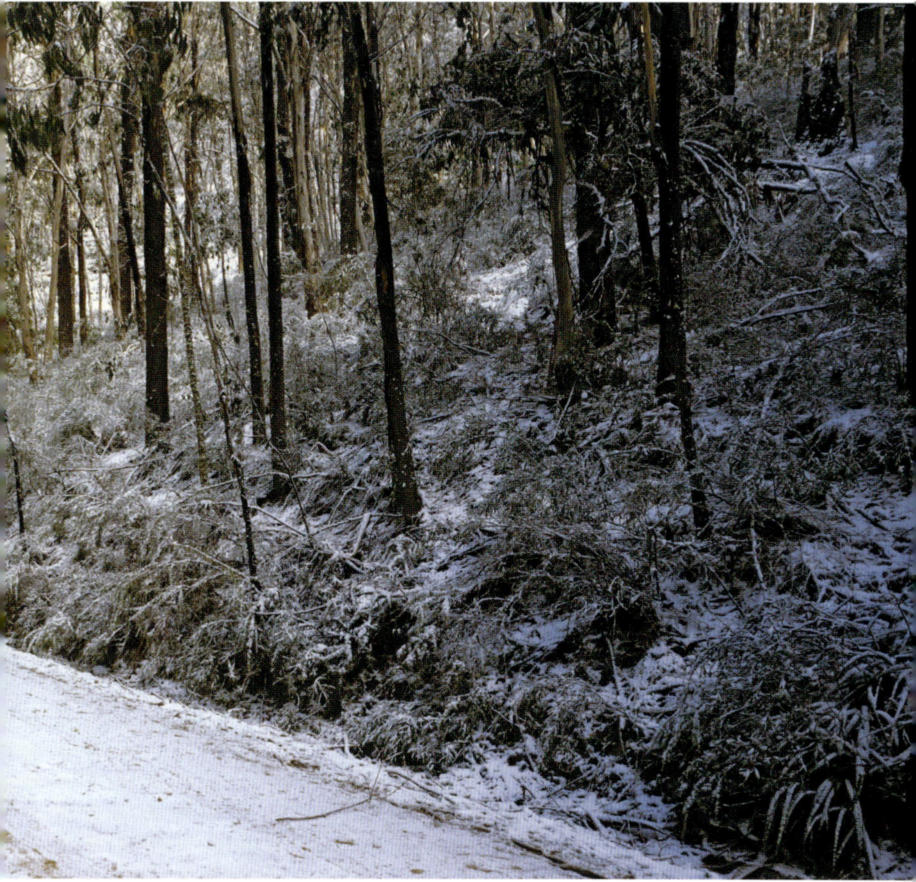

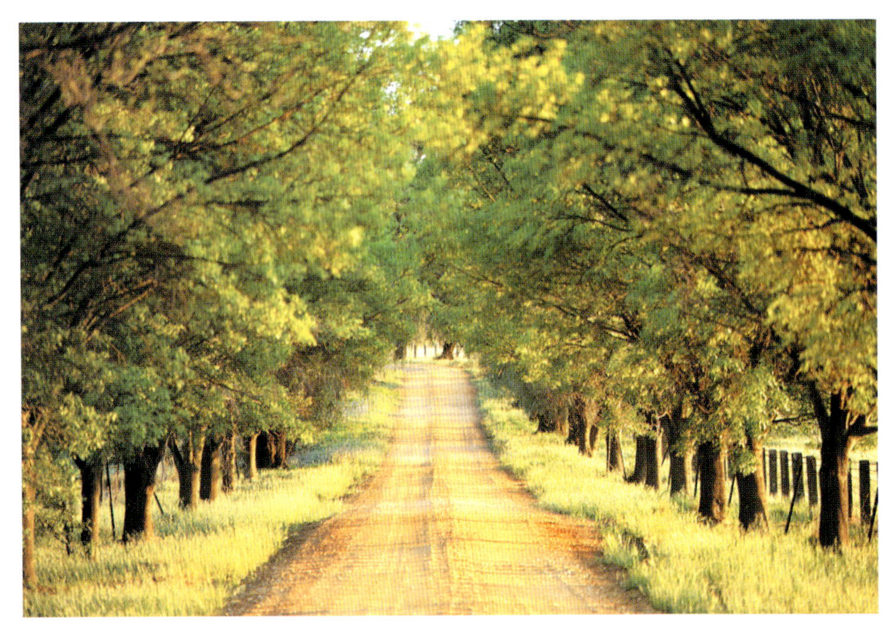

A country road through Cowra in New South Wales, Australia

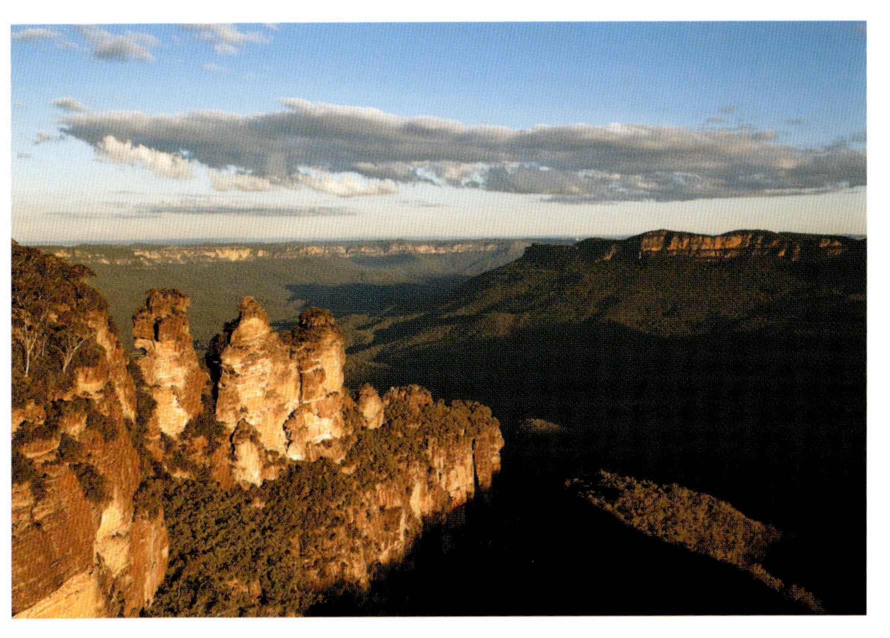

View of the Three Sisters in Blue Mountains National Park, New South Wales, Australia

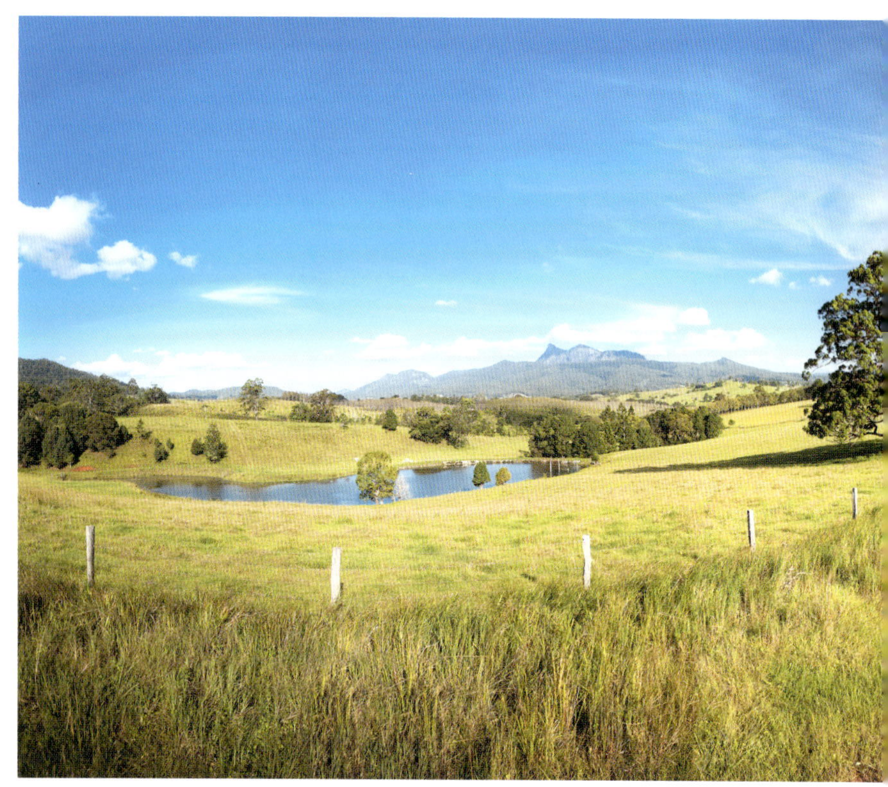

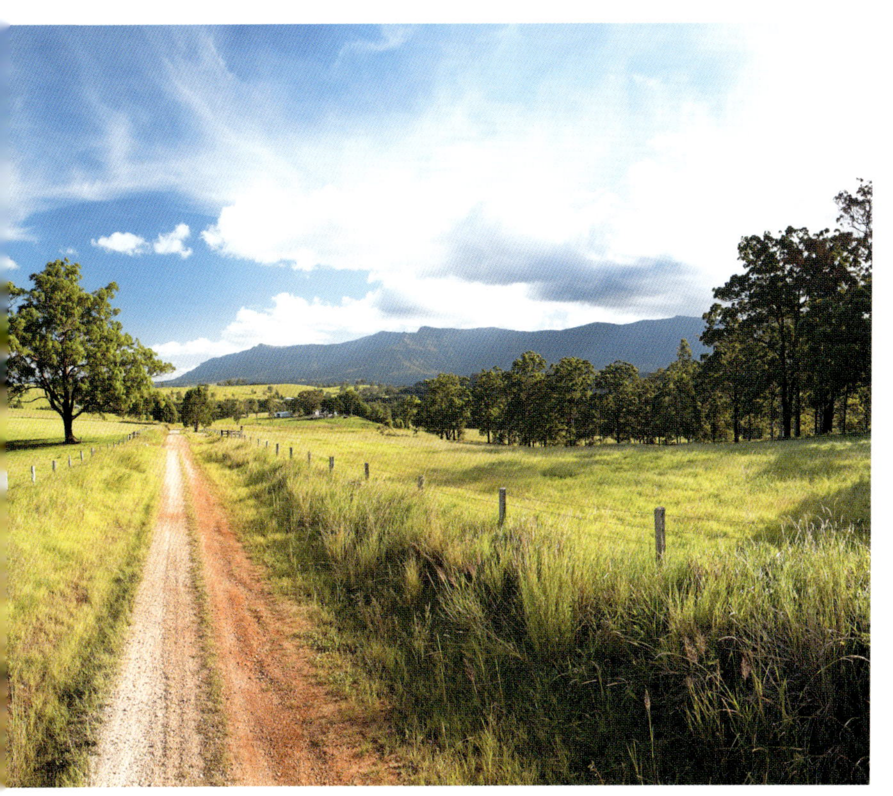

A dirt road near Tyalgum in Northern Rivers, New South Wales, Australia

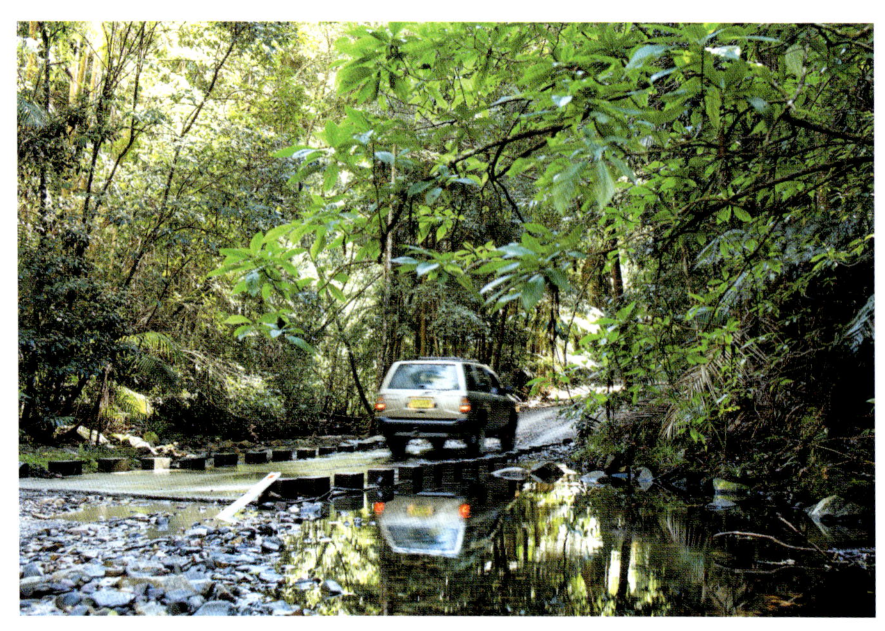

Four-wheel driving through Yarrahapinni in New South Wales, Australia

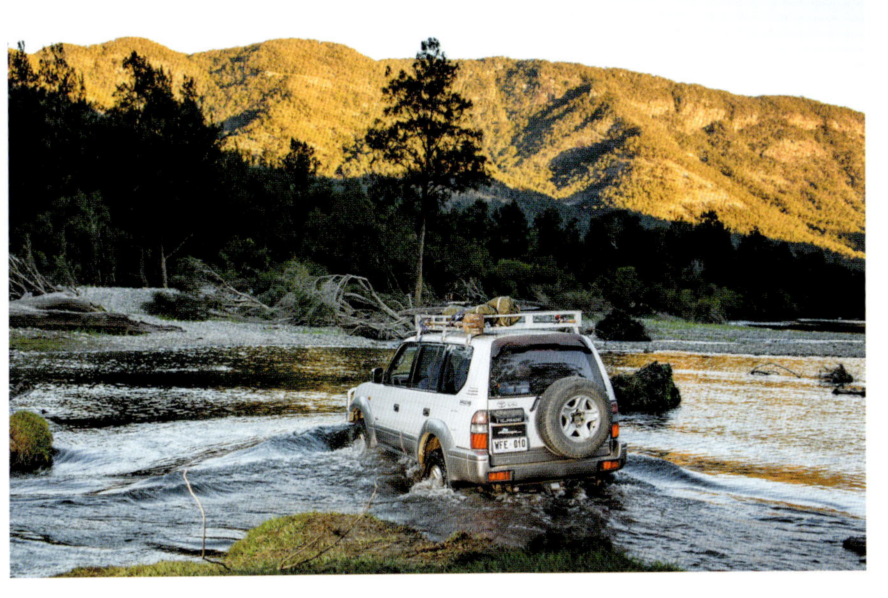

Fjording a river in the hinterland of Macleay Valley Coast, New South Wales, Australia

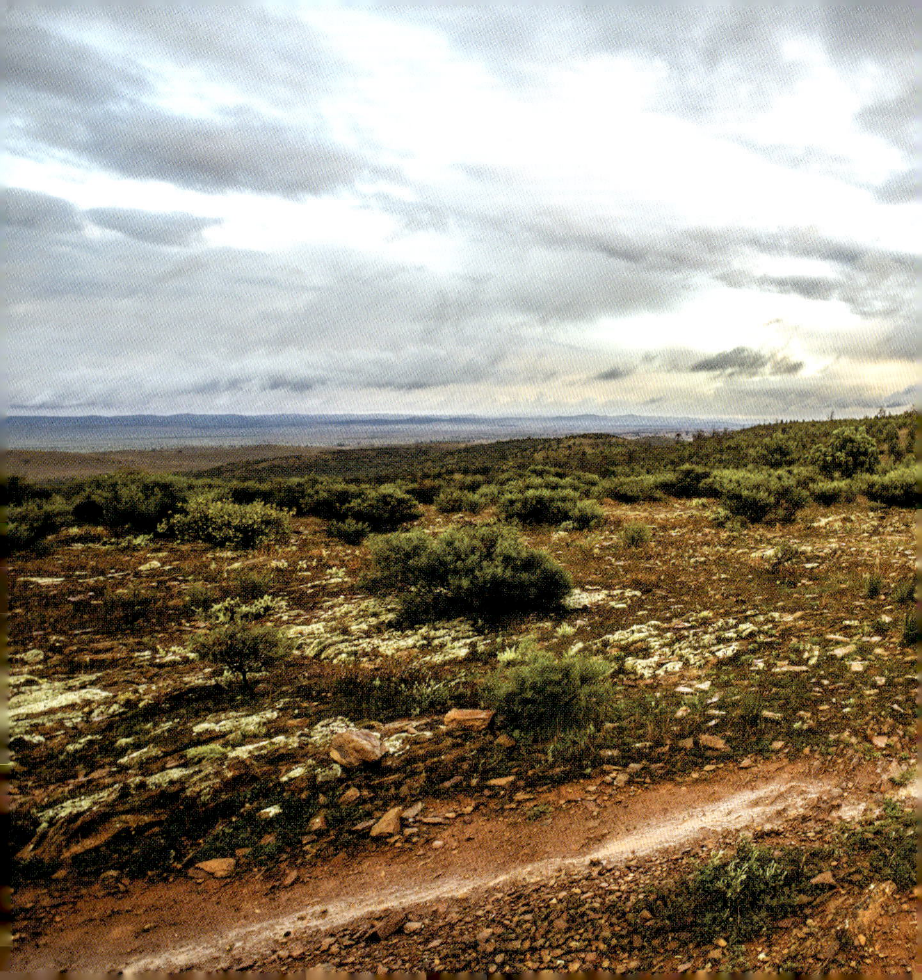

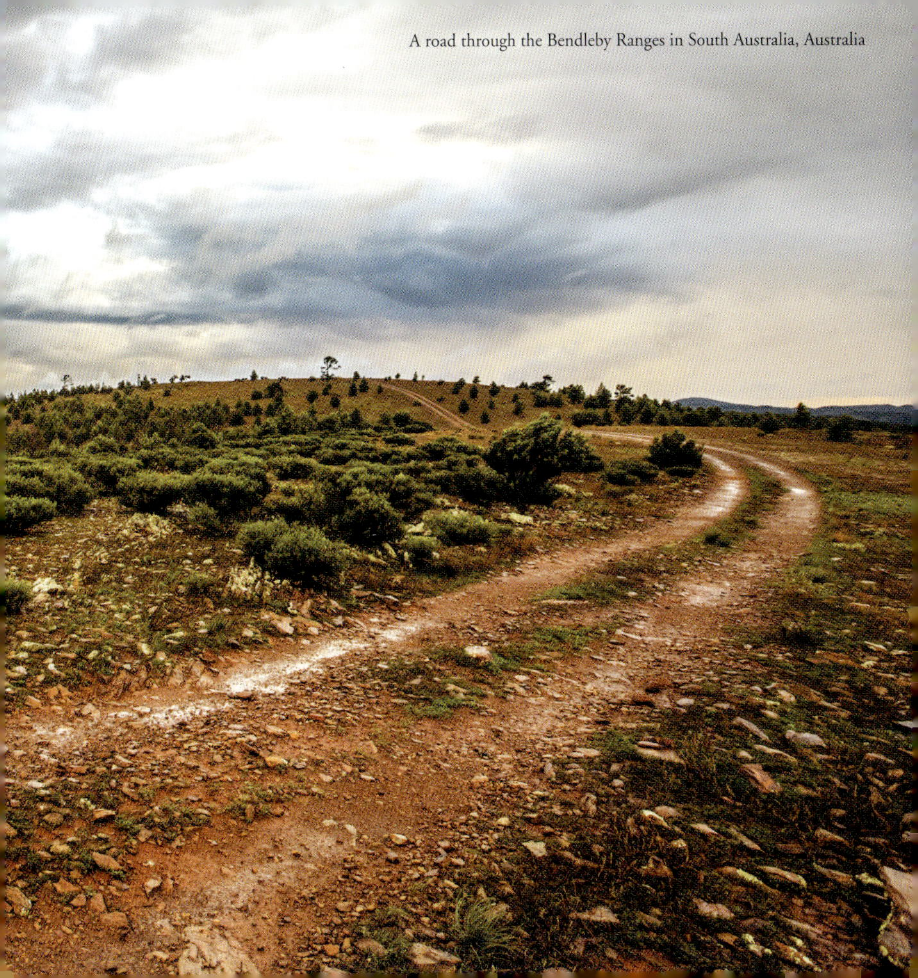

A road through the Bendleby Ranges in South Australia, Australia

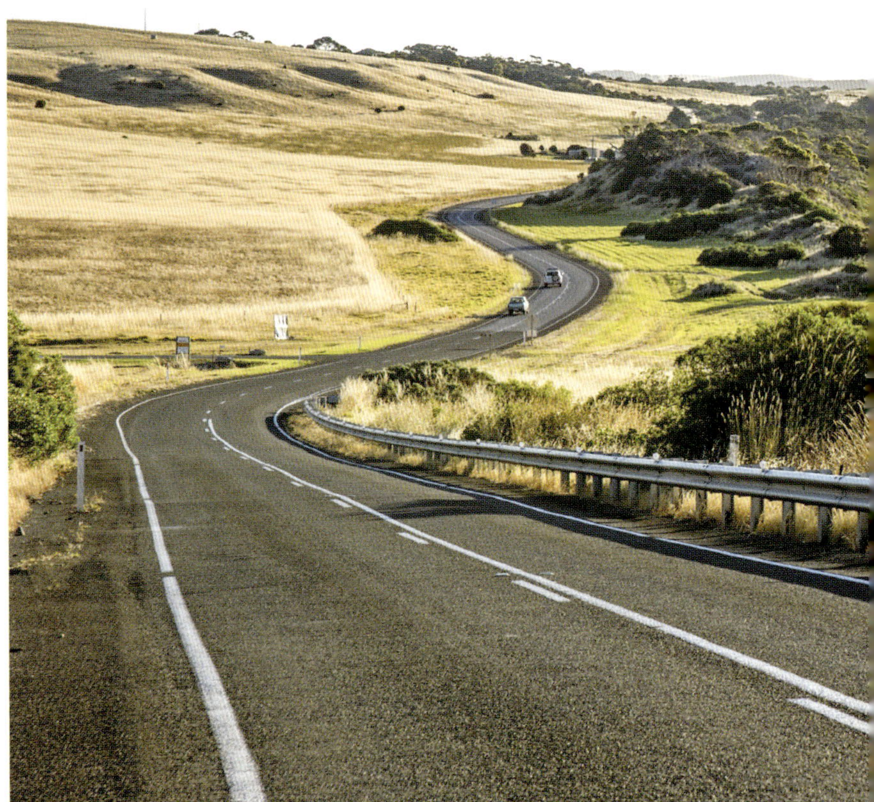

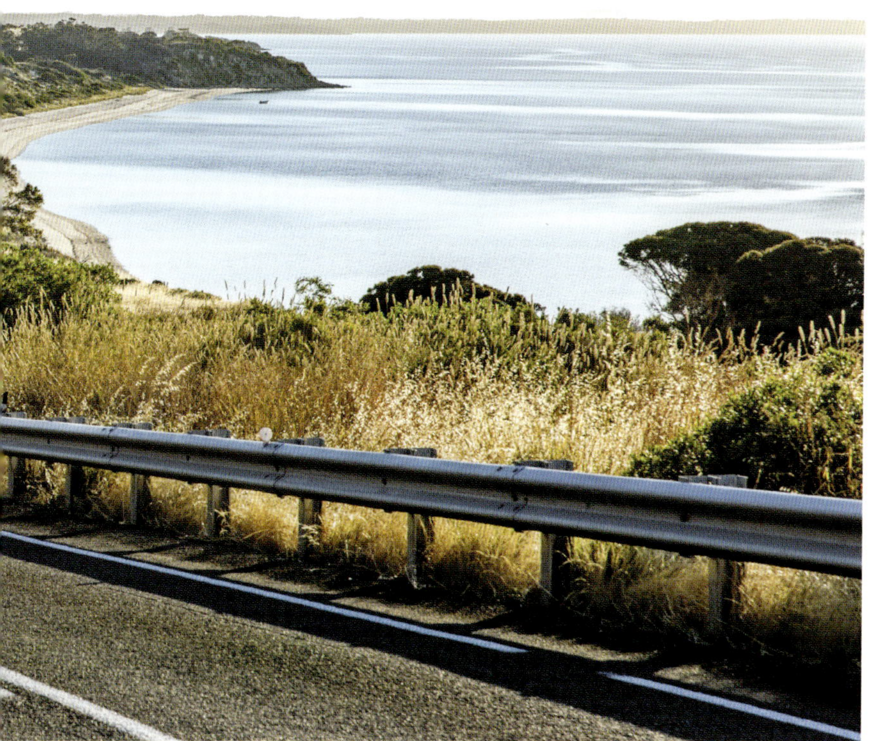

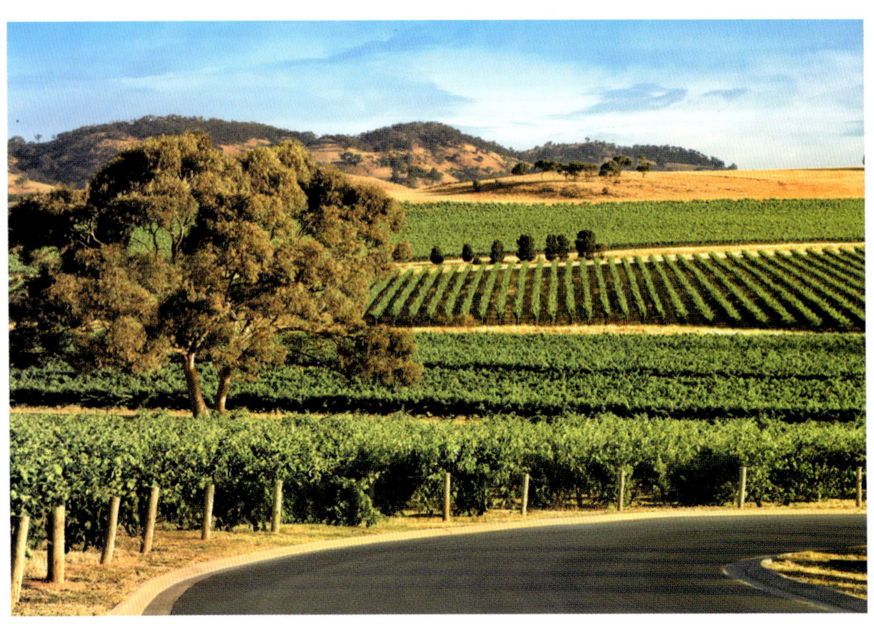

Meandering through the vineyards of the Barossa Valley in South Australia, Australia

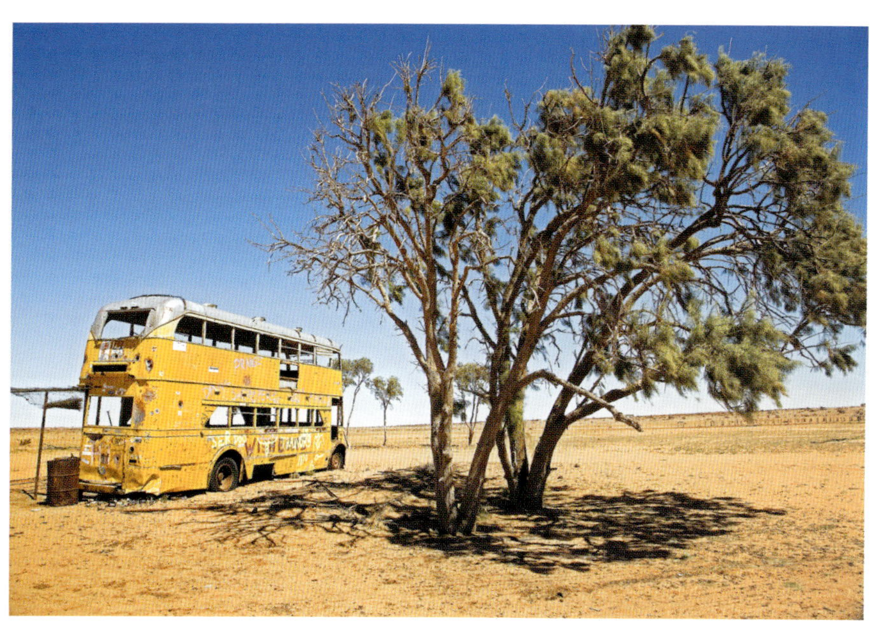

Lonely double-decker bus in the South Australian outback, Australia

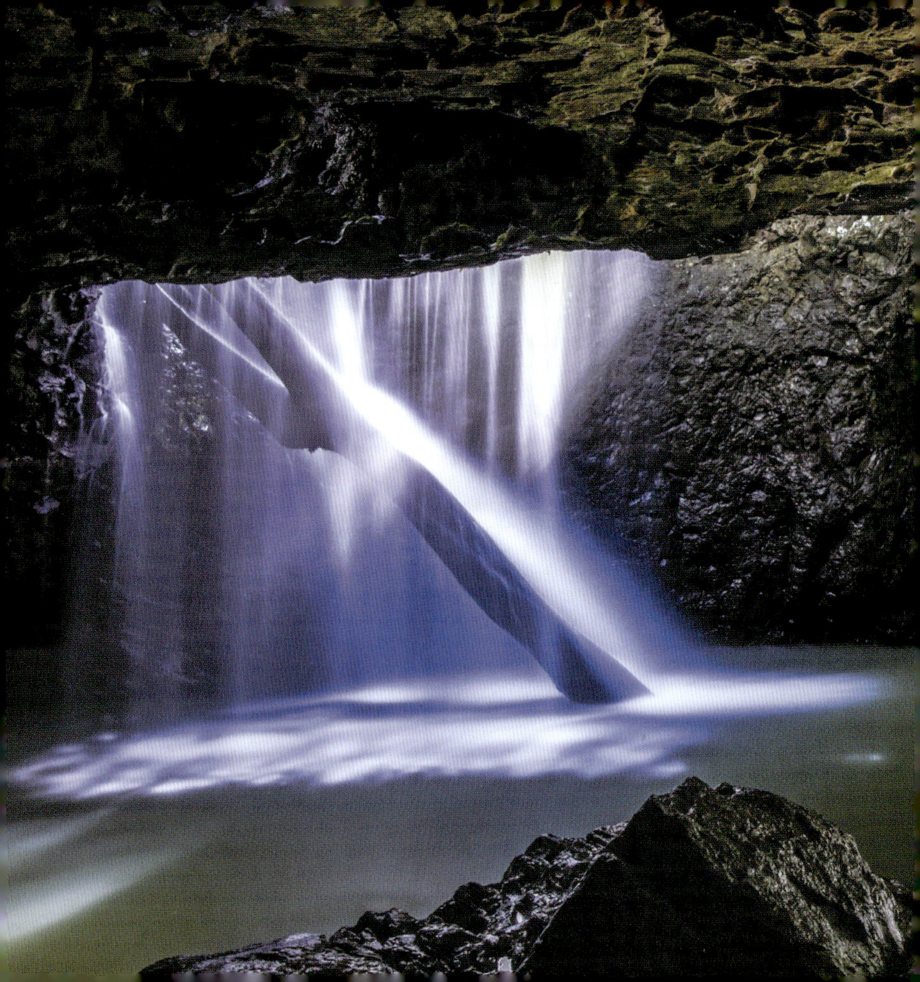

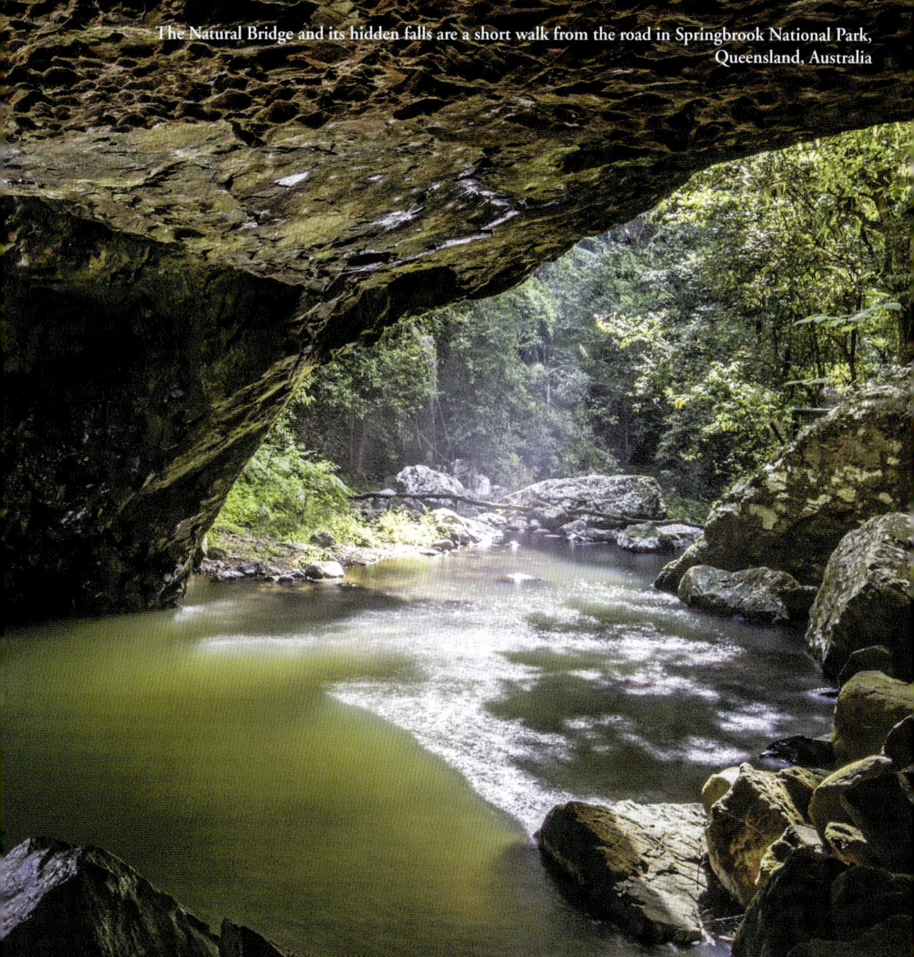

The Natural Bridge and its hidden falls are a short walk from the road in Springbrook National Park, Queensland, Australia

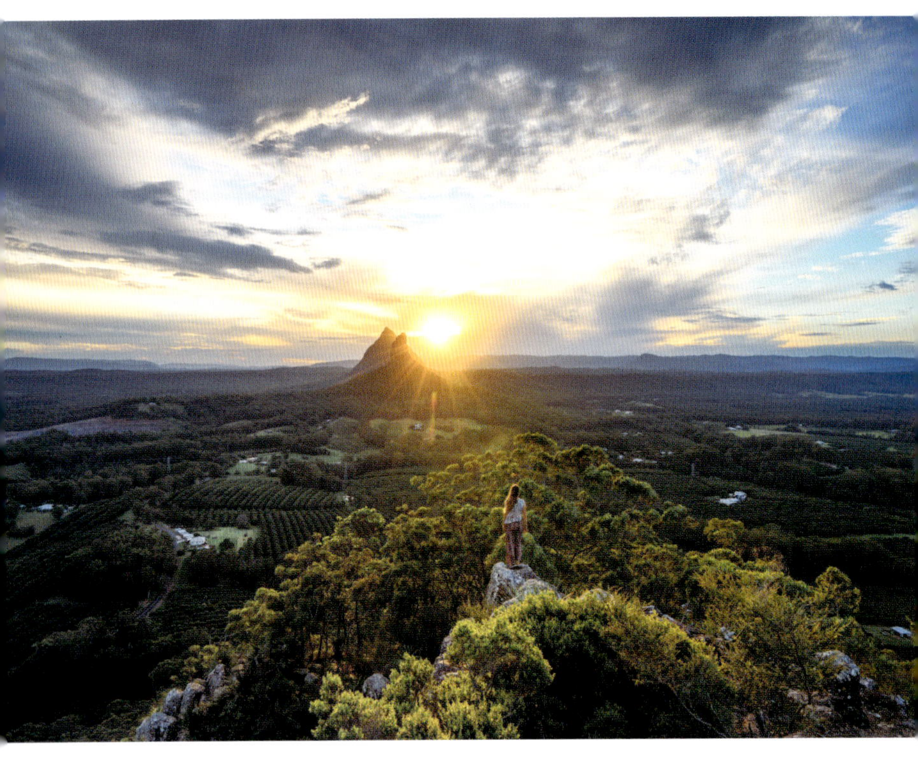

ABOVE The Glasshouse Mountains on the Sunshine Coast, Queensland, Australia
RIGHT Back road through Maleny with the Glasshouse Mountains in the distance, Queensland, Australia

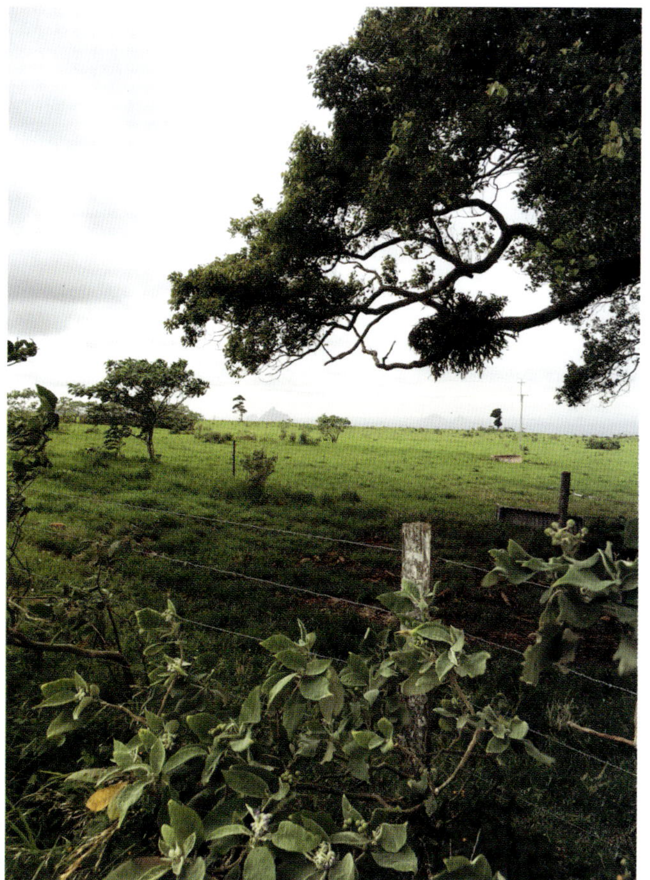

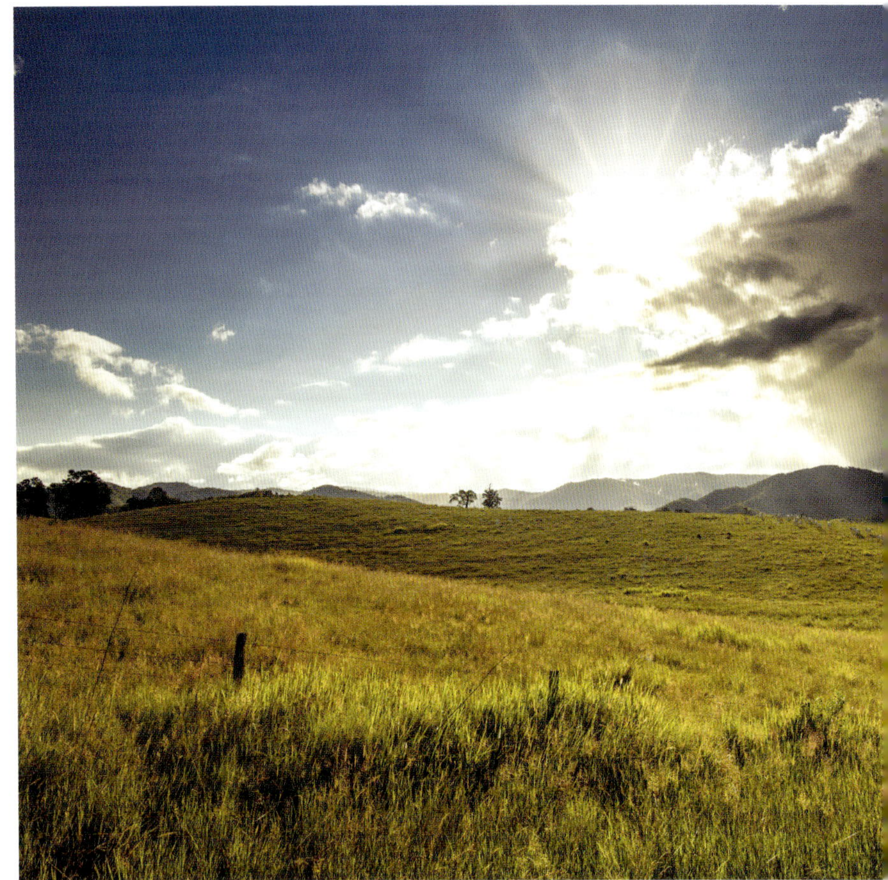

Driving through Curramore in Queensland, Australia

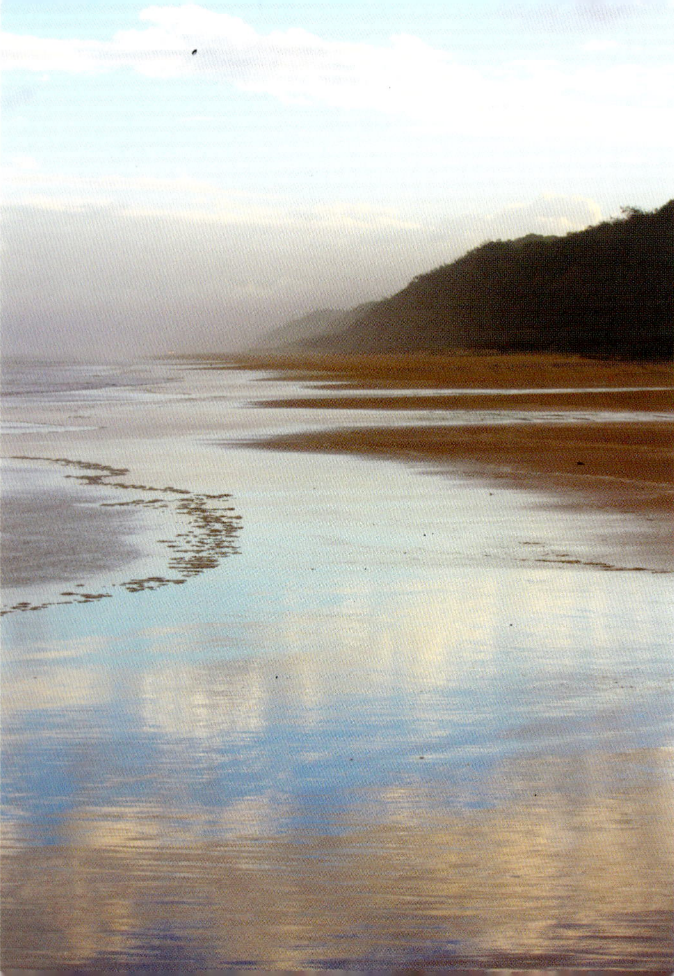

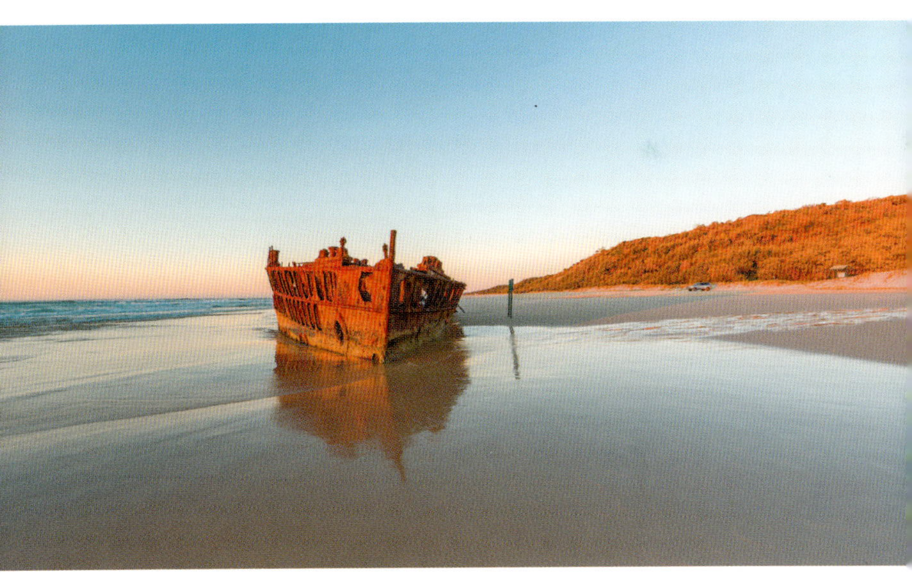

LEFT The beach is the road on Fraser Island in Queensland, Australia
ABOVE The remains of the SS *Maheno* on Fraser Island in Queensland, Australia

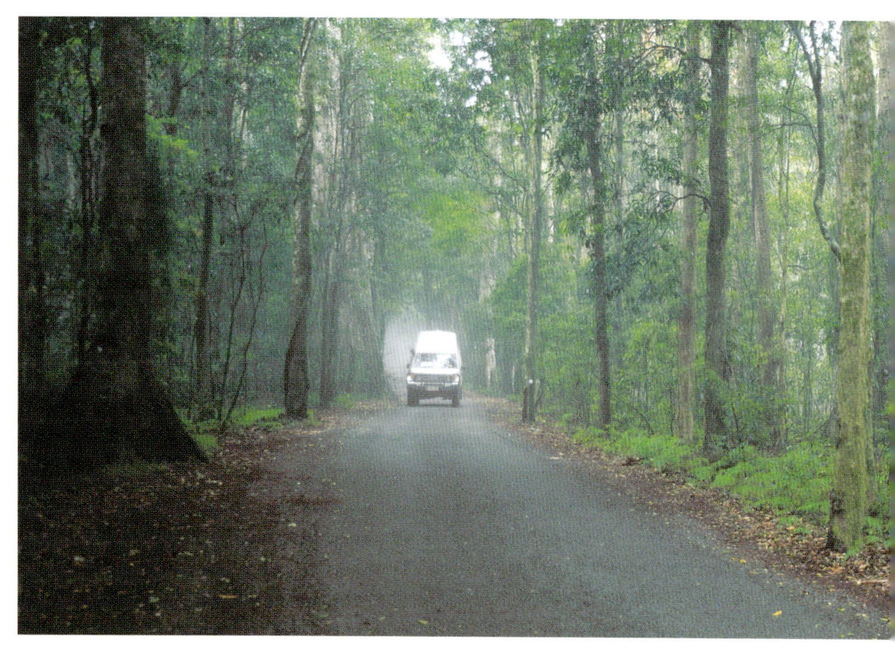

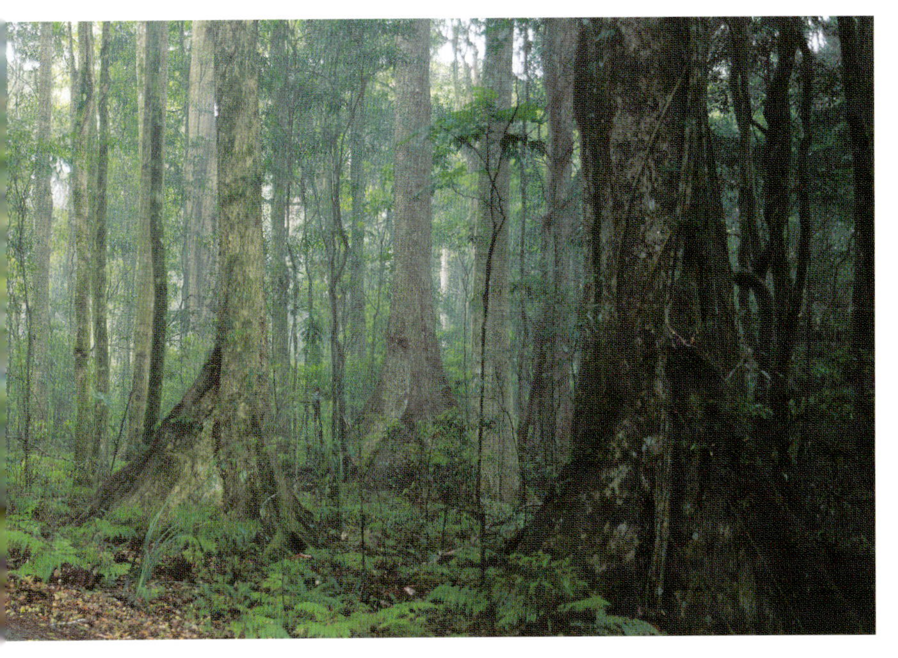

Winding through rainforest in Lamington National Park, Queensland, Australia

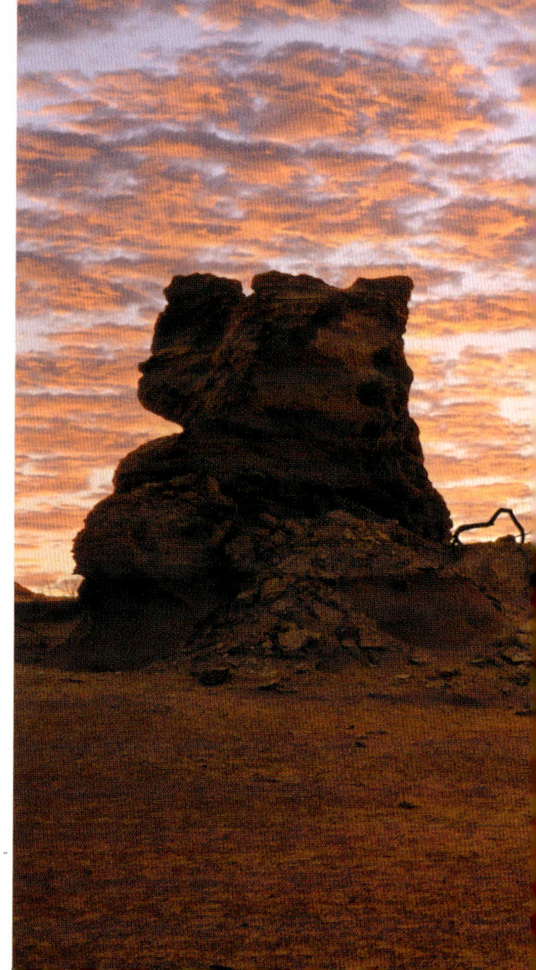

Sunset blooms over the Pinnacles in
Western Australia, Australia

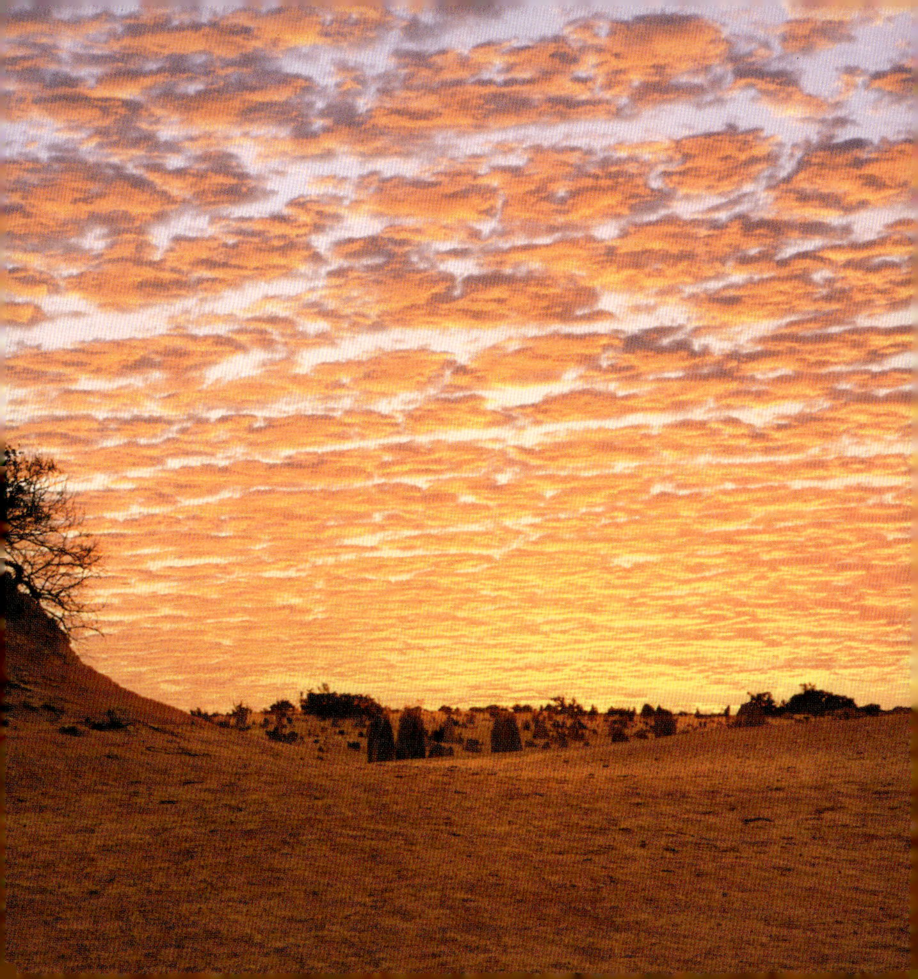

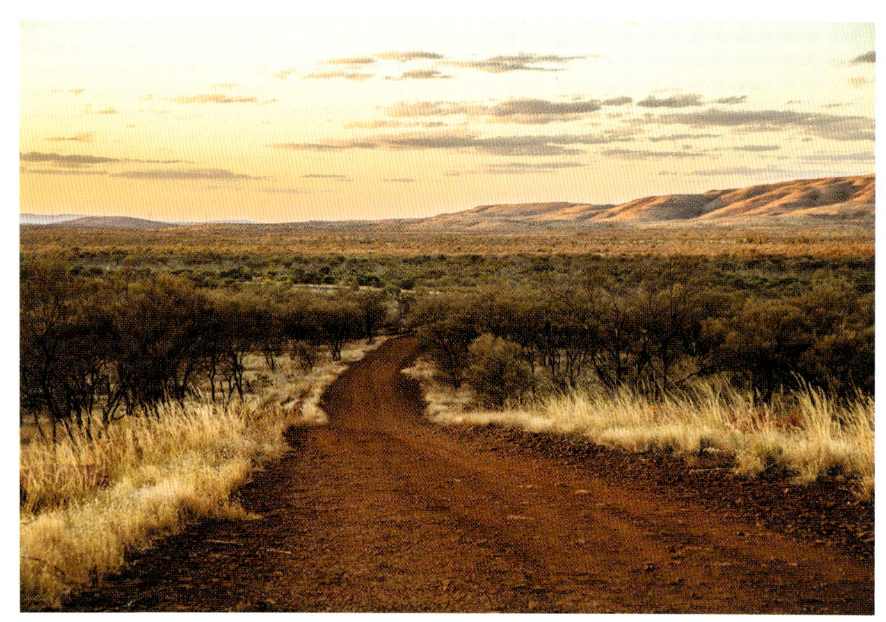

The road to Karijini National Park in Western Australia, Australia

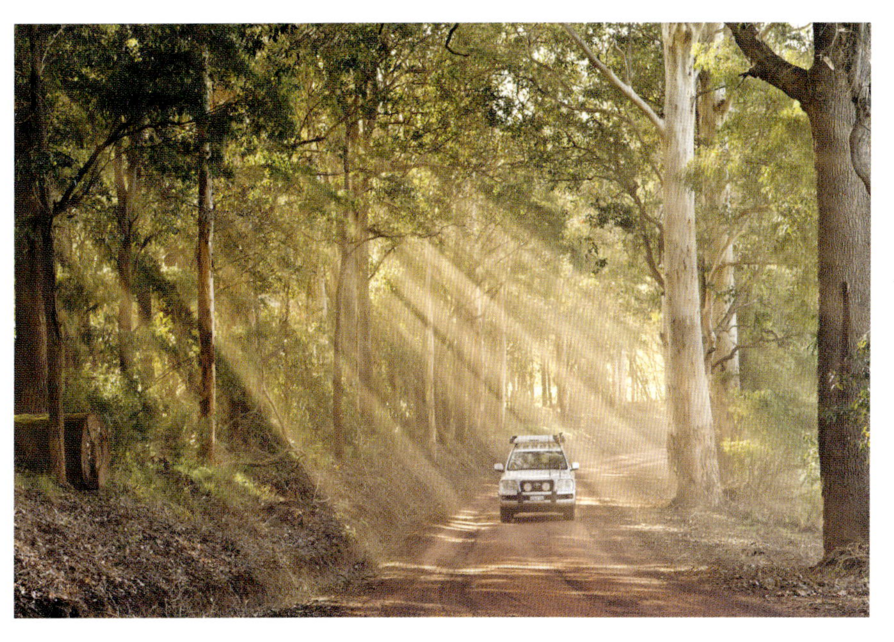

A dusty, forested road near Walpole in Western Australia, Australia

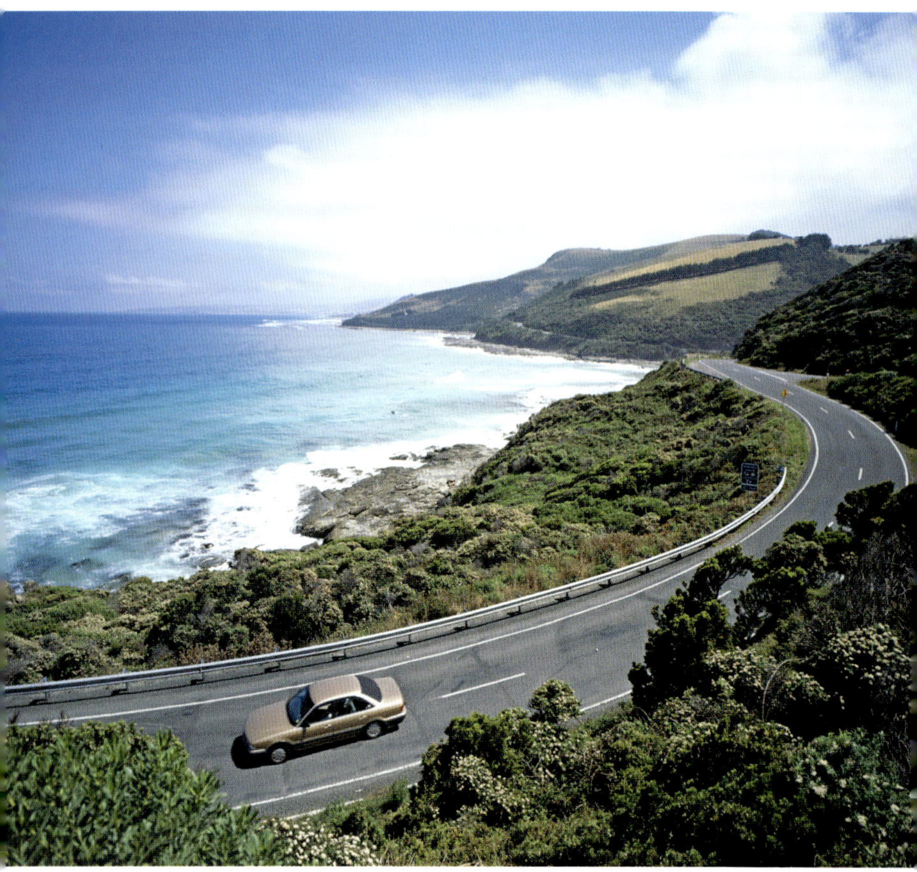

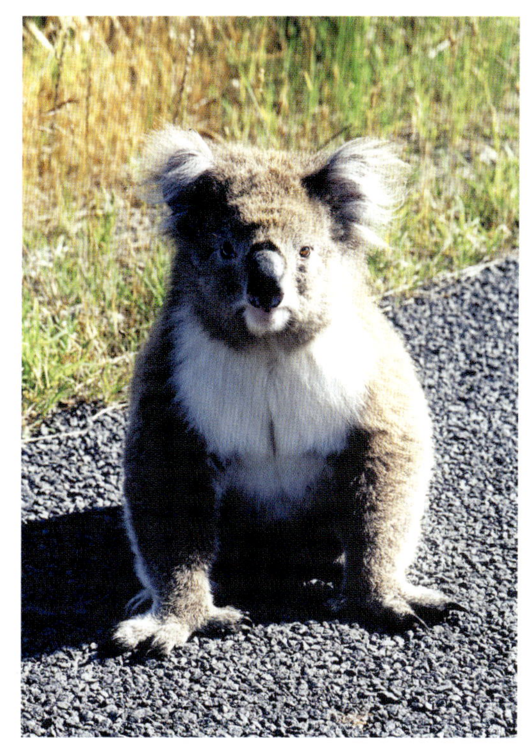

LEFT Driving along Great Ocean Road in Victoria, Australia
ABOVE A koala suns itself on Great Ocean Road in Victoria, Australia

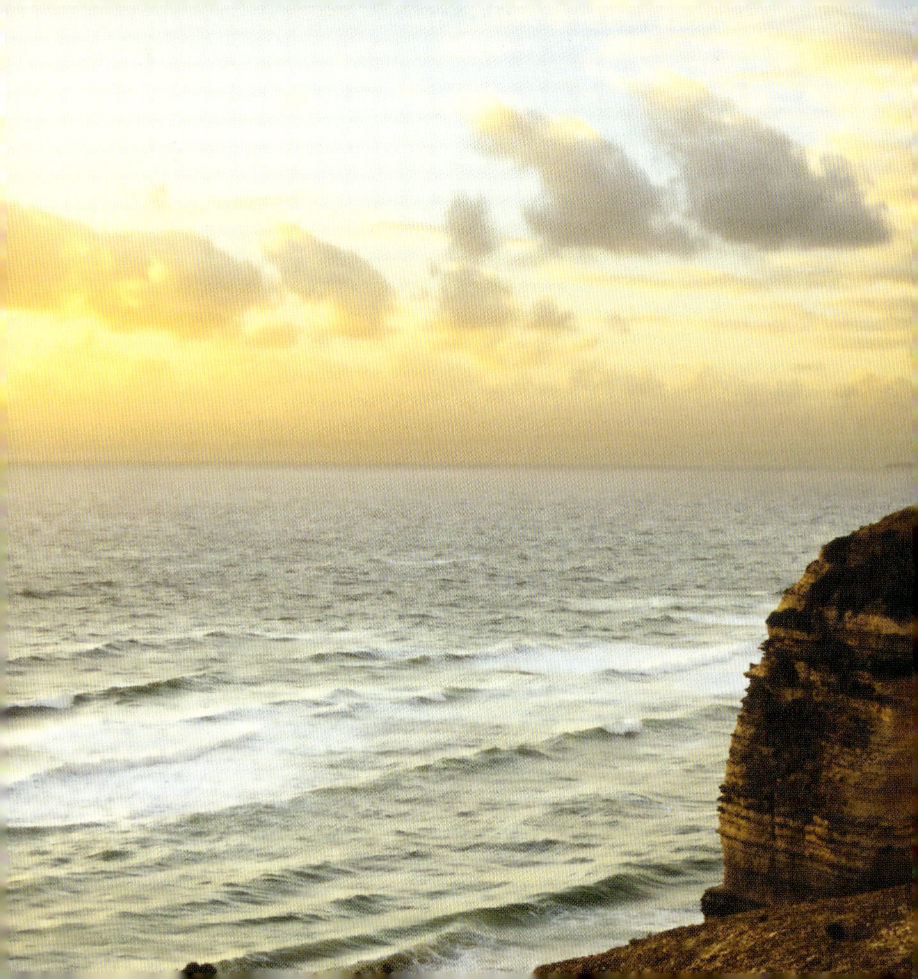

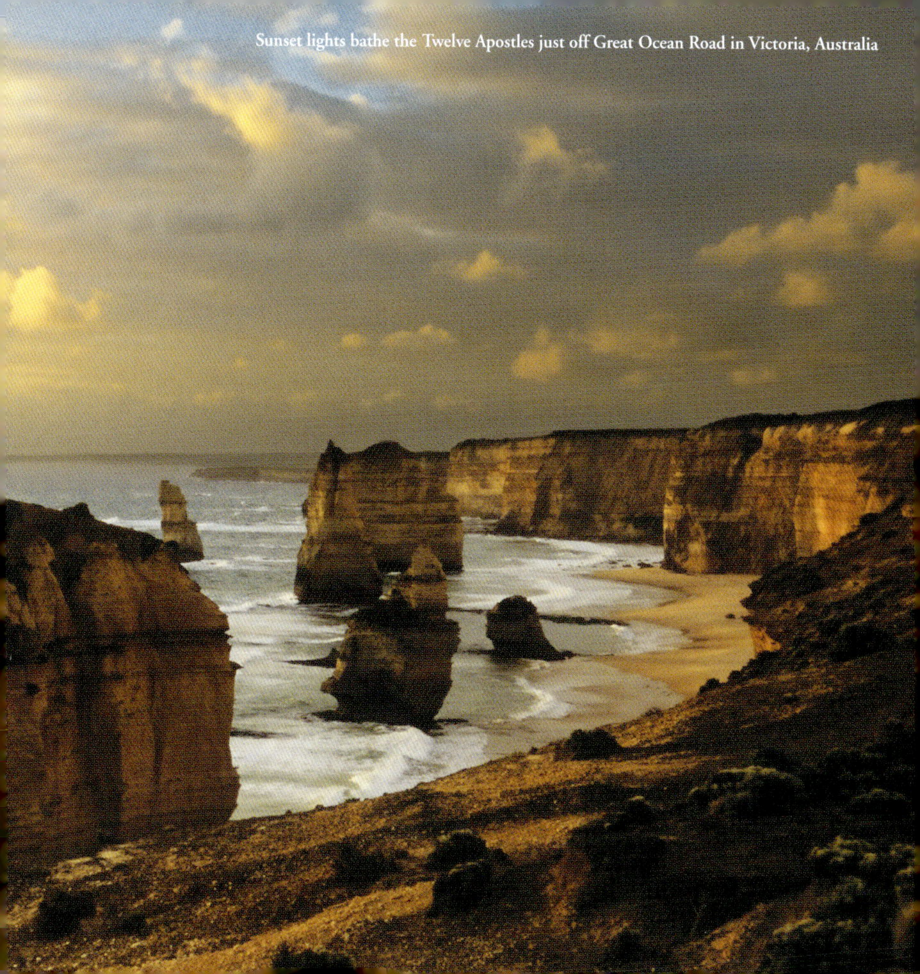

Sunset lights bathe the Twelve Apostles just off Great Ocean Road in Victoria, Australia

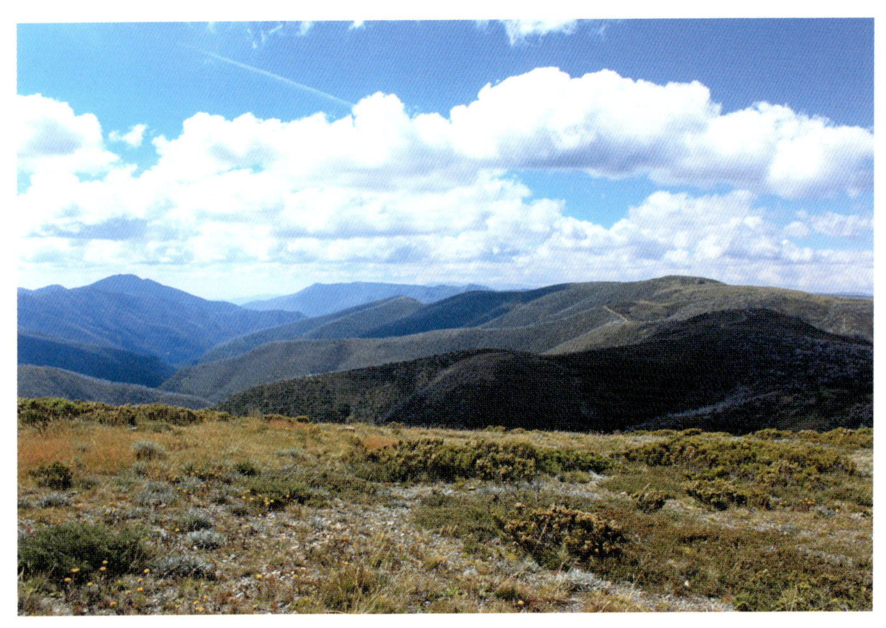

ABOVE The mountains of Alpine National Park as seen from Great Alpine Road in Victoria, Australia
RIGHT The mountainous Great Alpine Road running through the High Country in Victoria, Australia

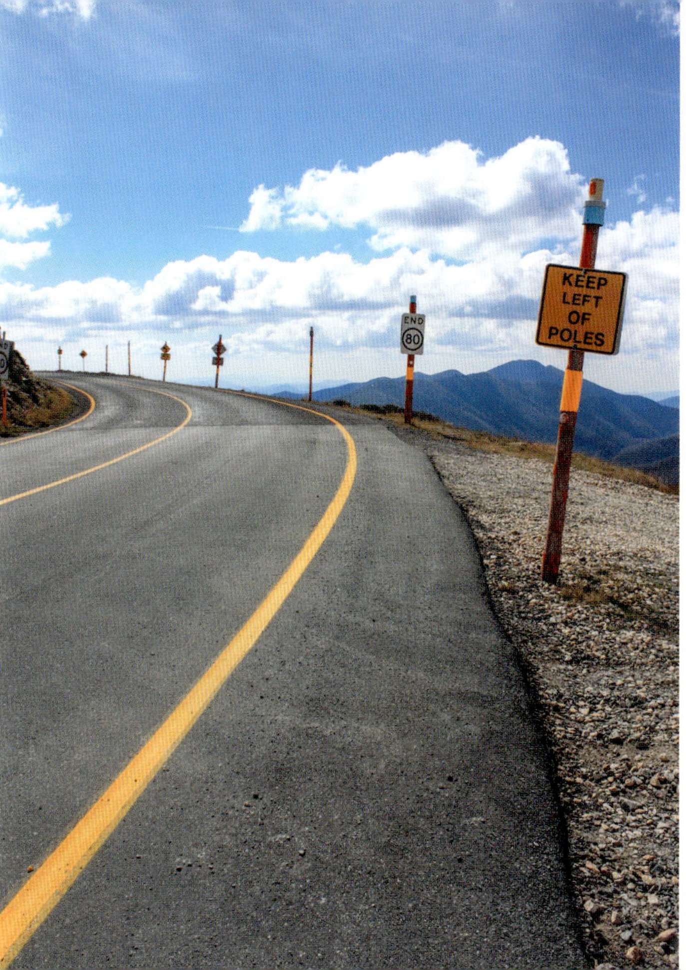
KEEP
LEFT
OF
POLES
END
80

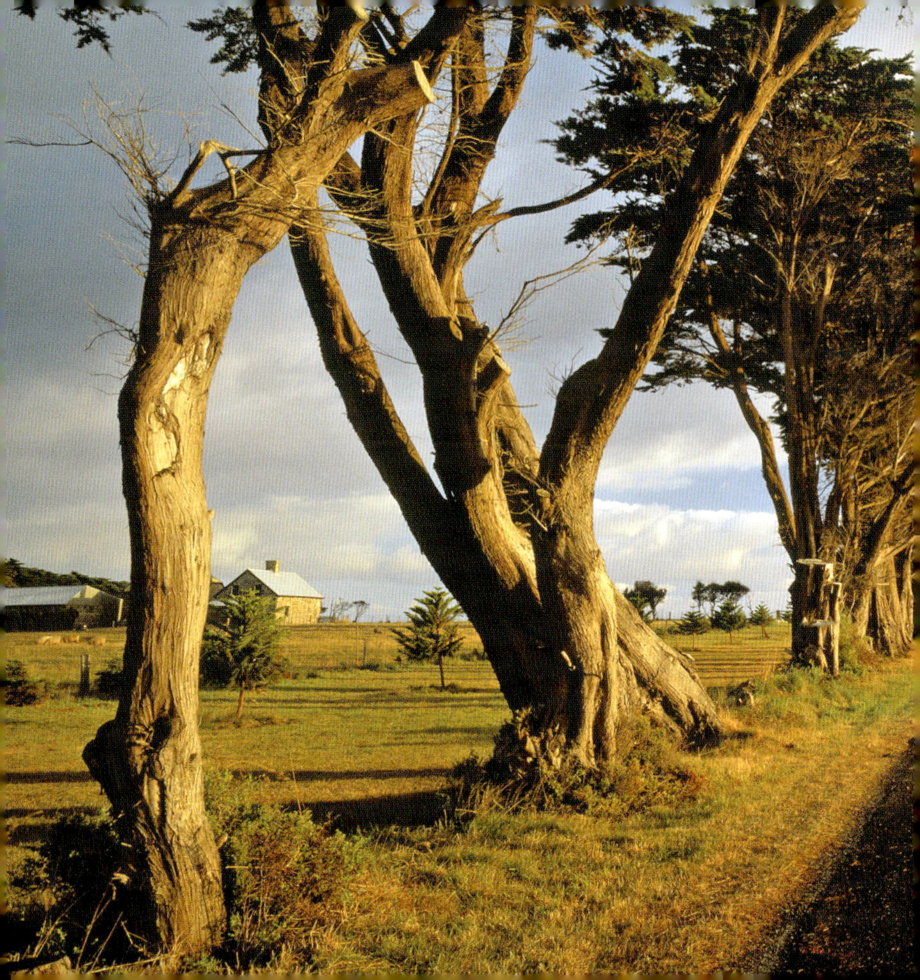

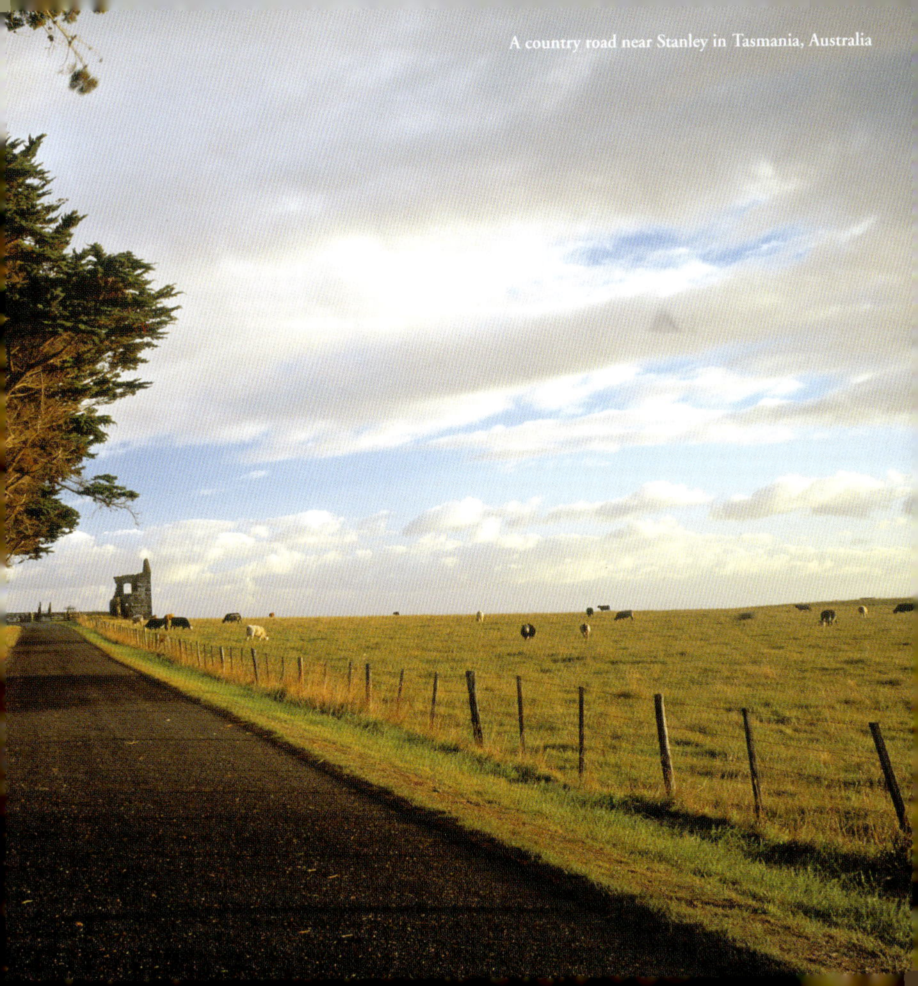
A country road near Stanley in Tasmania, Australia

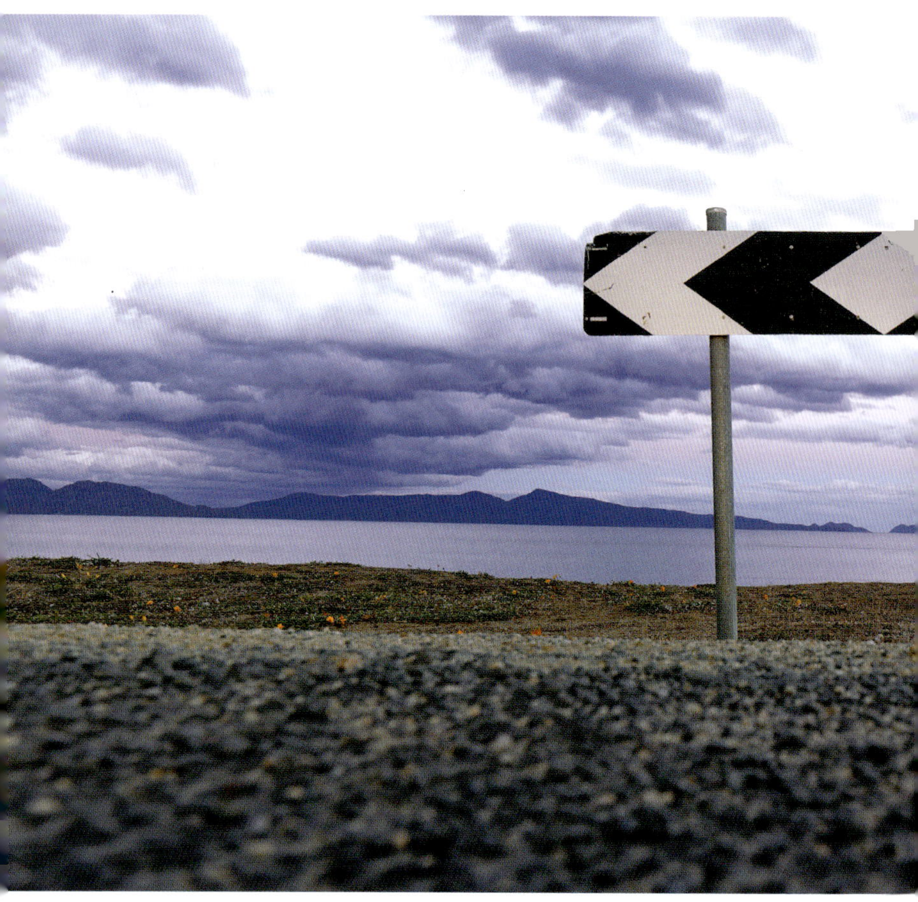

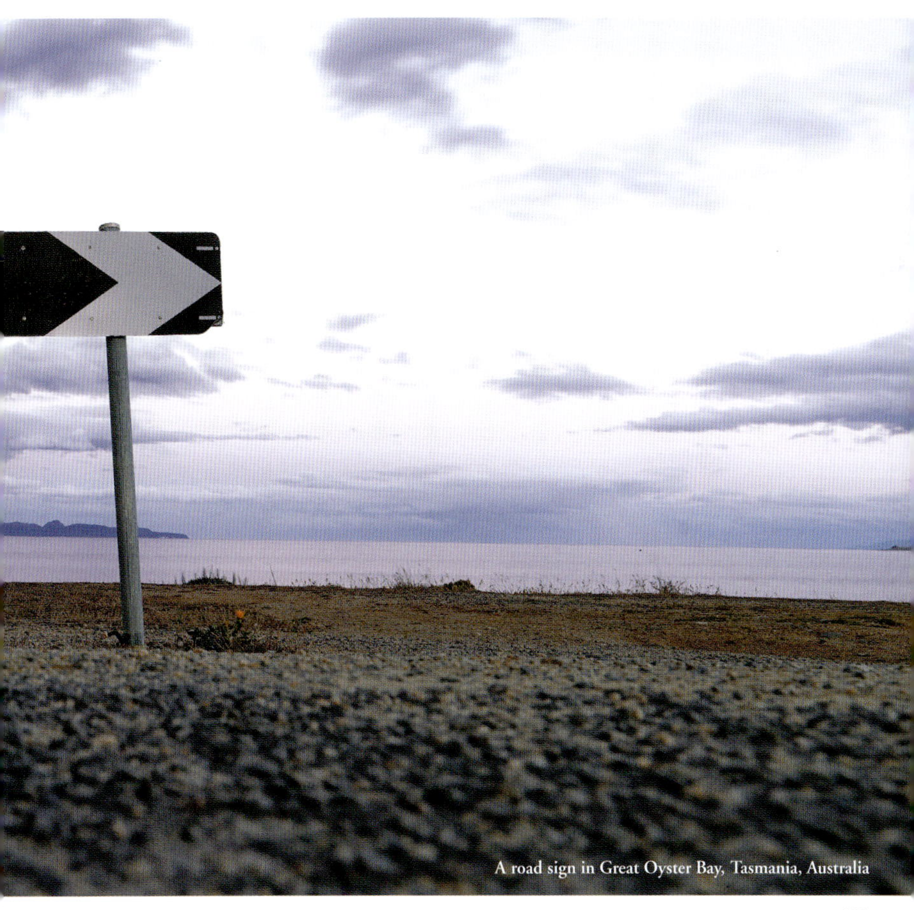
A road sign in Great Oyster Bay, Tasmania, Australia

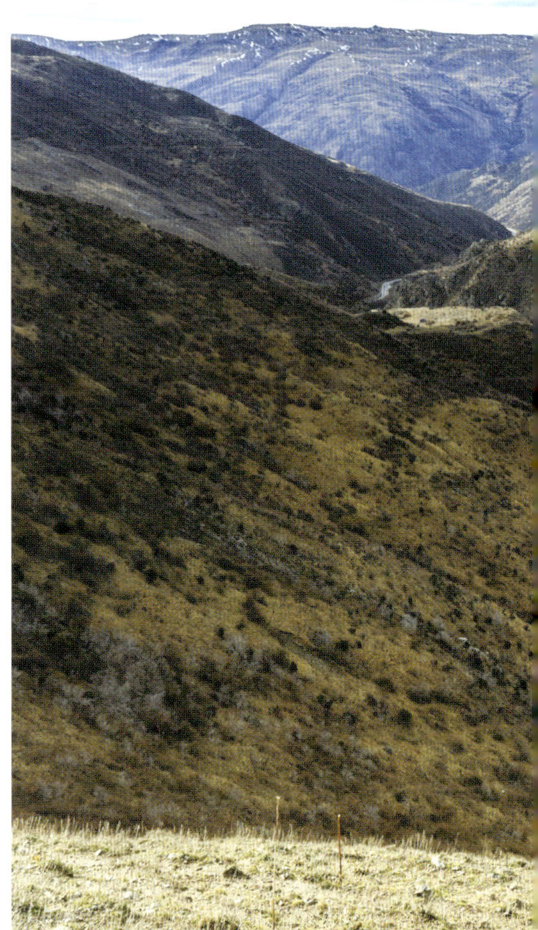

A road winds towards Queenstown on the
South Island, New Zealand

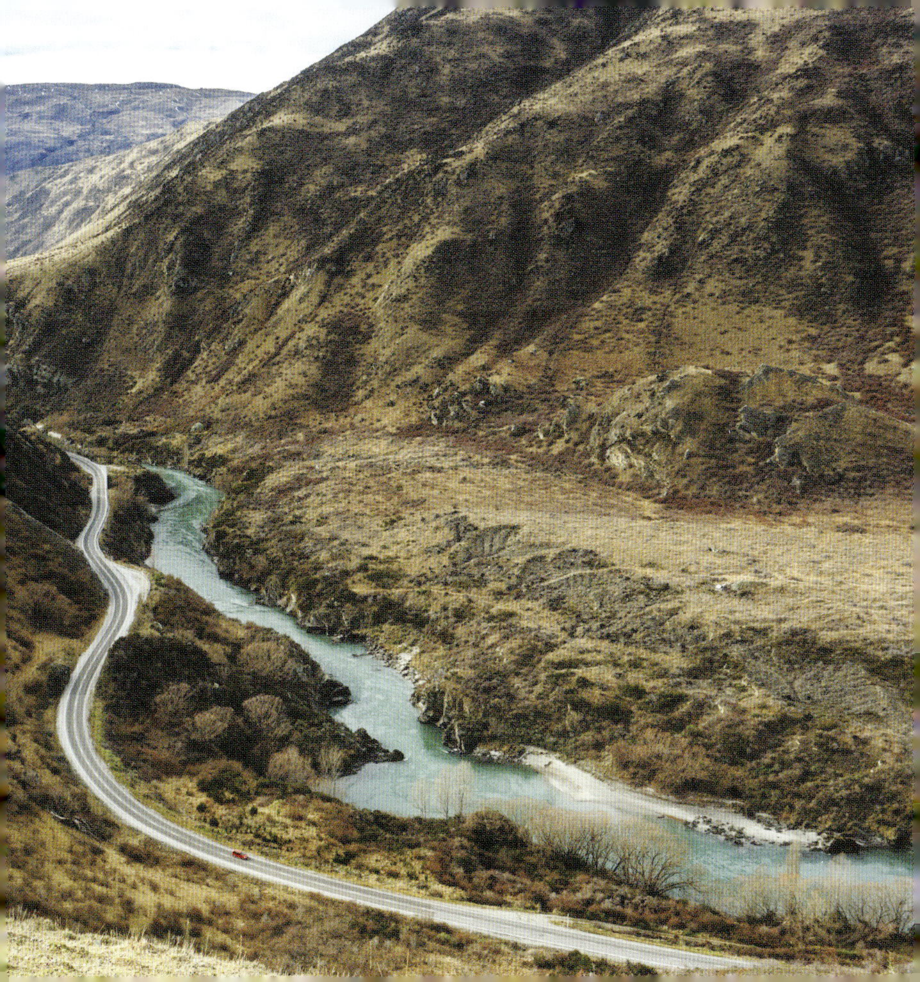

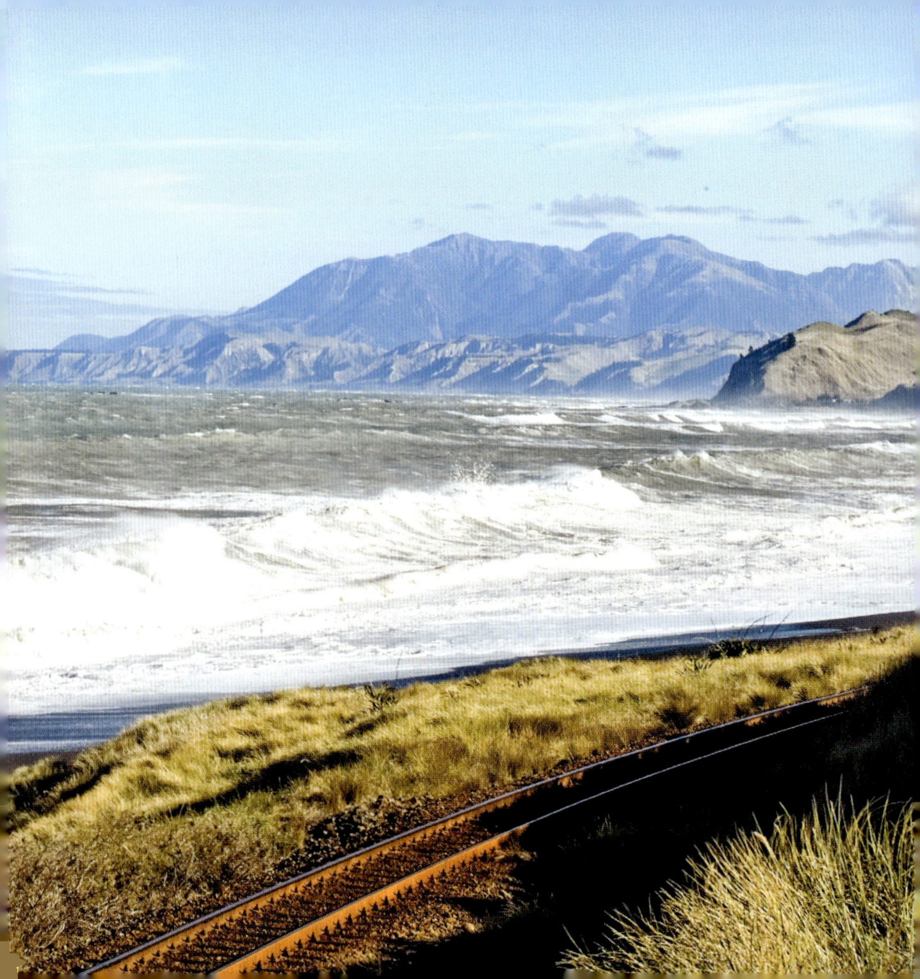

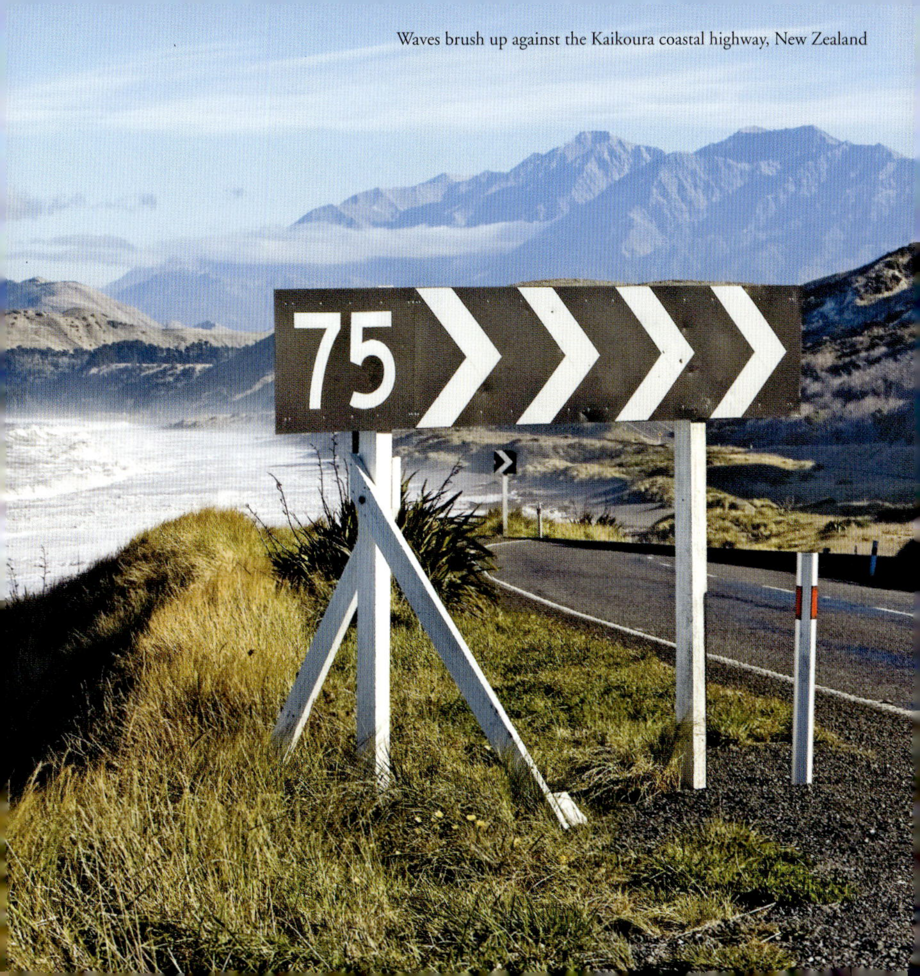

Waves brush up against the Kaikoura coastal highway, New Zealand

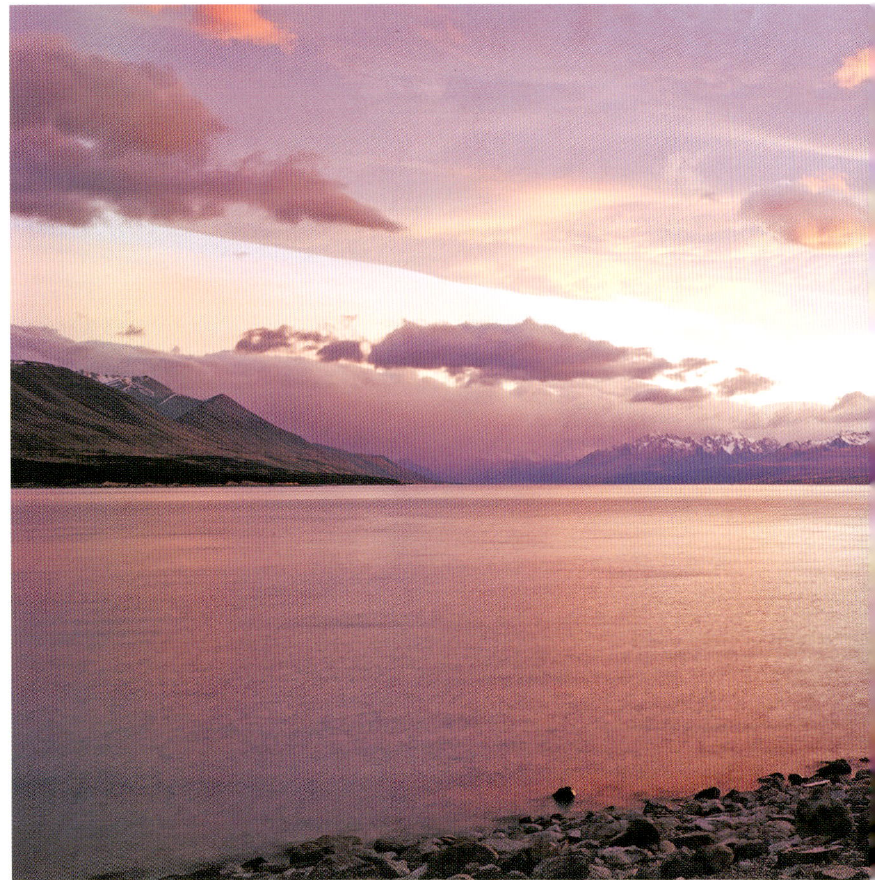

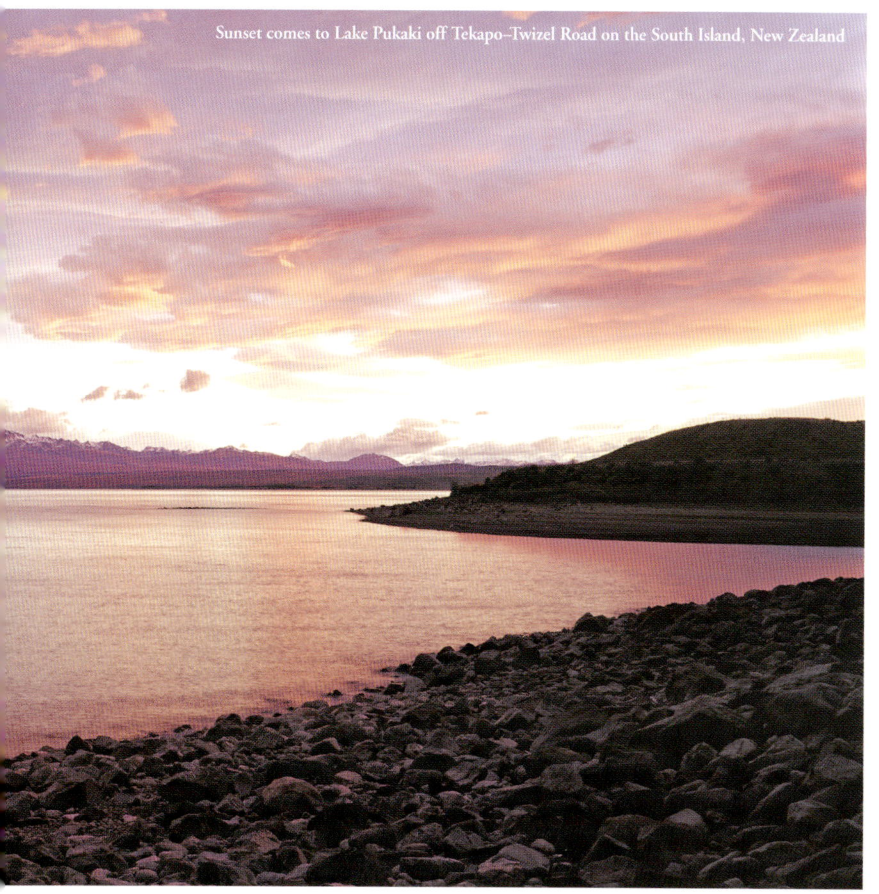

Sunset comes to Lake Pukaki off Tekapo–Twizel Road on the South Island, New Zealand

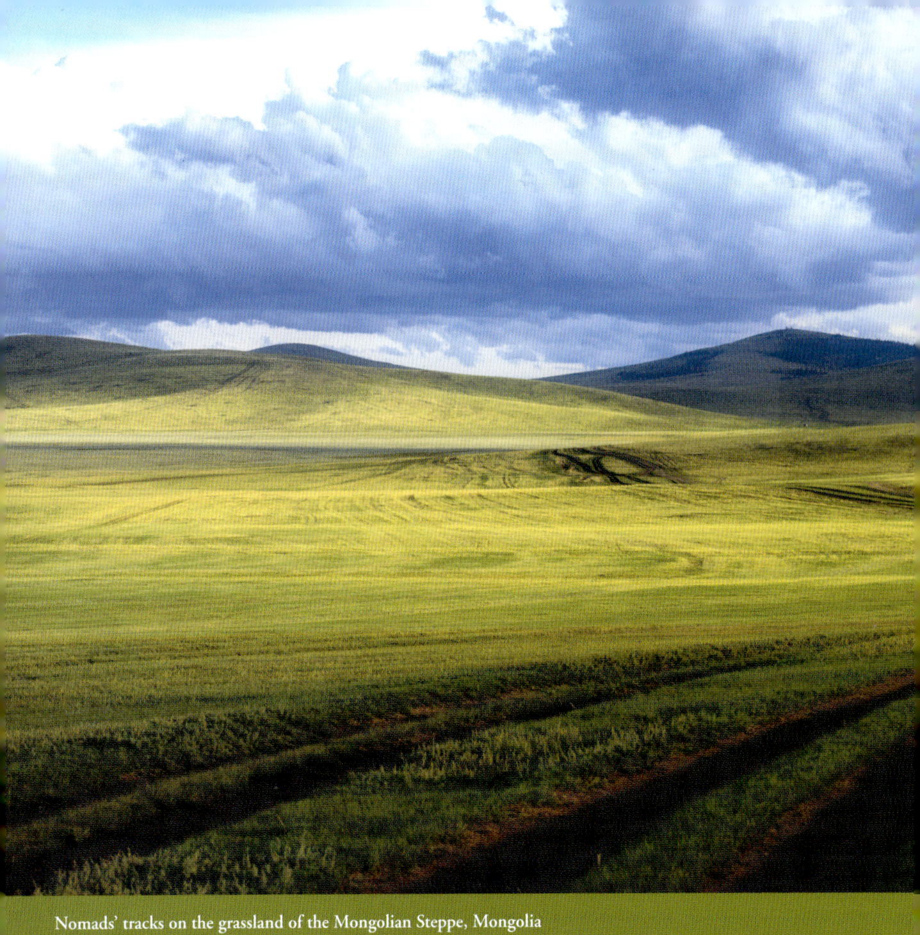

Nomads' tracks on the grassland of the Mongolian Steppe, Mongolia

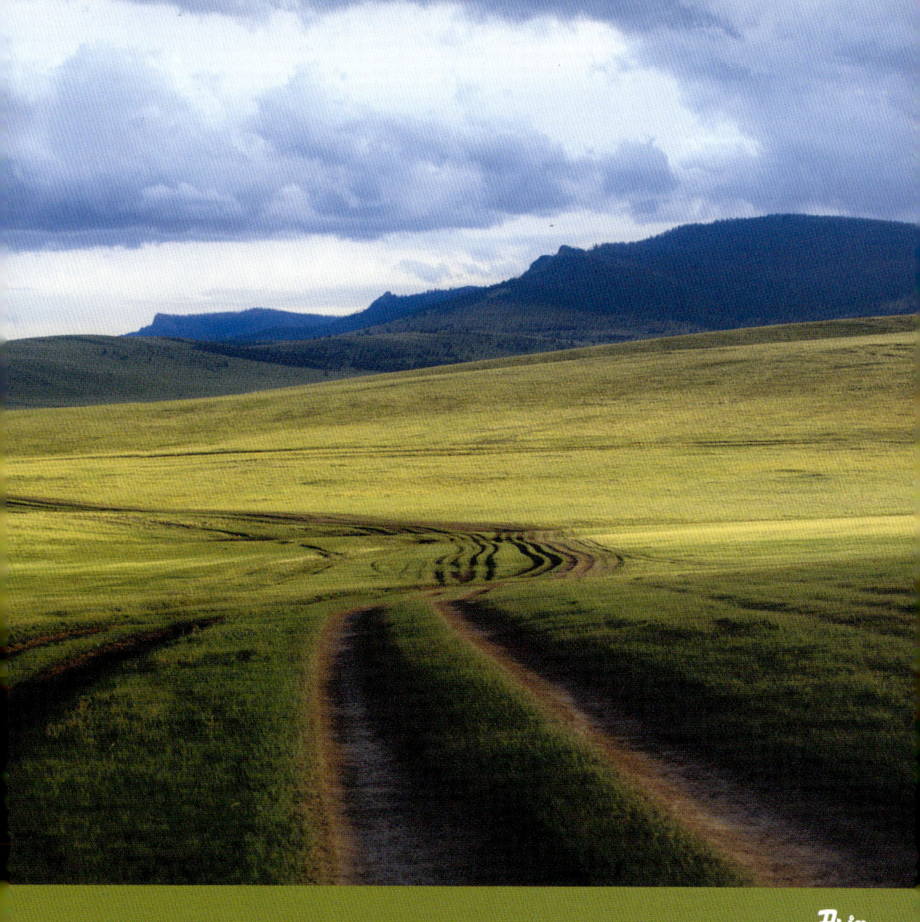
Asia

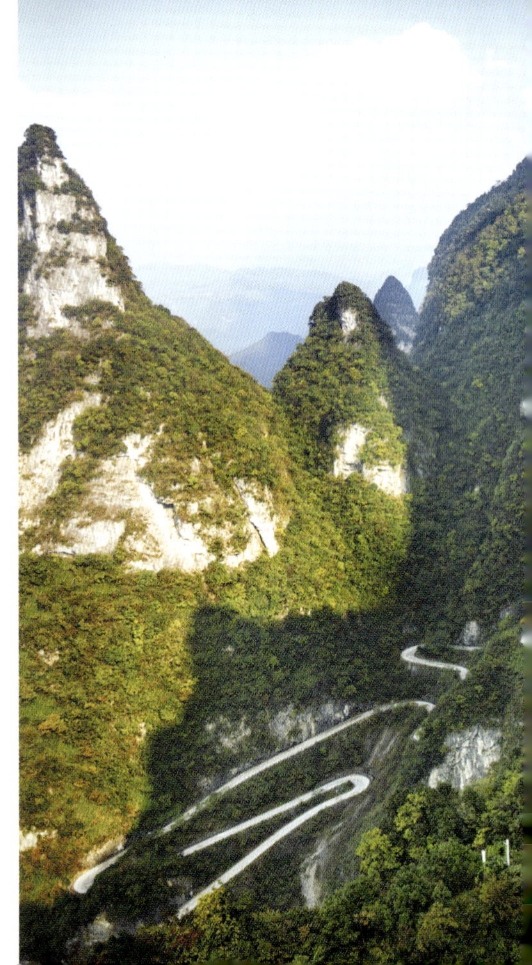

This serpentine road winds through Tianmen
Mountain National Park, China

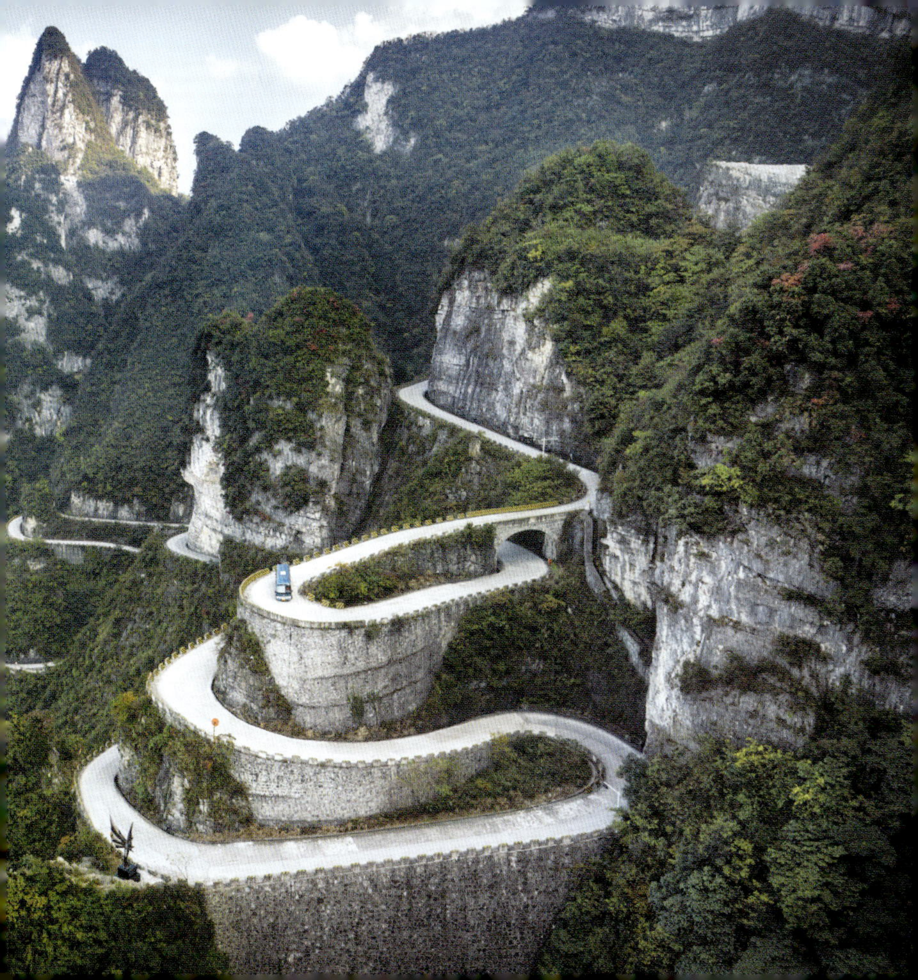

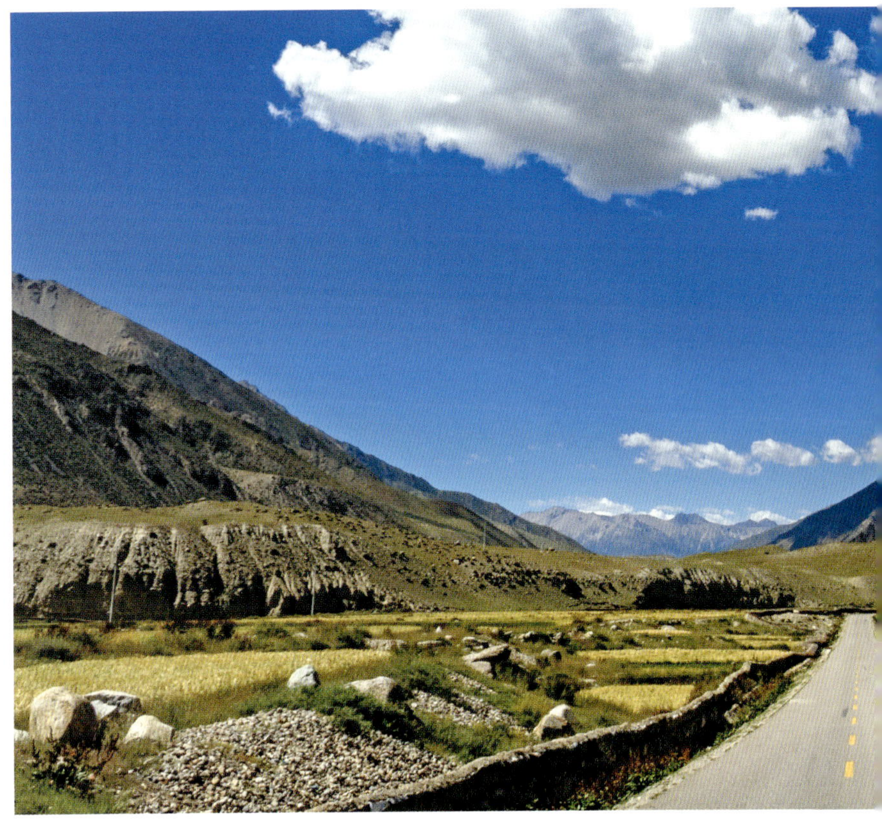

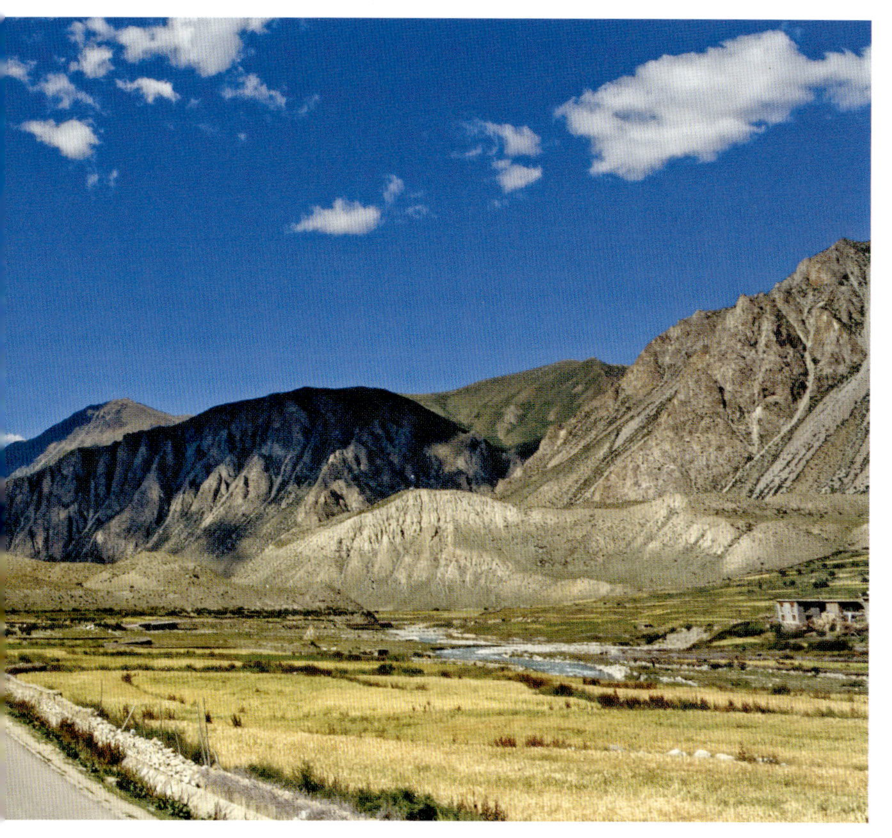

Long stretch of China National Highway 318, China

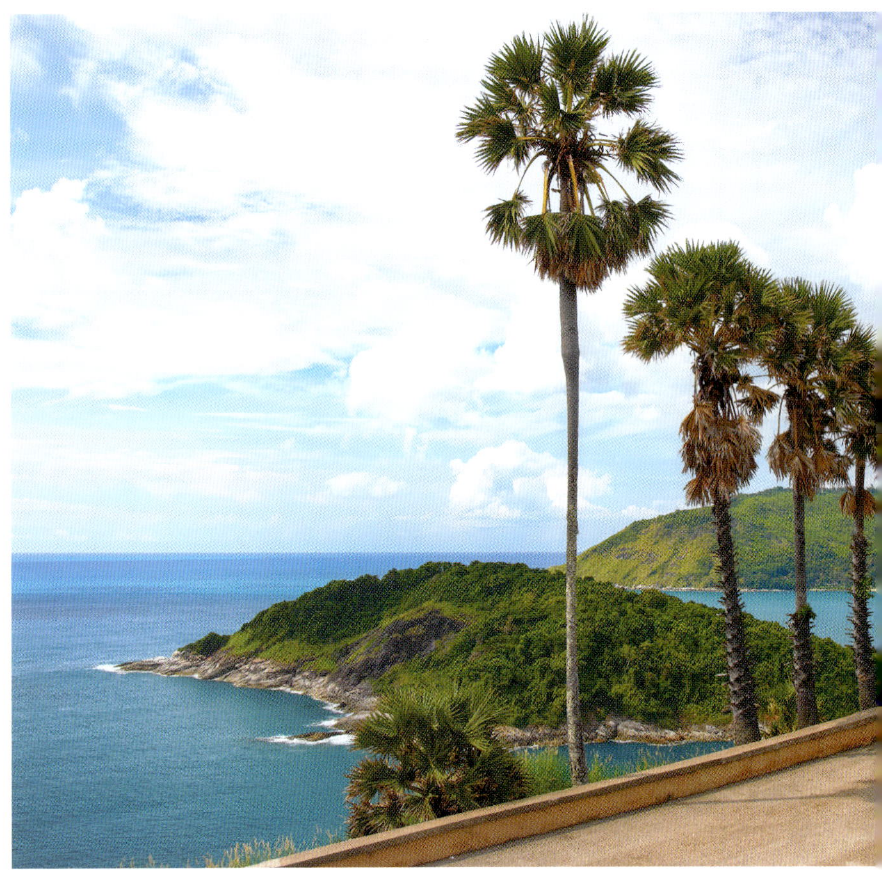

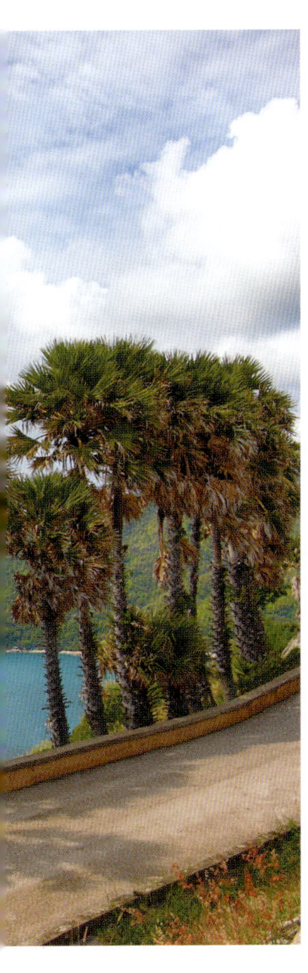

Promthep Cape on the island of Phuket, Thailand

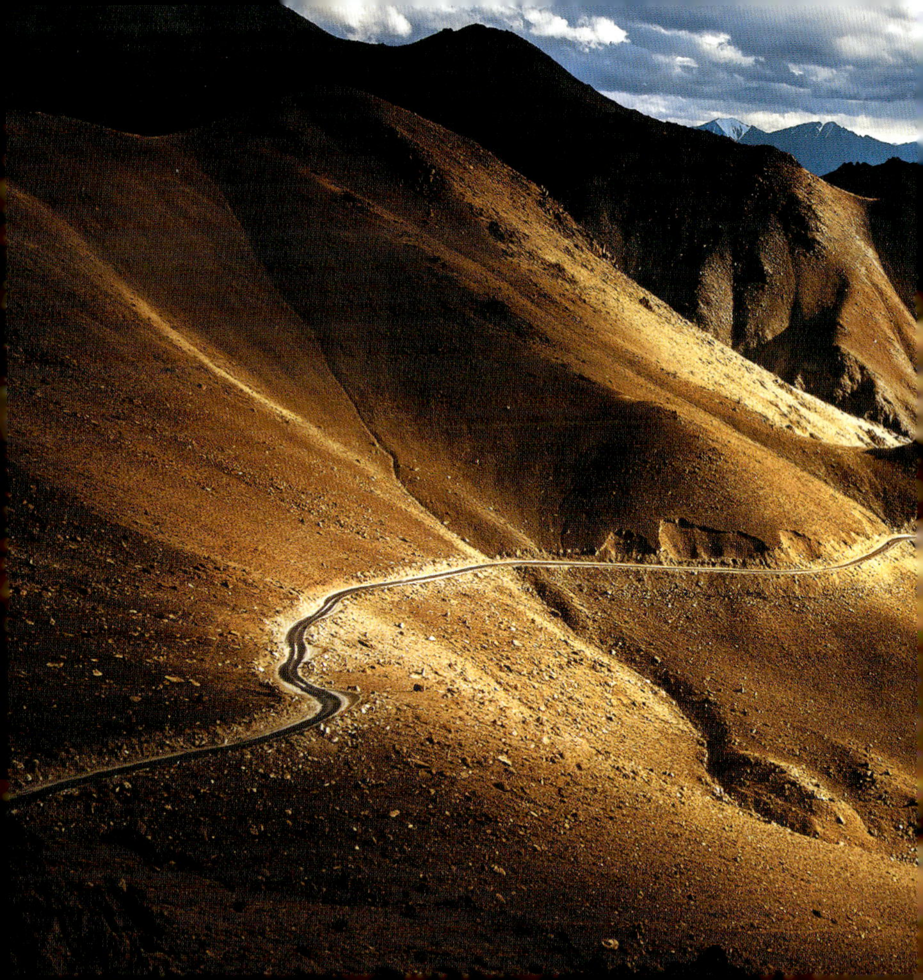

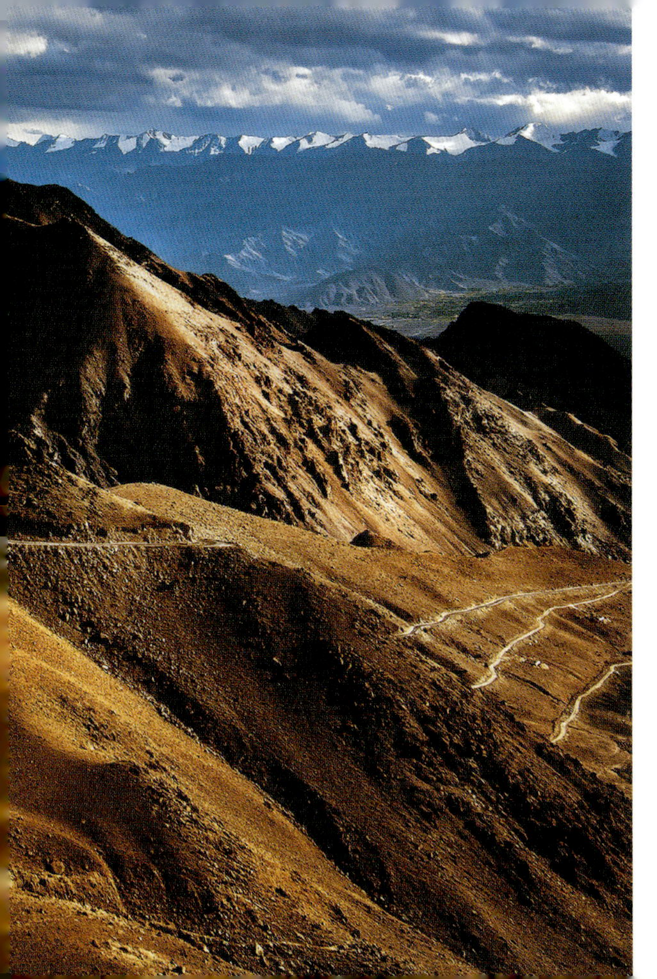

A winding road through
mountains in Ladakh, India

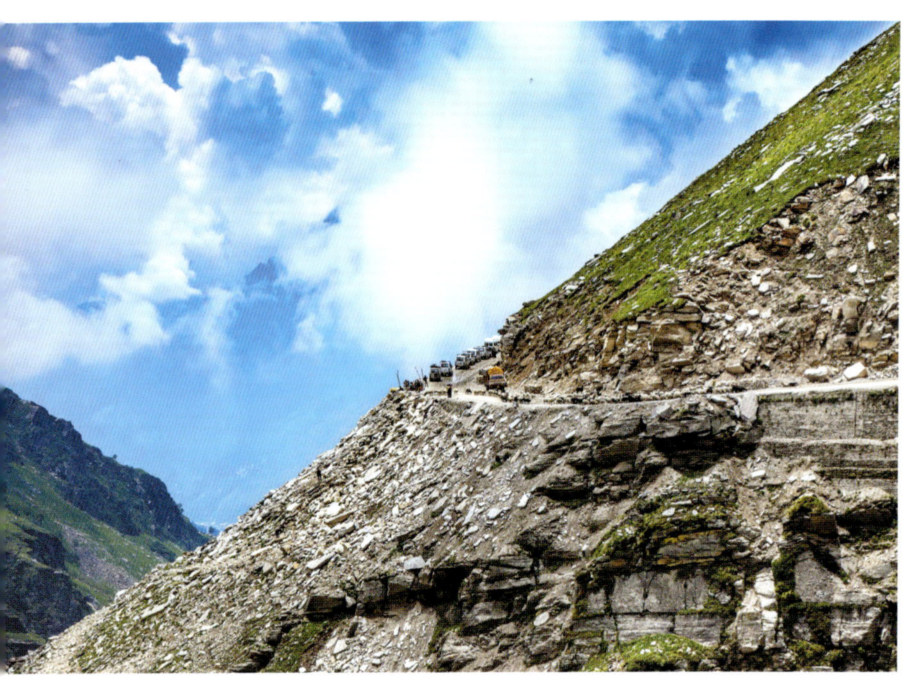

Traffic jam on the Rohtang Pass in Himachal Pradesh, India

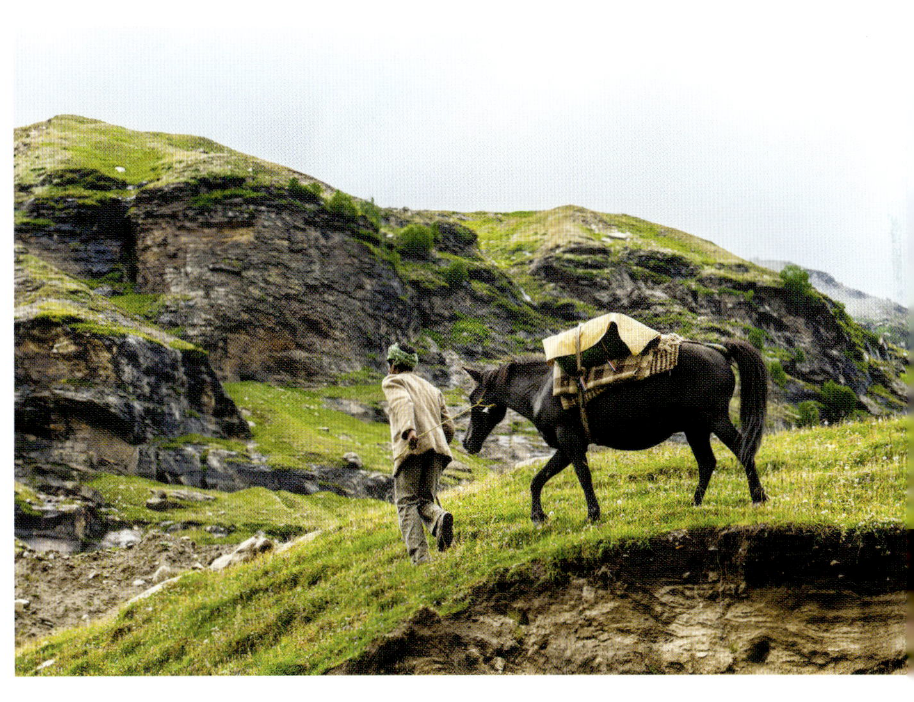

A man walks beside a road through lofty Rohtang Pass in Himachal Pradesh, India

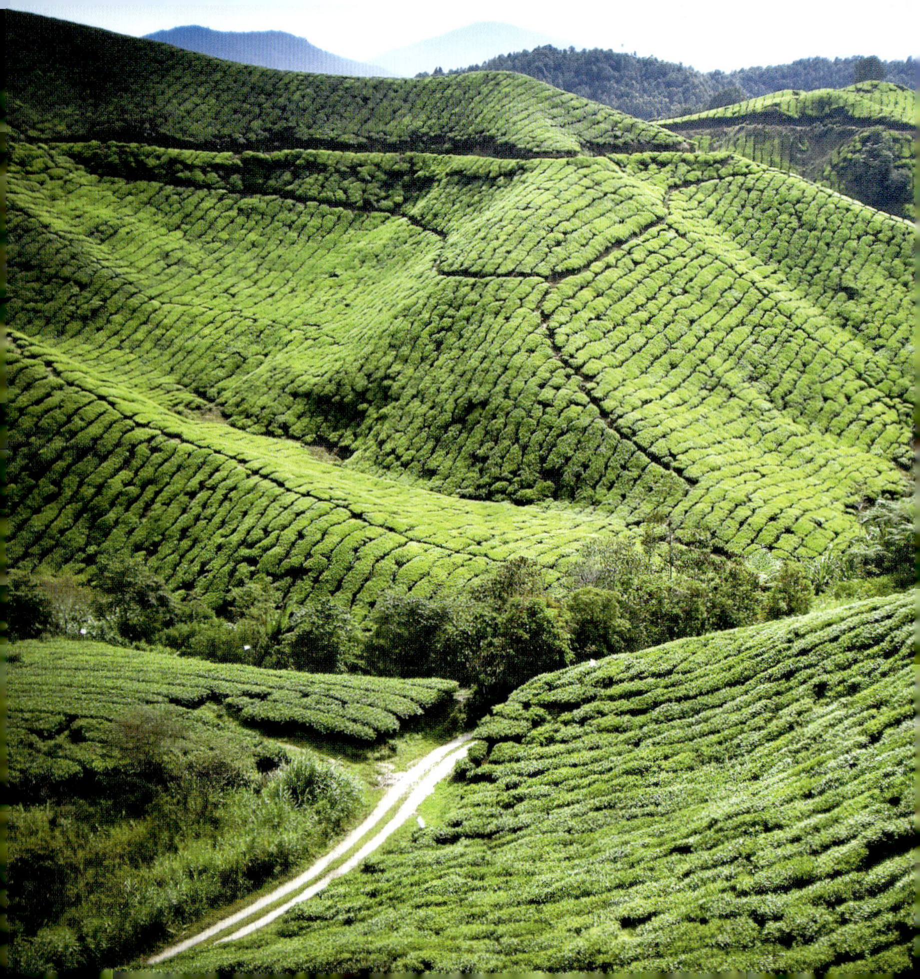

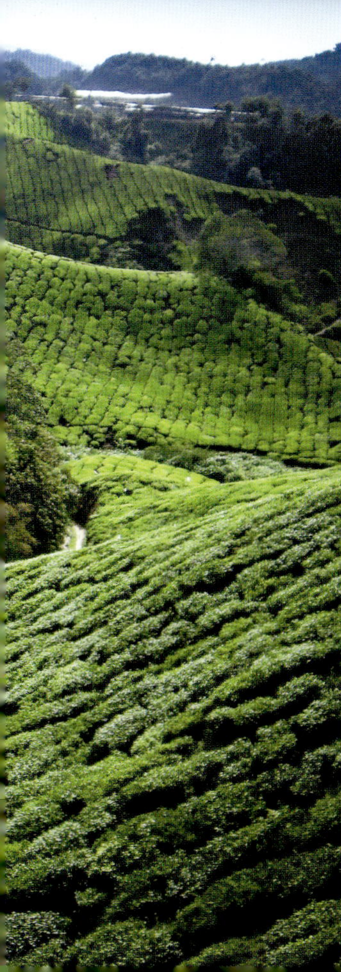

Plantation and tea house along the main road in Kampung Kuala Terla,
between Tringkap and Kampung Raja, Malaysia

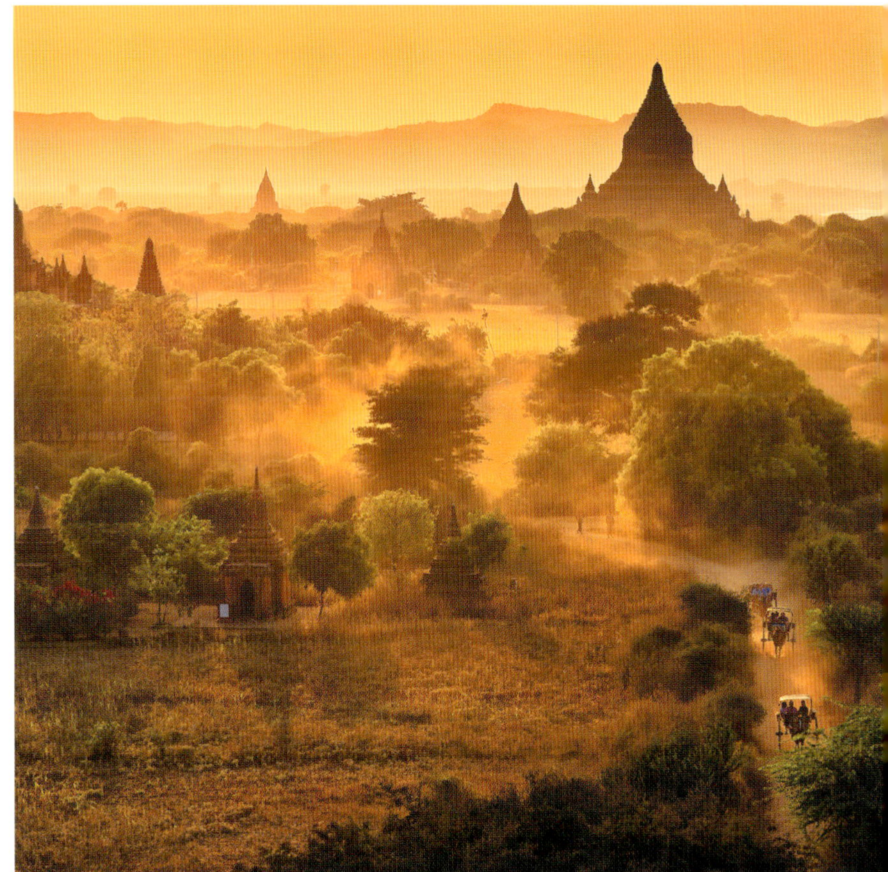

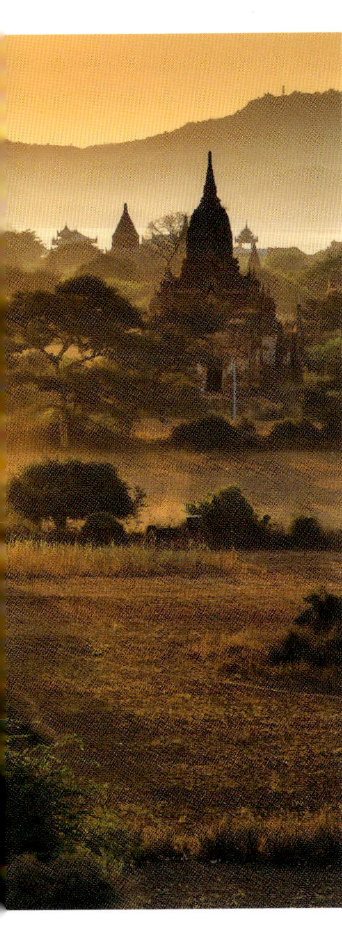

The dusty road into the ancient city of Bagan, Mayanmar (Burma)

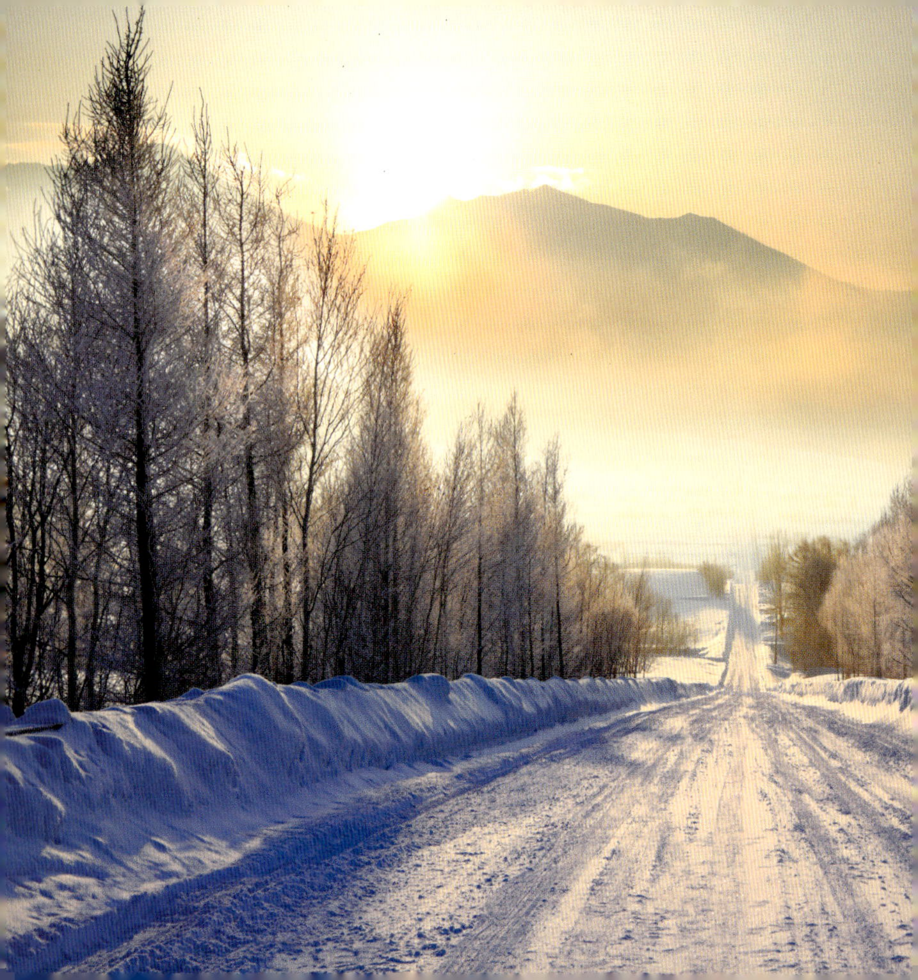

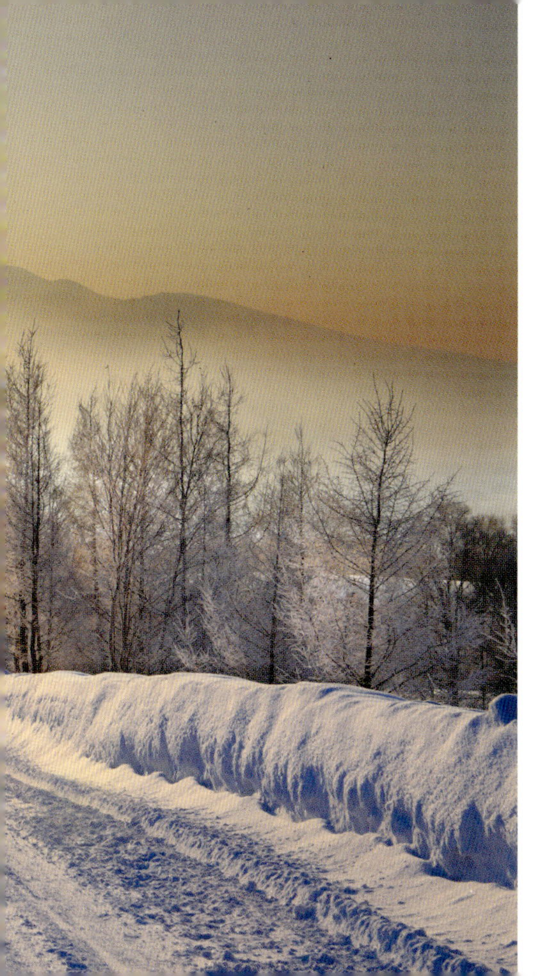

Snow-covered road towards Tokachidake
mountain range, Japan

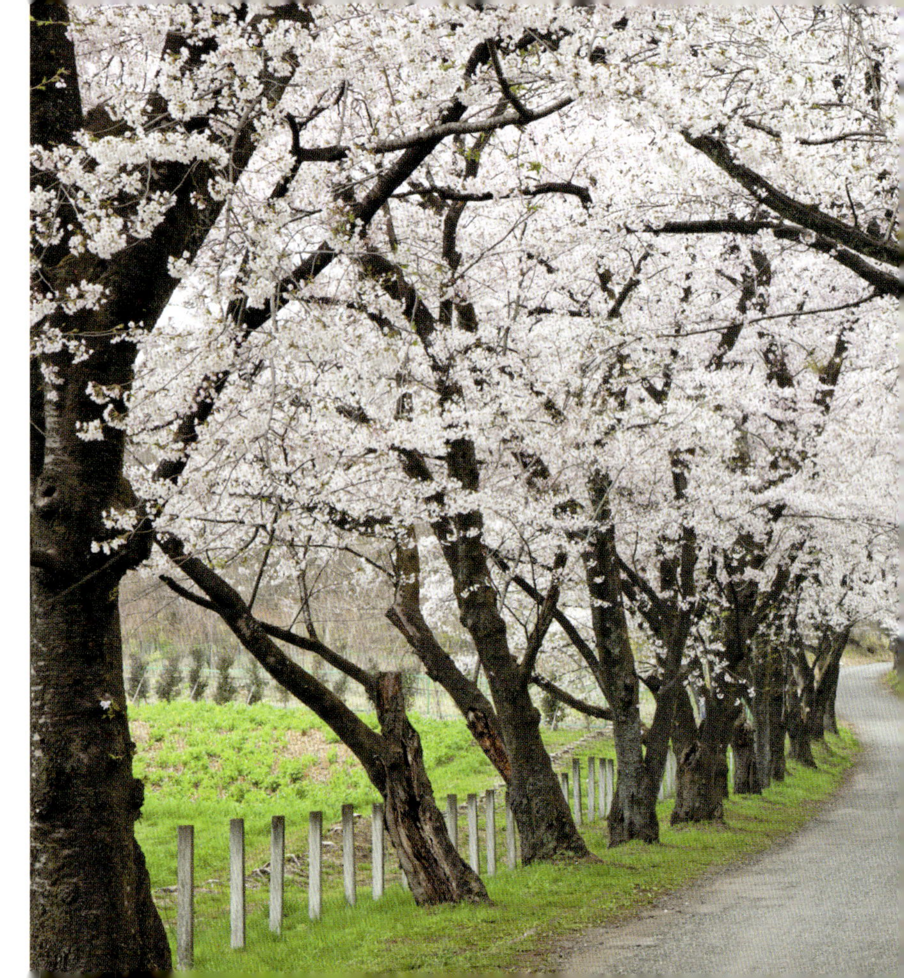

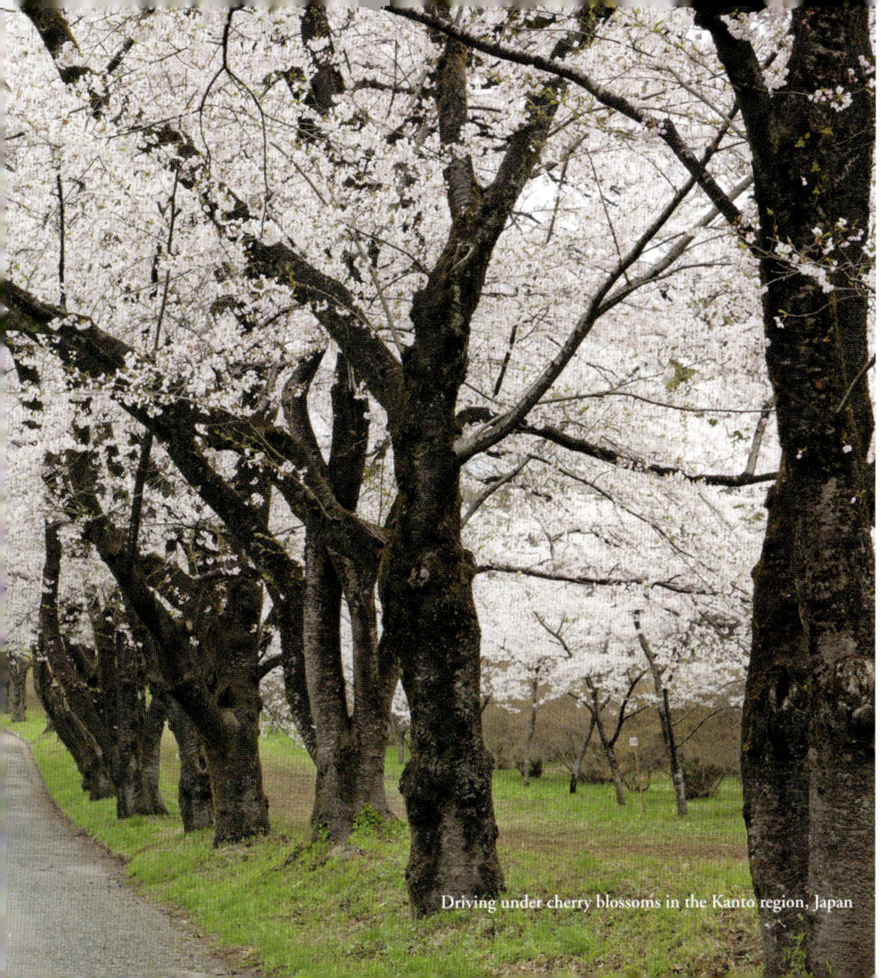

Driving under cherry blossoms in the Kanto region, Japan

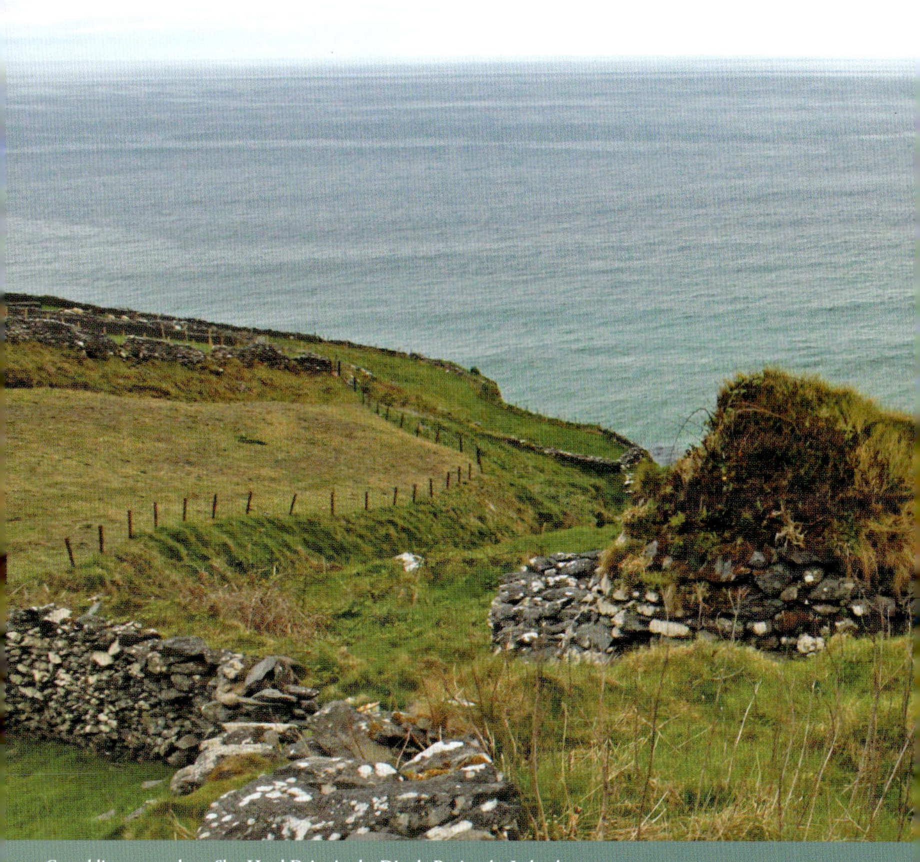

Crumbling stone along Slea Head Drive in the Dingle Peninsula, Ireland

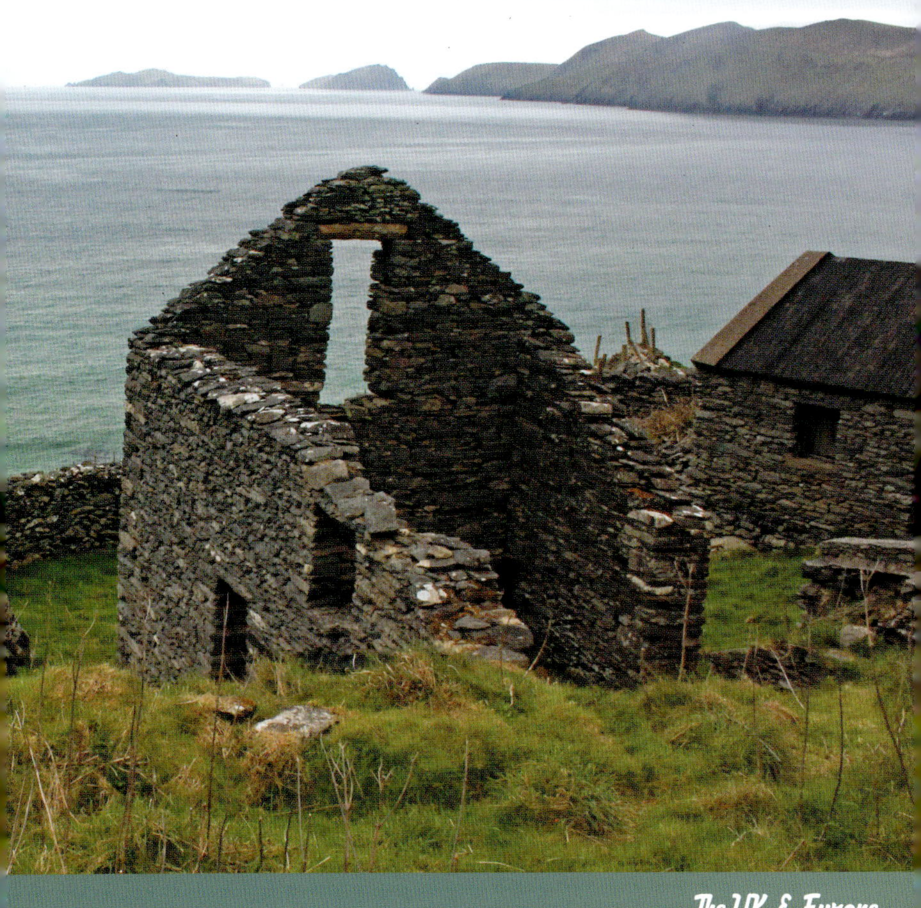
The UK & Europe

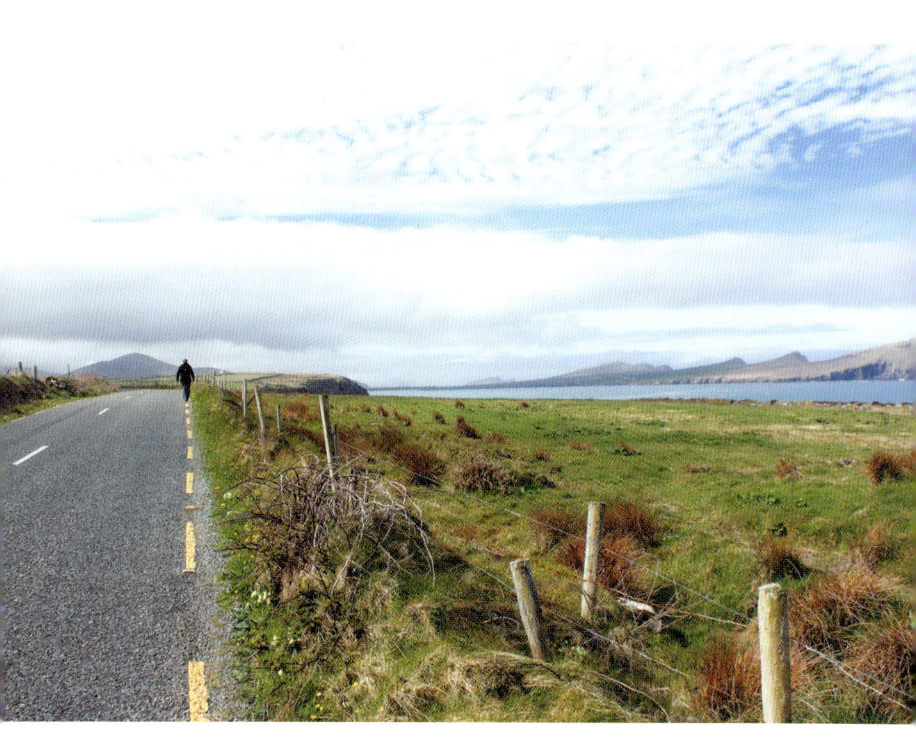

Cliffside road through Dingle in County Kerry, Ireland

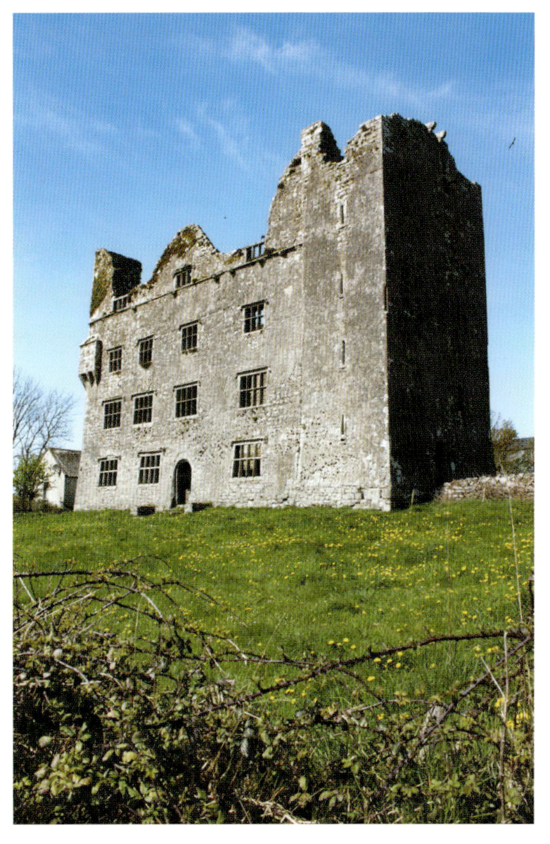

Old roadside castle in the Burren, Ireland

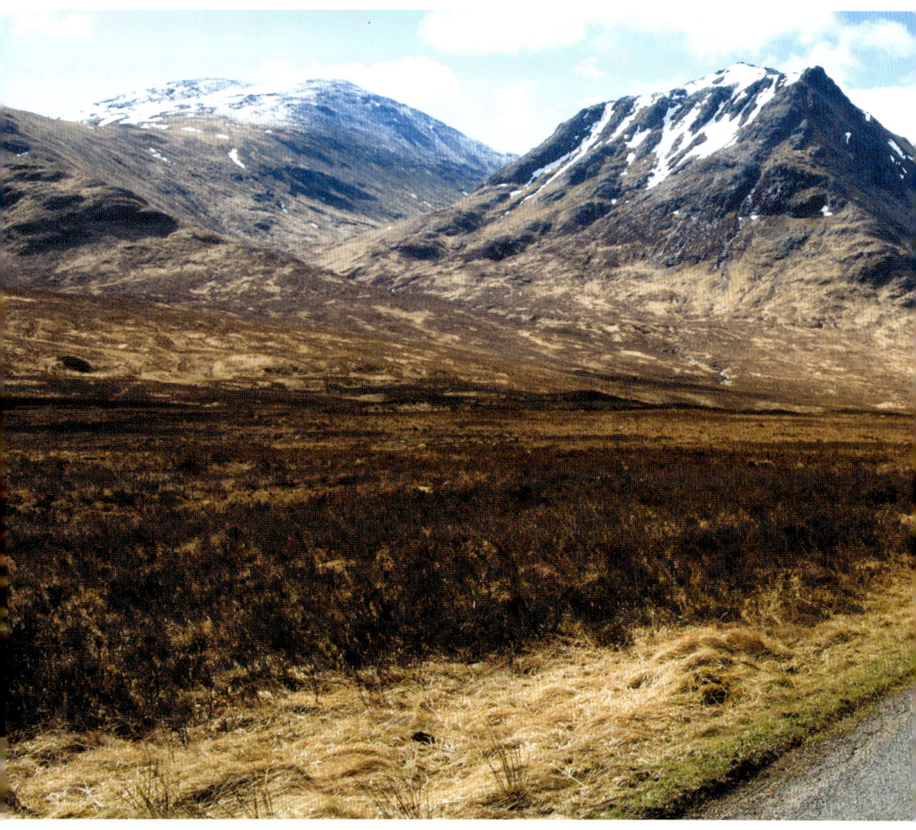

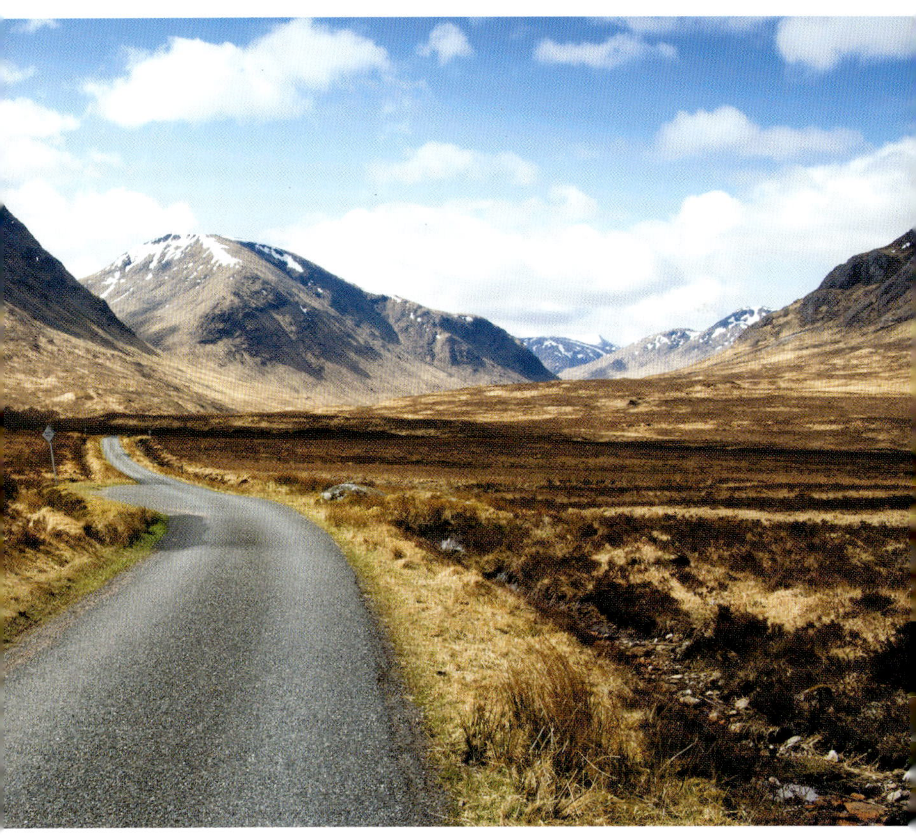

Cuillin mountains on the Isle of Skye in the Hebrides, Scotland, UK

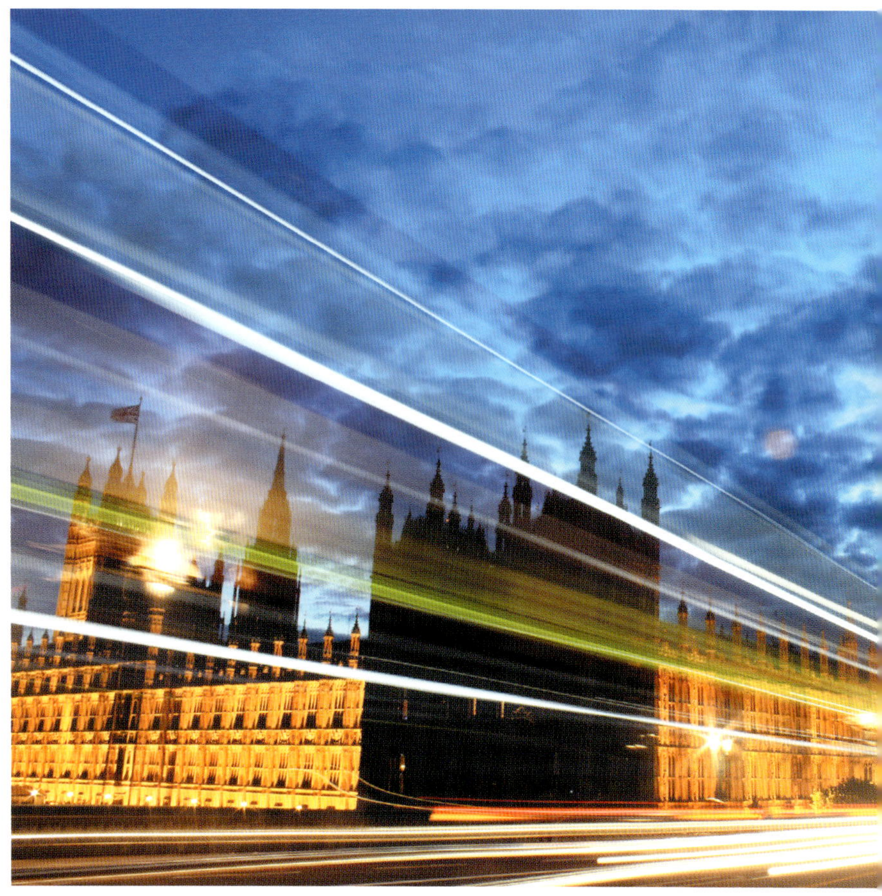

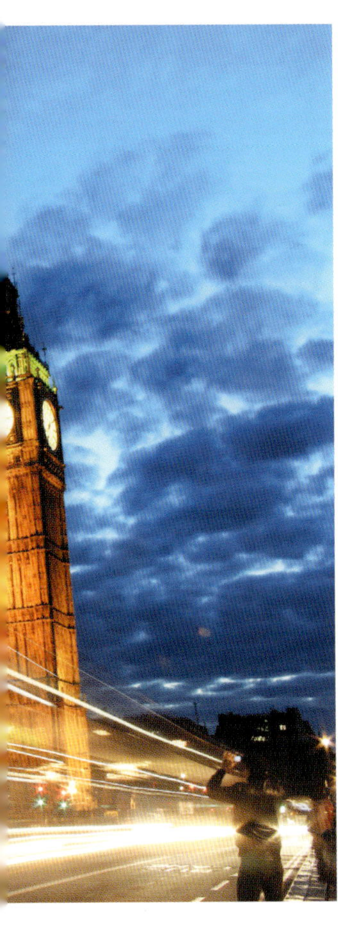

Headlights streak past the Palace of Westminster in London, England, UK

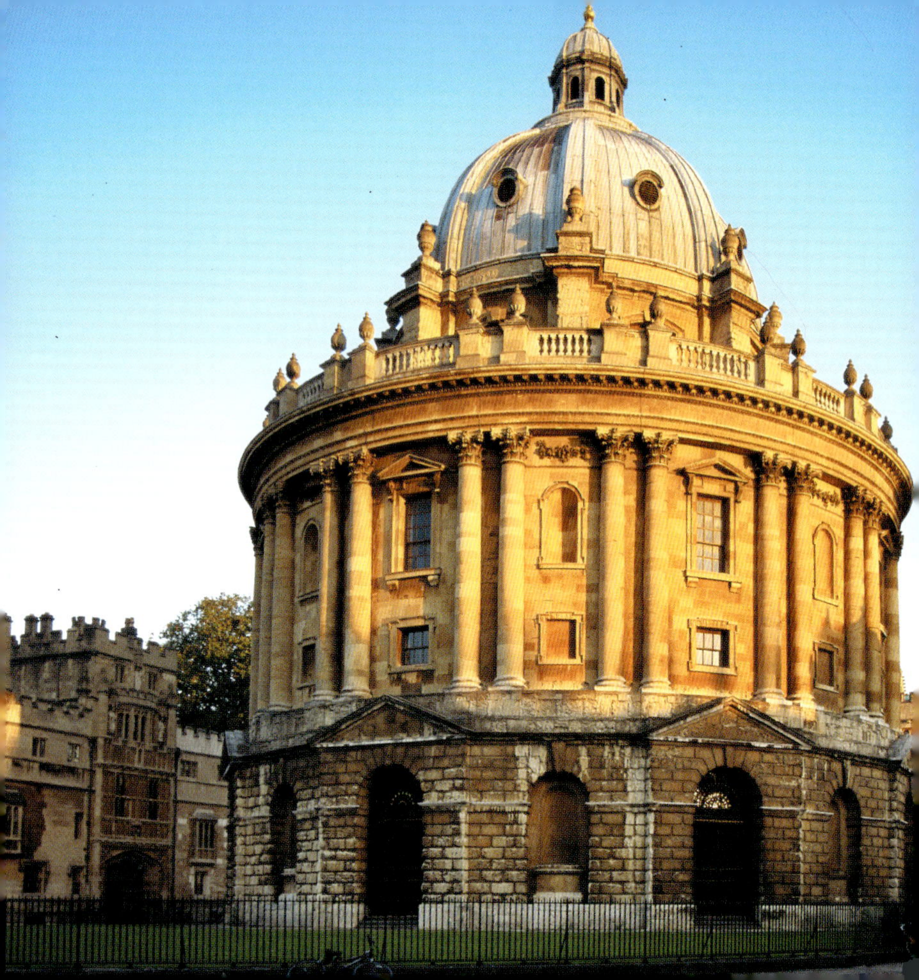

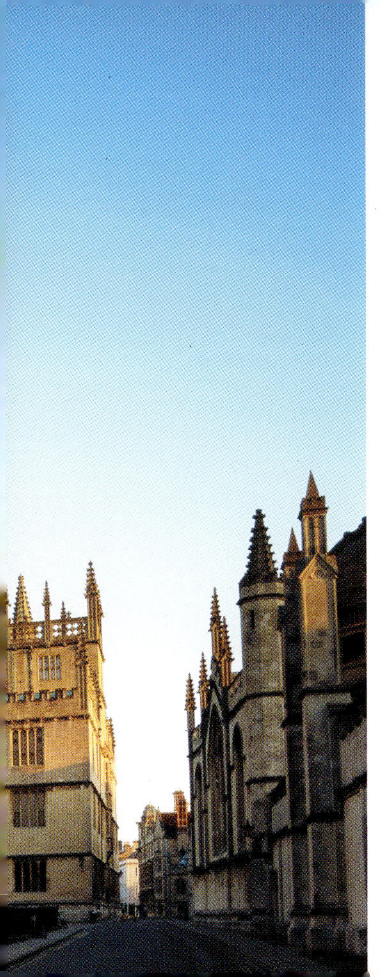

Driving by Radcliffe Camera in Oxford, England, UK

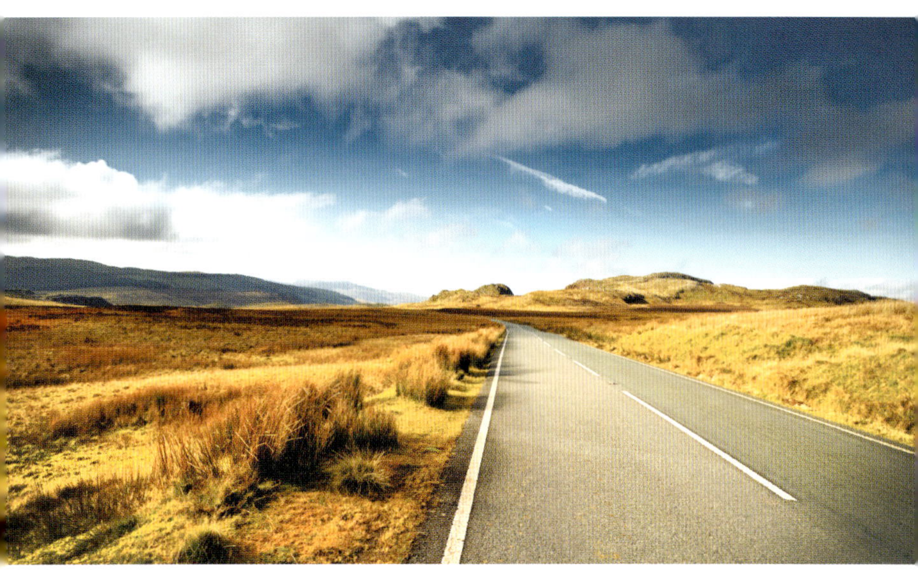

The road between Itsby Ifan and Festiniog in Snowdonia National Park, Wales, UK

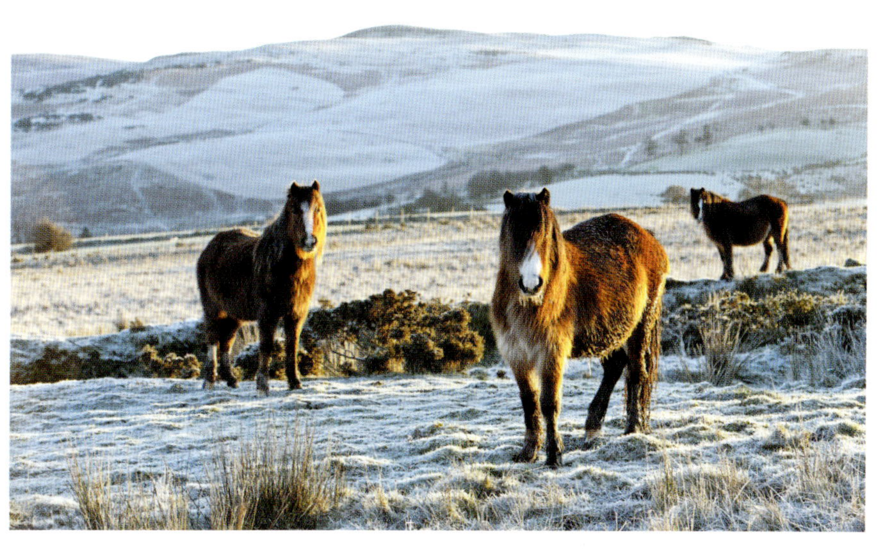

Welsh ponies on the high moorland in Powys, Wales, UK

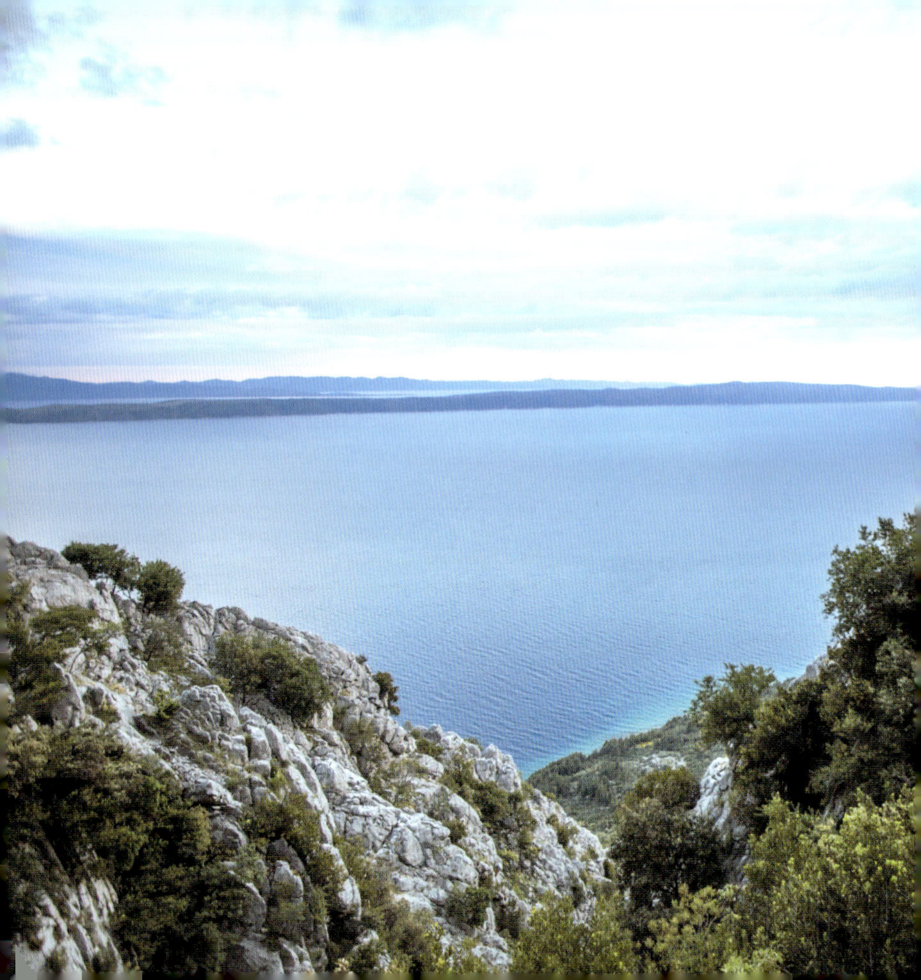

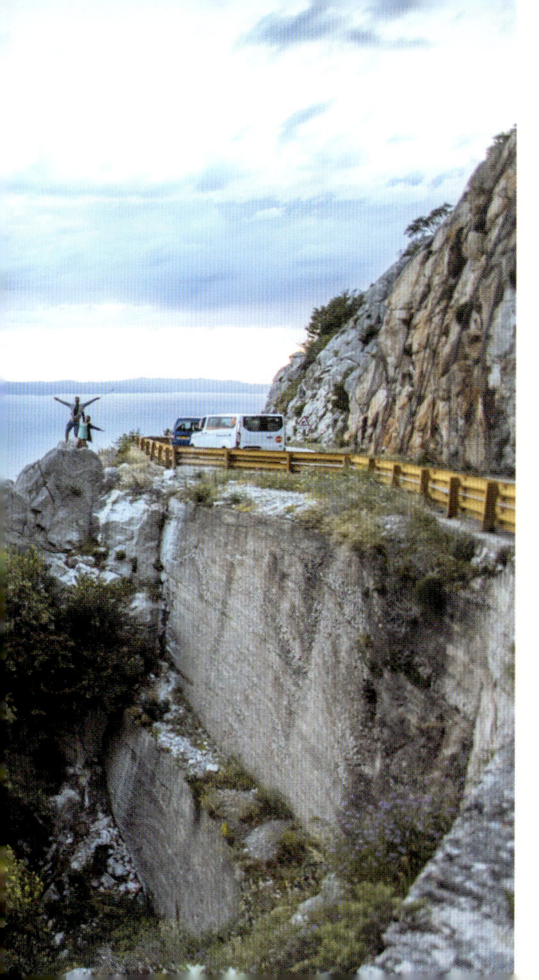

A high altitude cliffside road, Croatia

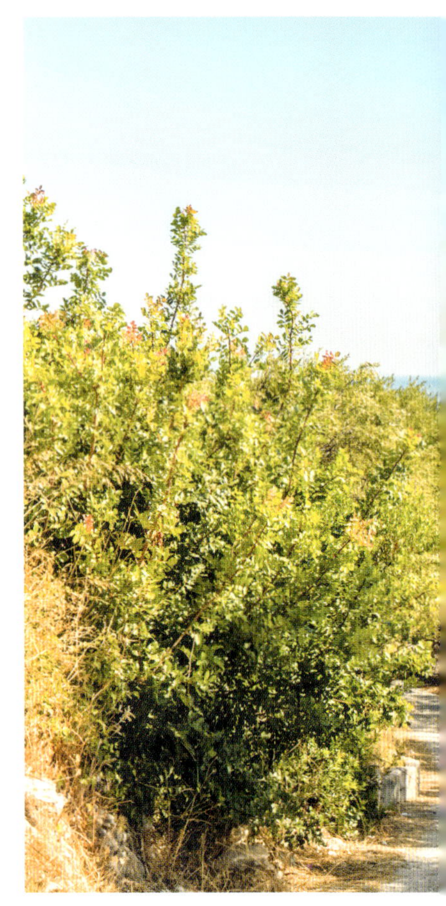

Road to a church on the island of Kefalonia, Greece

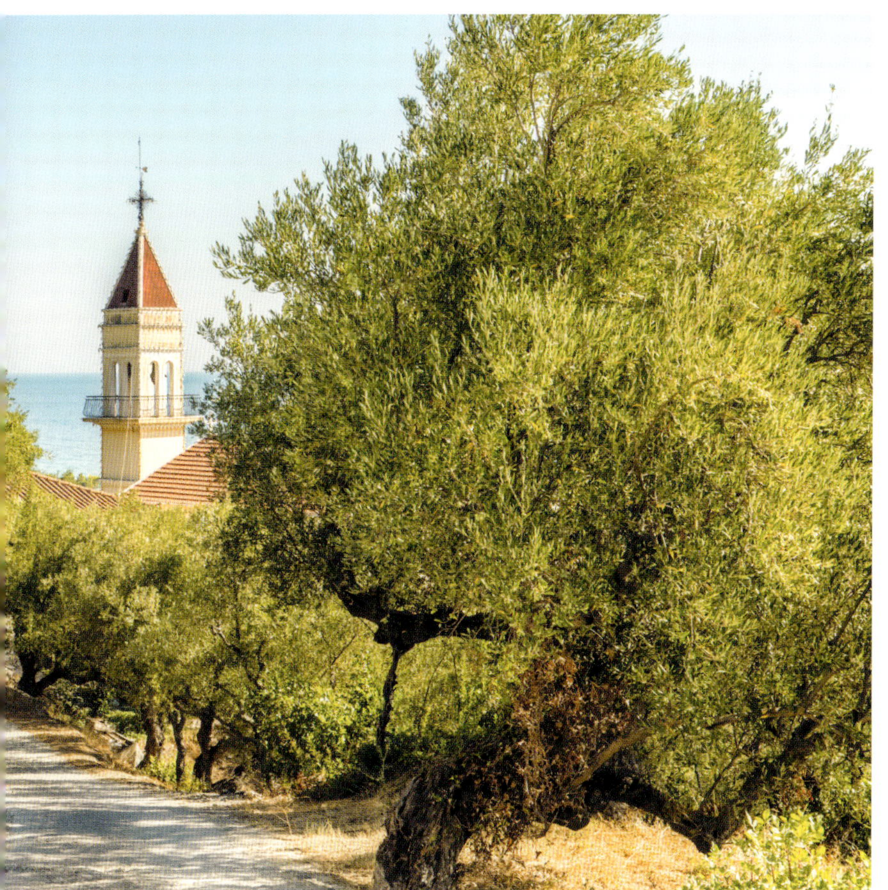

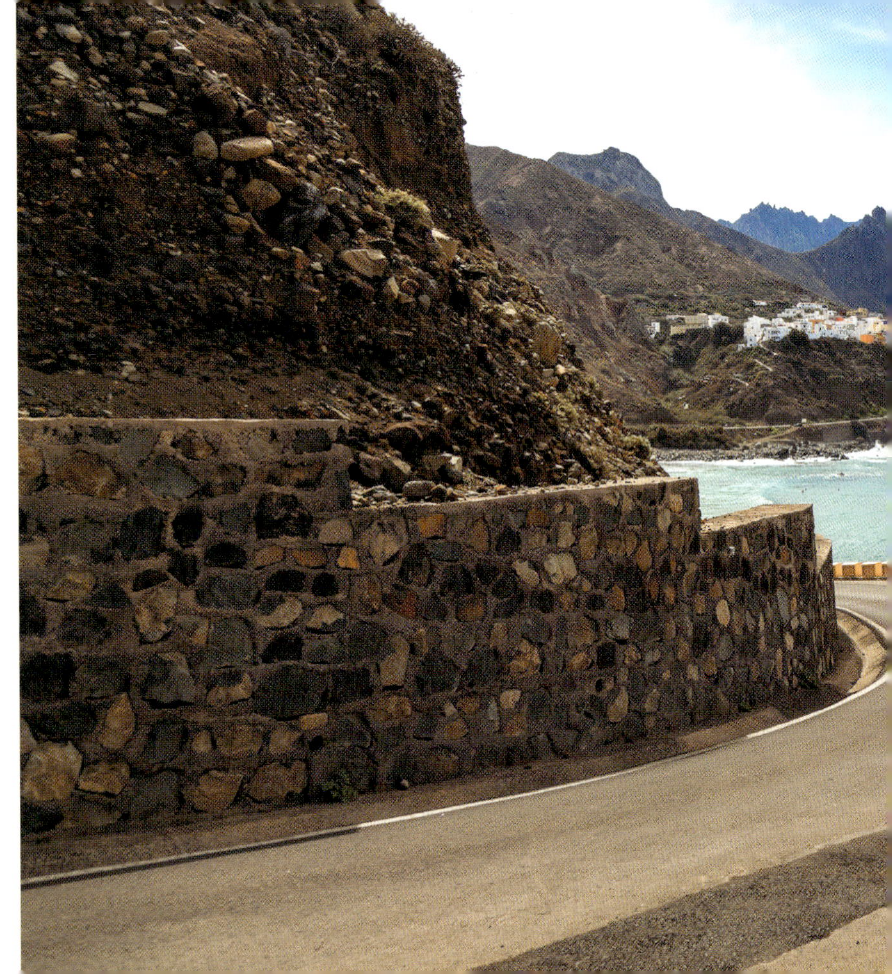

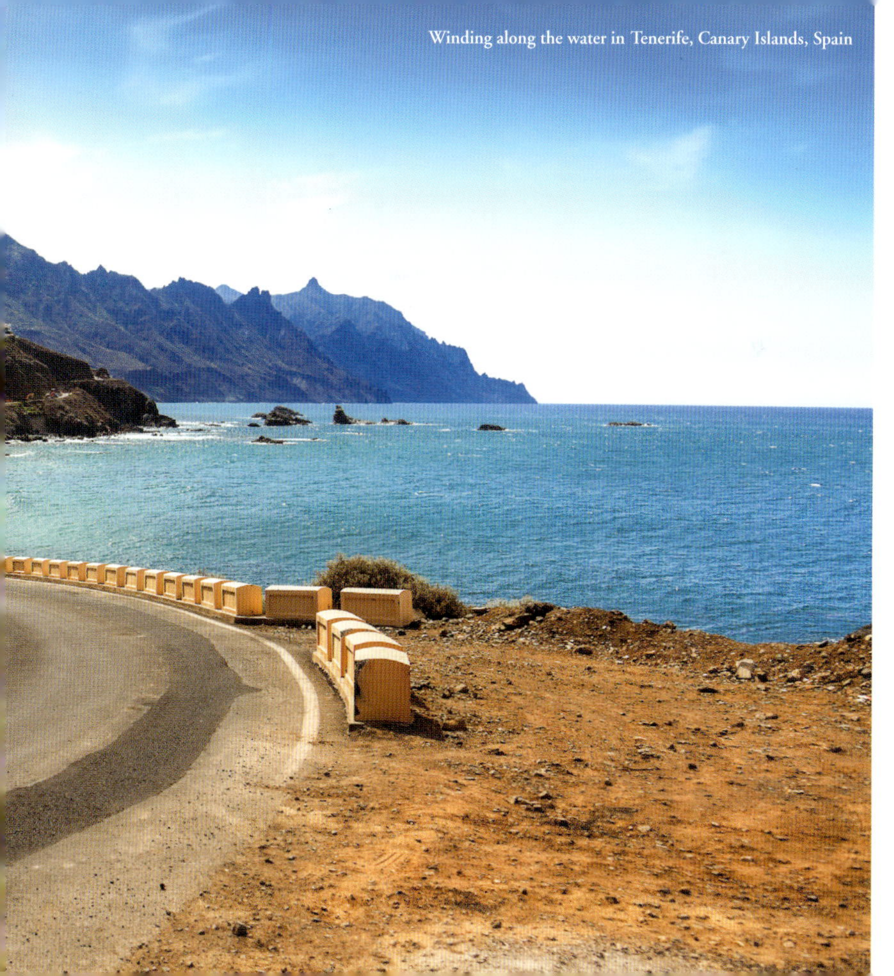

Winding along the water in Tenerife, Canary Islands, Spain

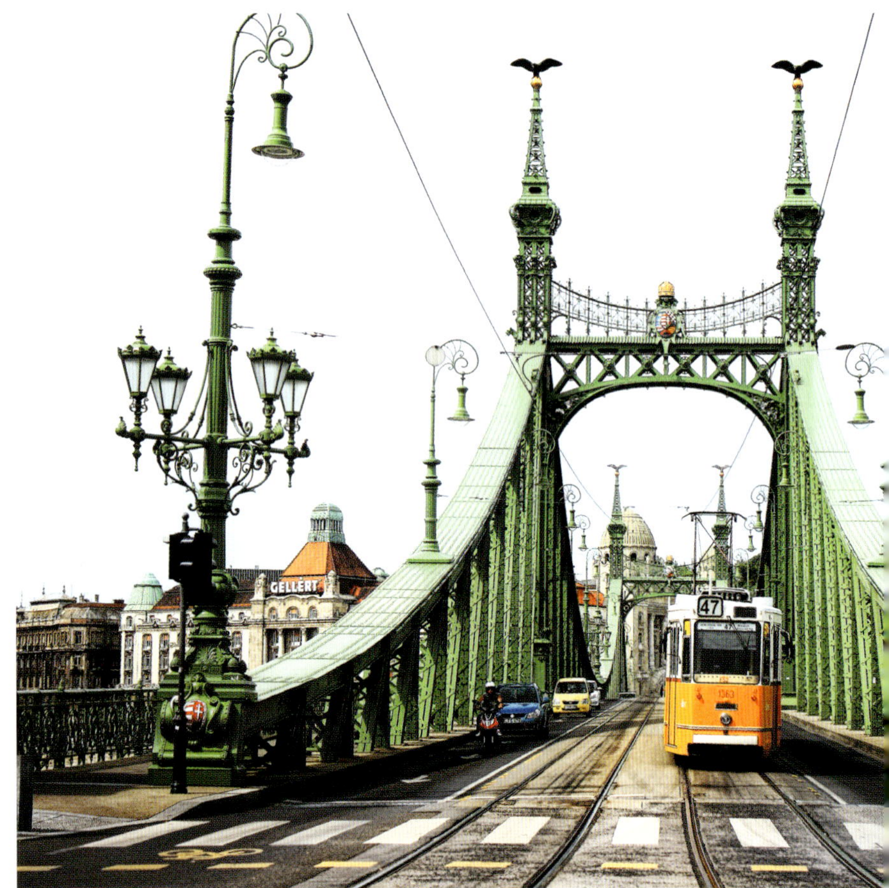

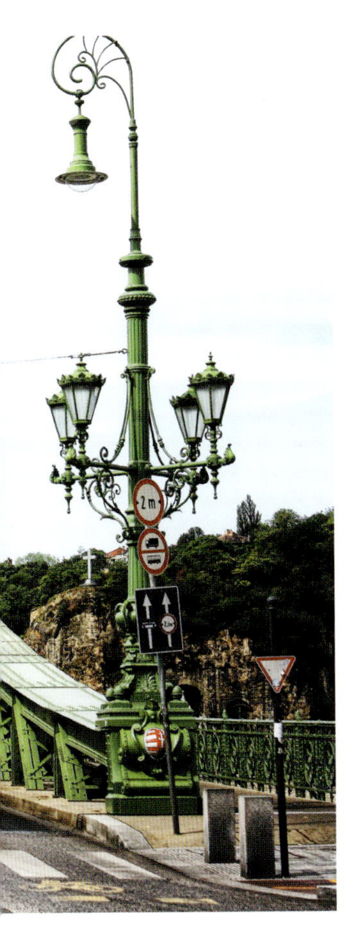

An old bridge in Budapest, Hungary

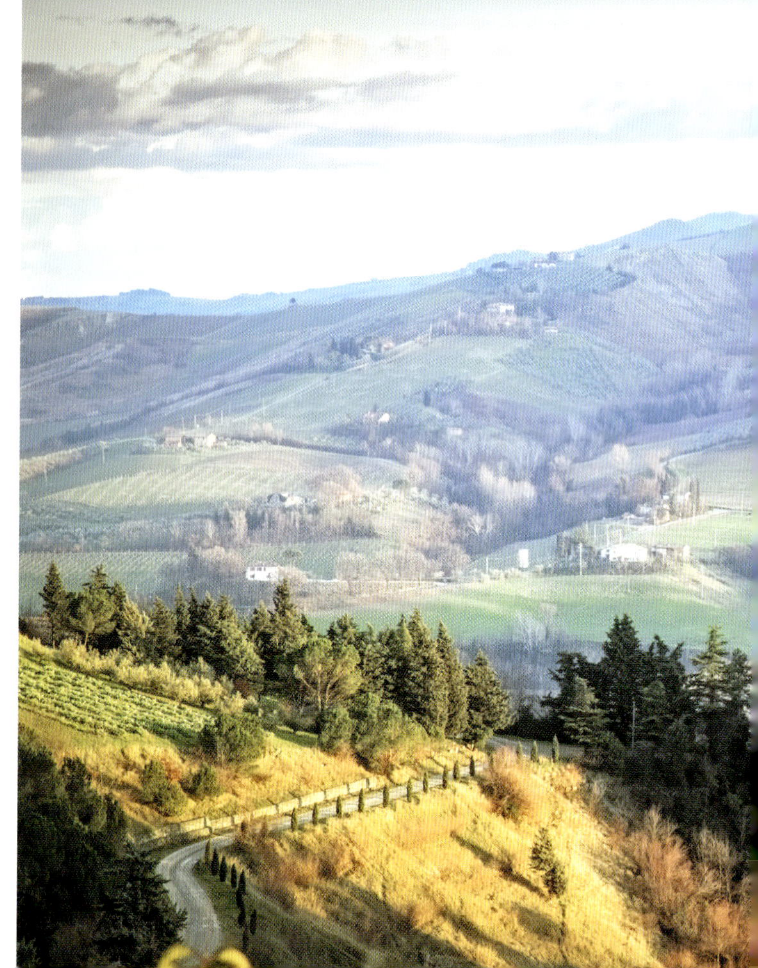

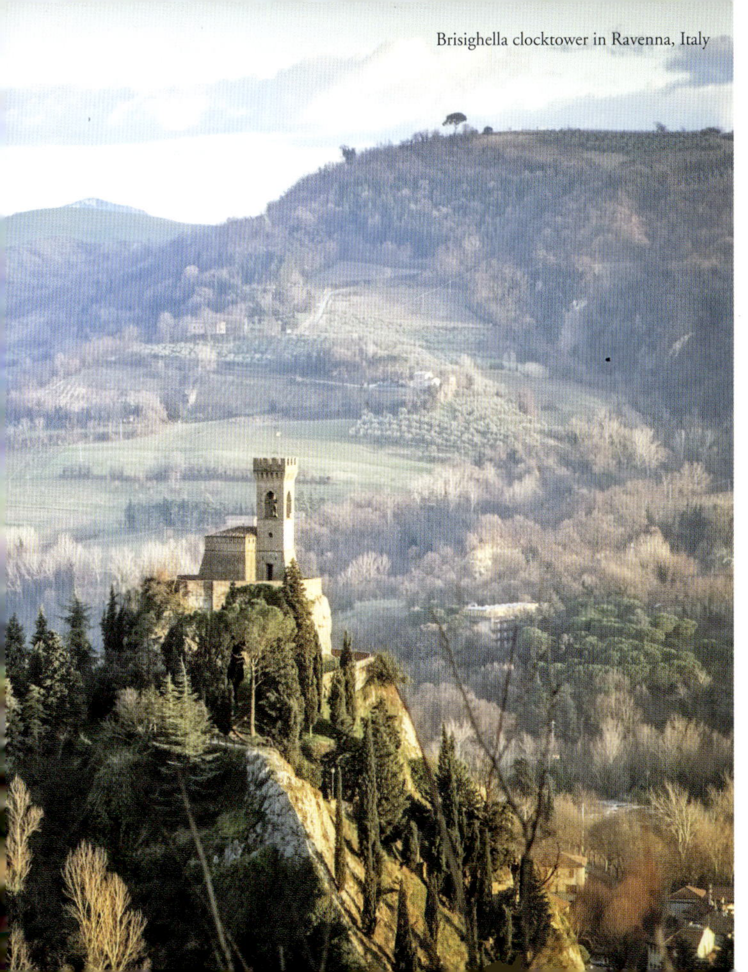

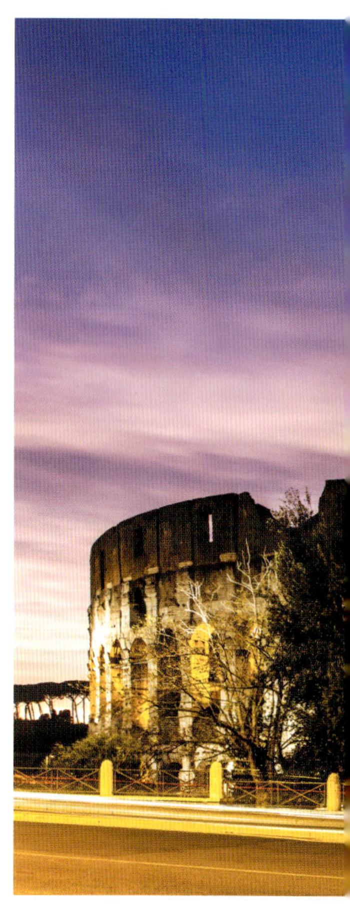

Colosseum in Rome, Italy

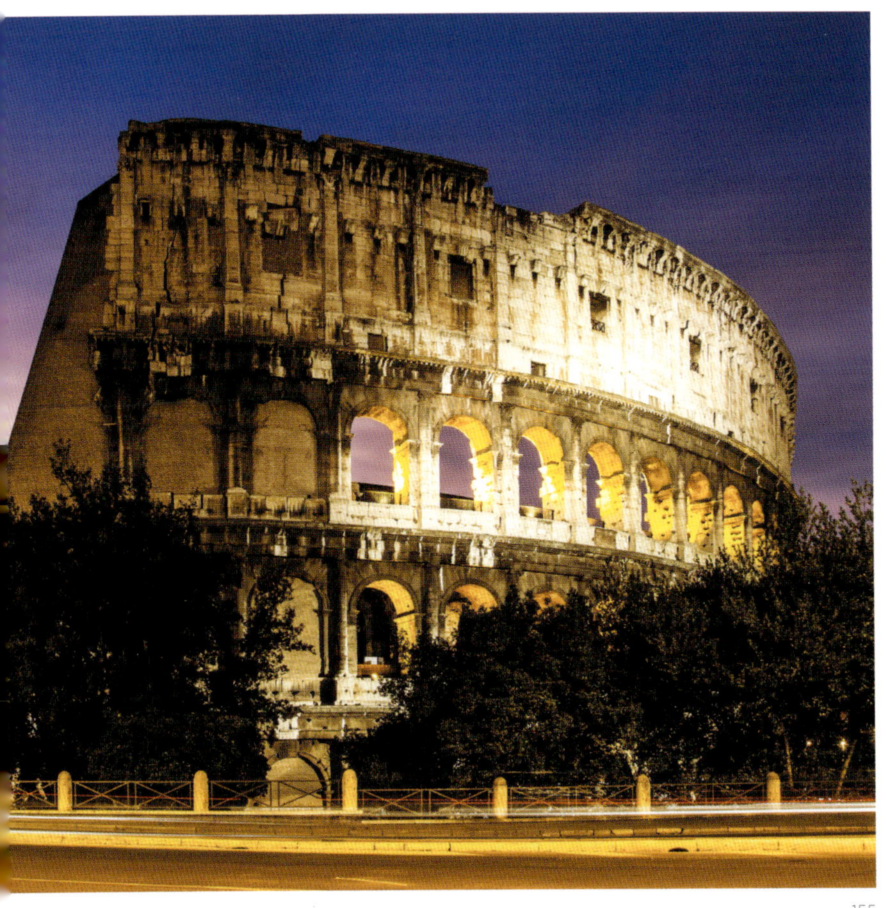

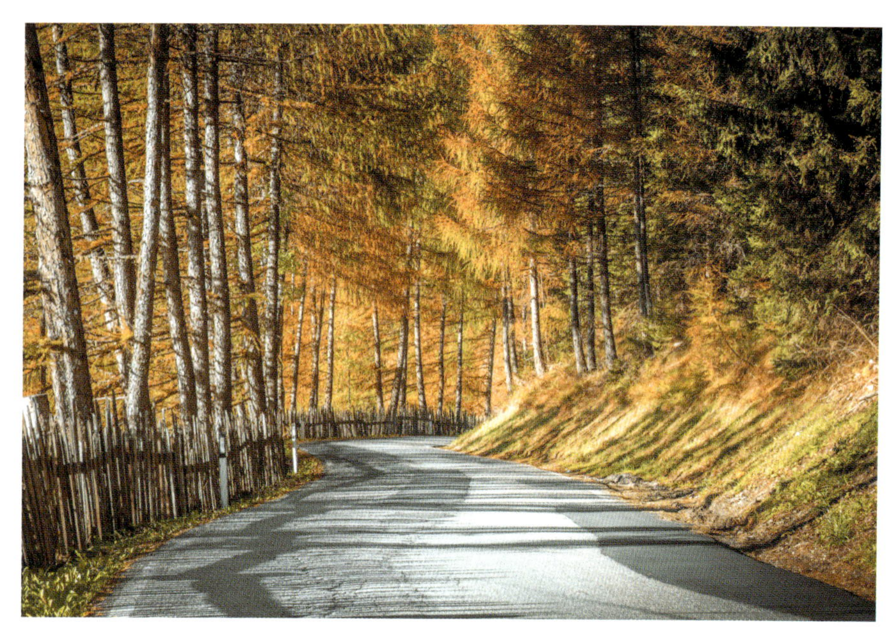

ABOVE Autumn colours in Trentino–Alto Adige, Italy
RIGHT A laneway in Monforte d'Alba in the Piedmont region, Italy

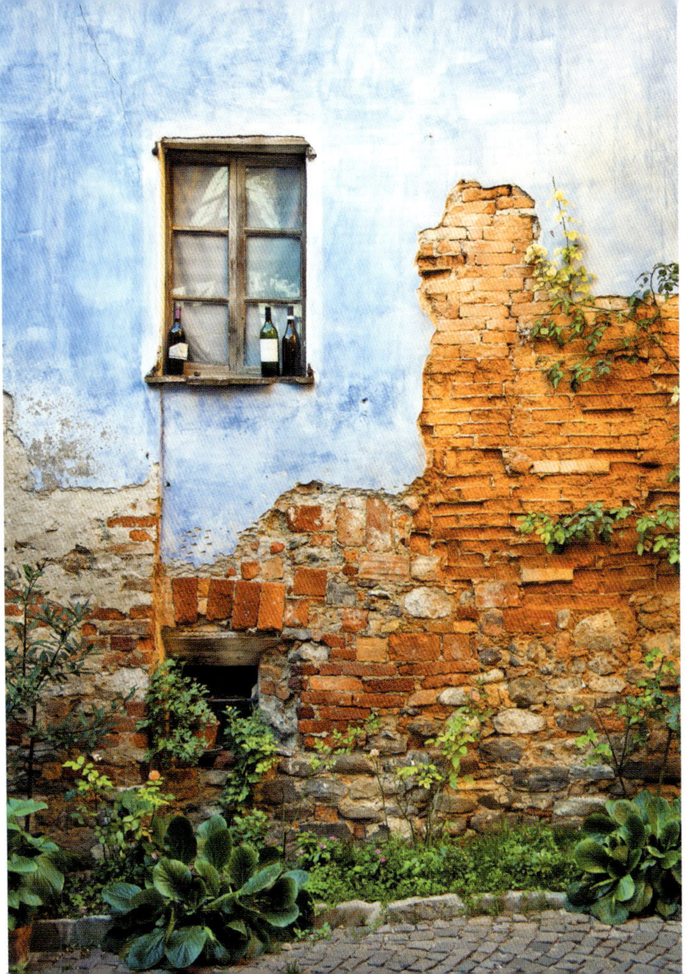

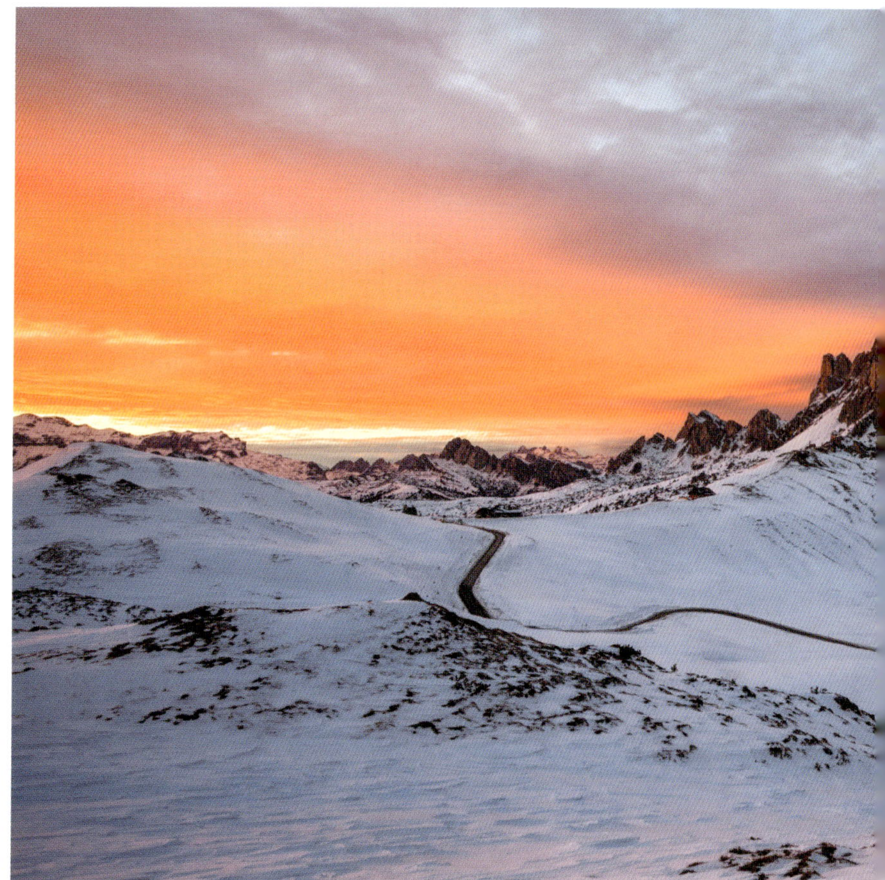

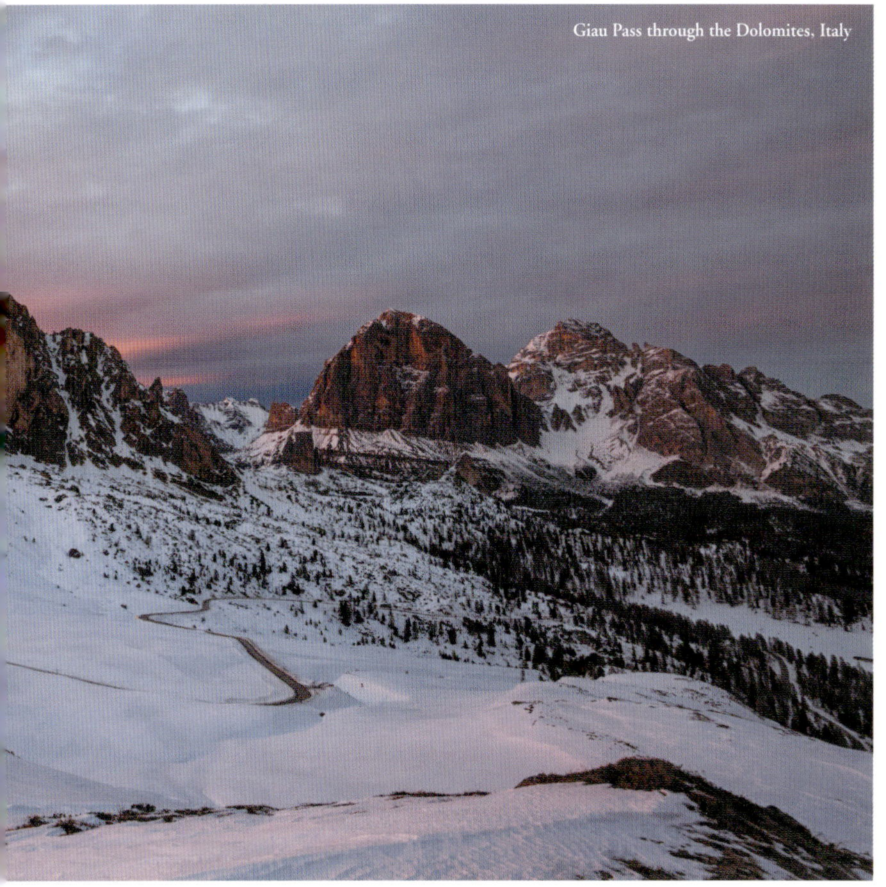
Giau Pass through the Dolomites, Italy

A foggy road through Burgundy, France

Arc de Triomphe with the Eiffel Tower in the distance in Paris, France

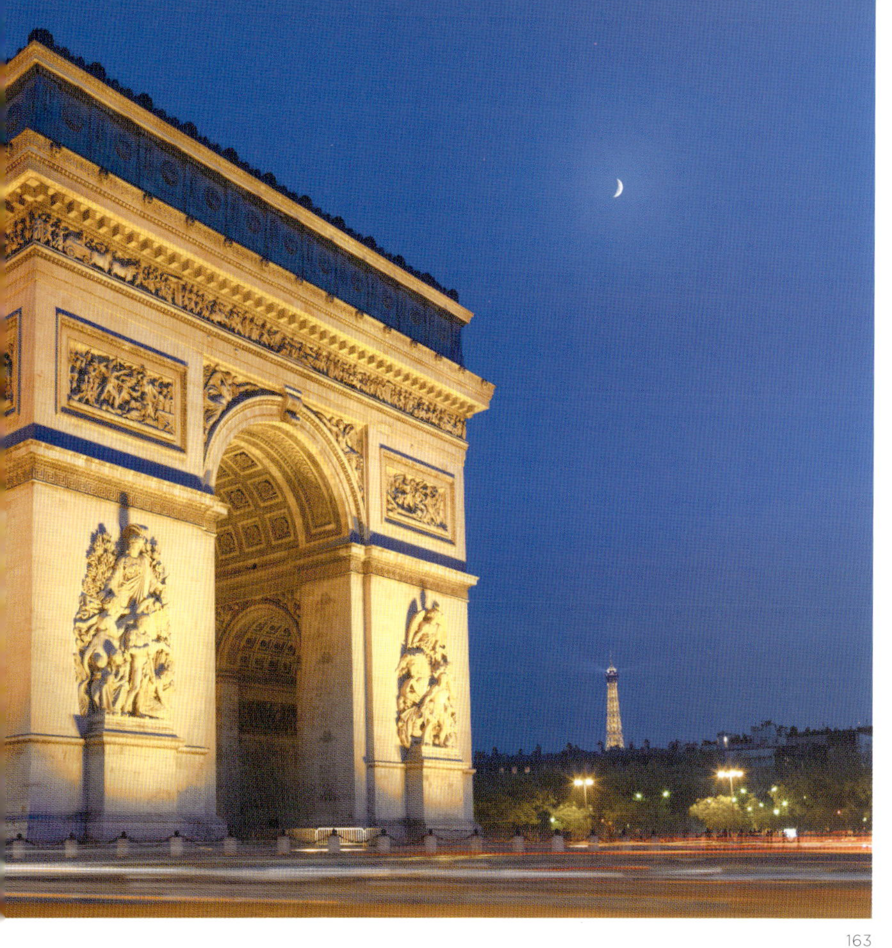

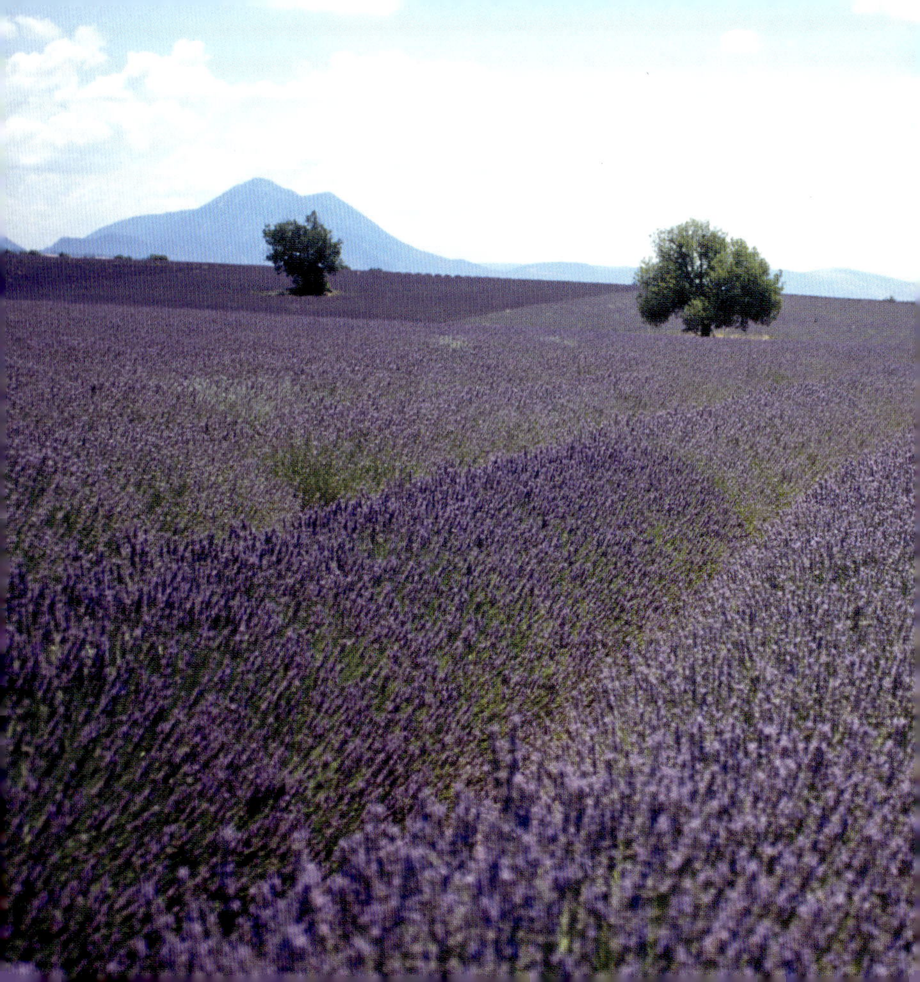

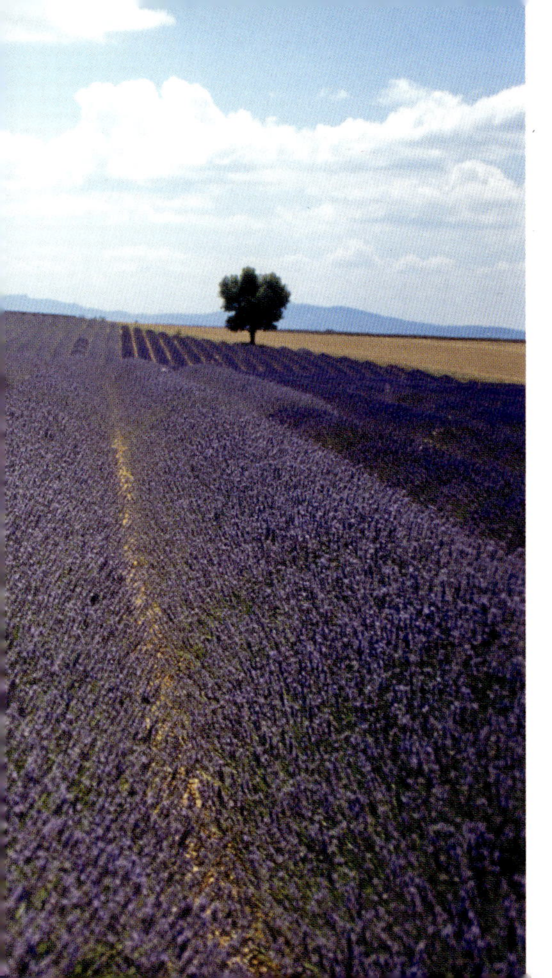

Lavender field along the D8 road in
Valensole, France

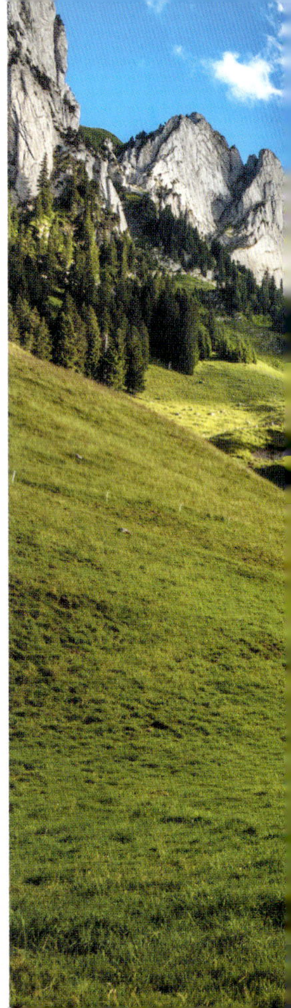

A path through the Alps, Switzerland

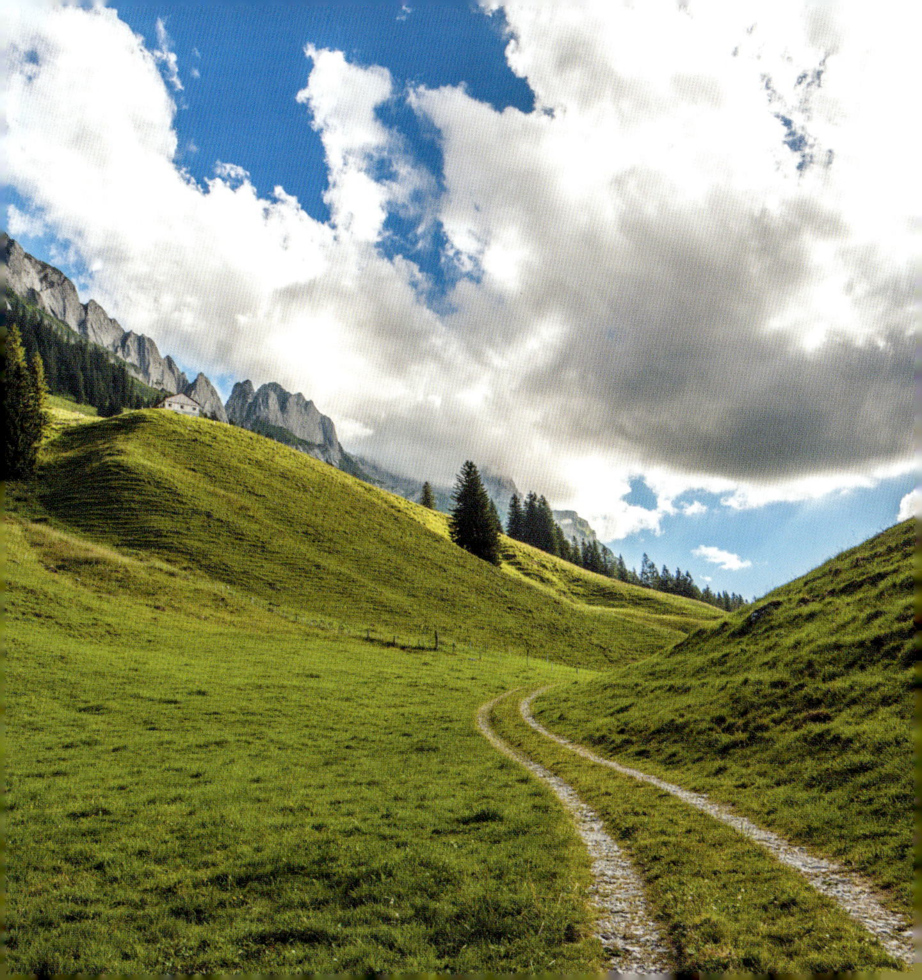

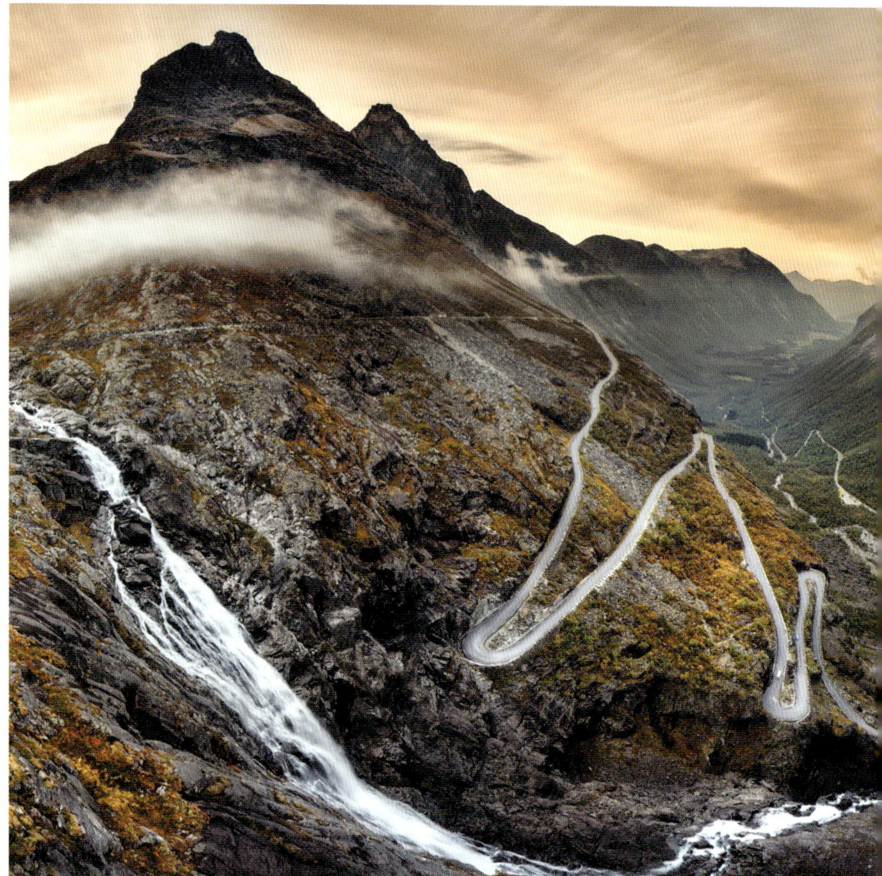

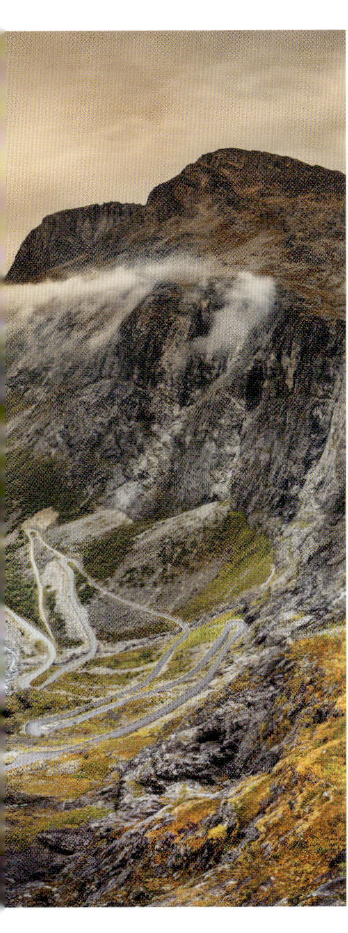

The winding Trollstigen mountain road, Norway

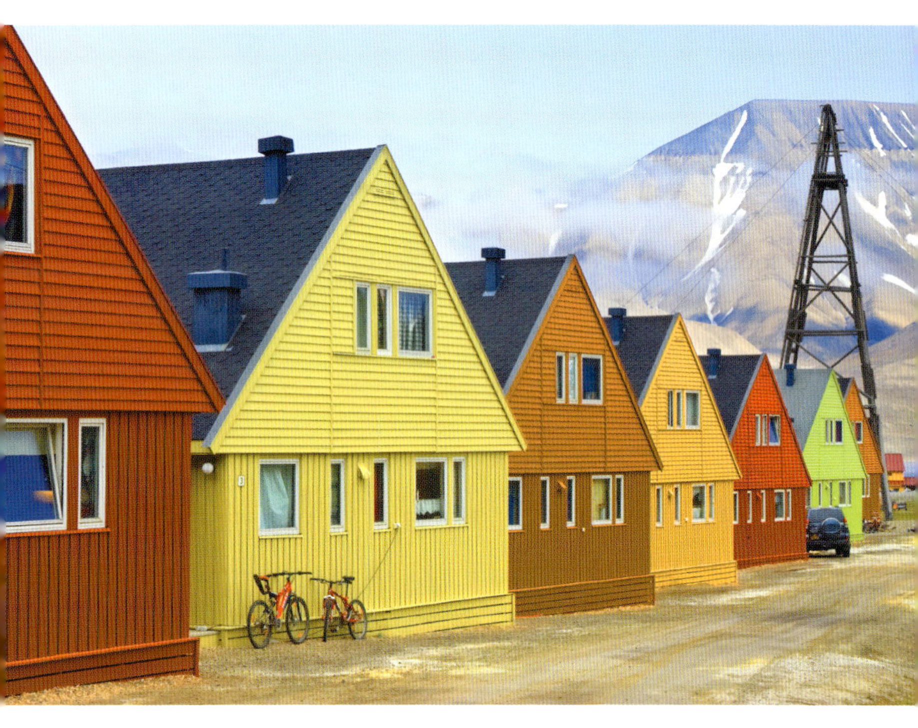

ABOVE Colourful houses in Longyearbyen on the island of Svalbard, Norway
RIGHT Watch out for bears on the roads through Svalbard, Norway

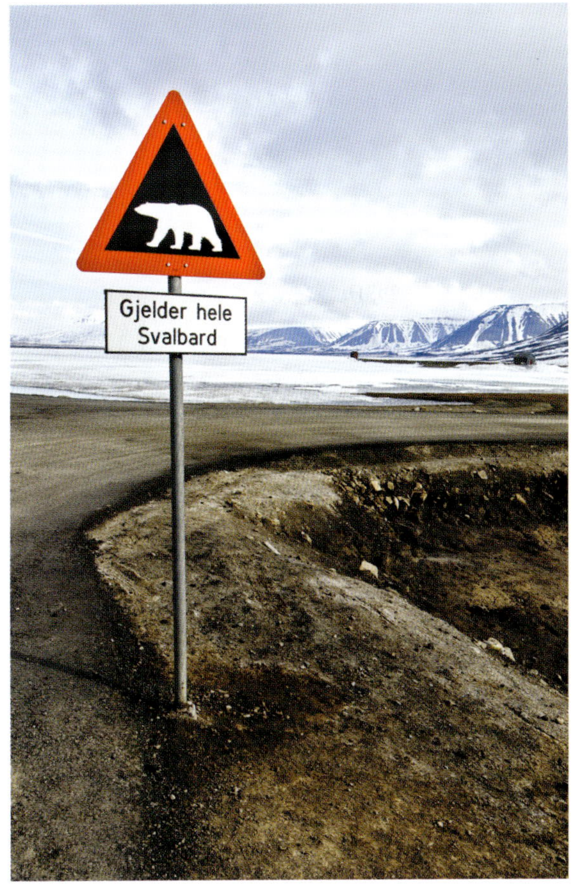

Gjelder hele
Svalbard

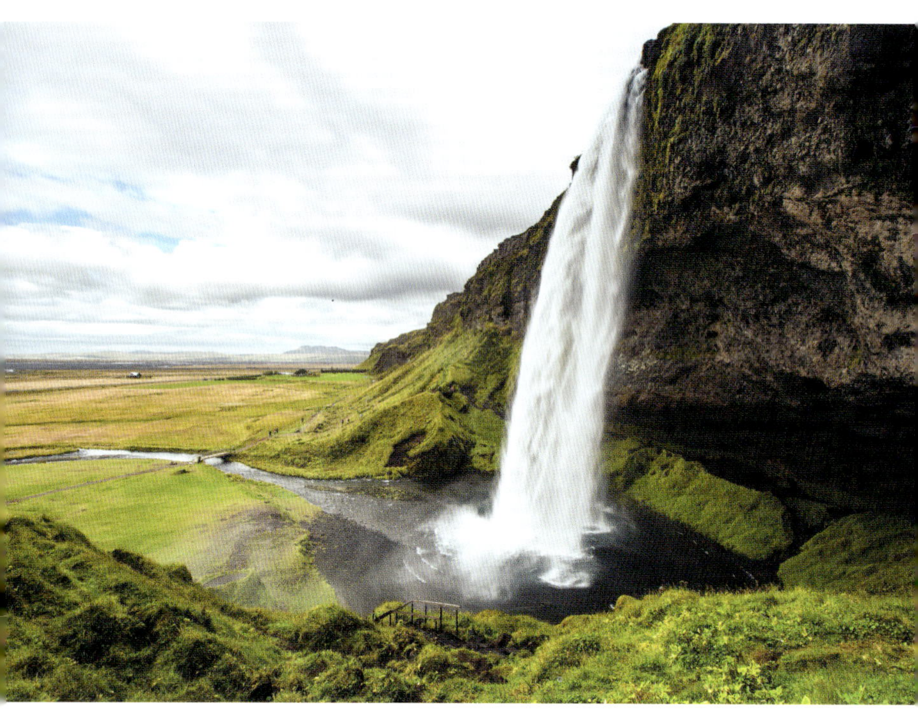

Seljalandsfoss waterfall near the Route 1 ring road, Iceland

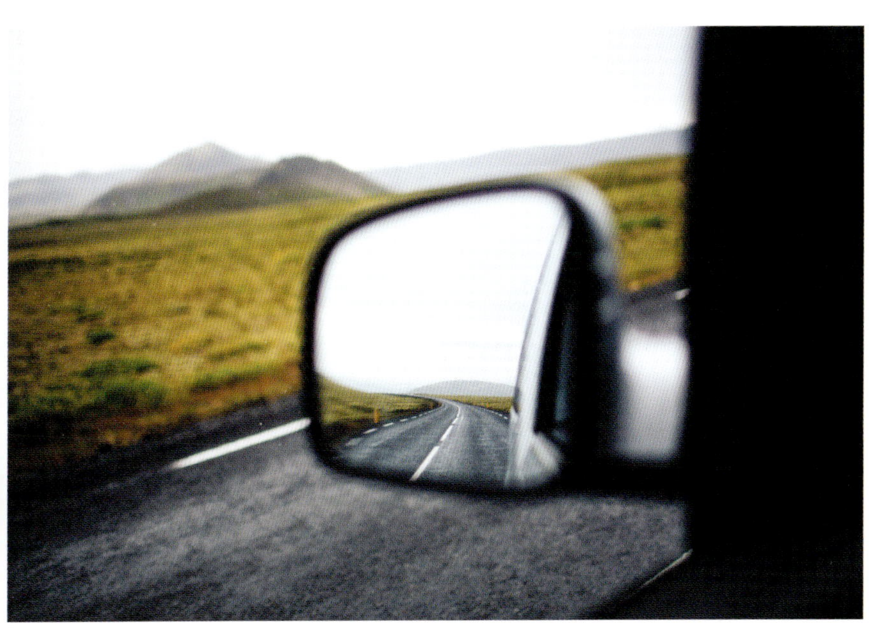

Moody Iceland reflection captured in a sideview mirror

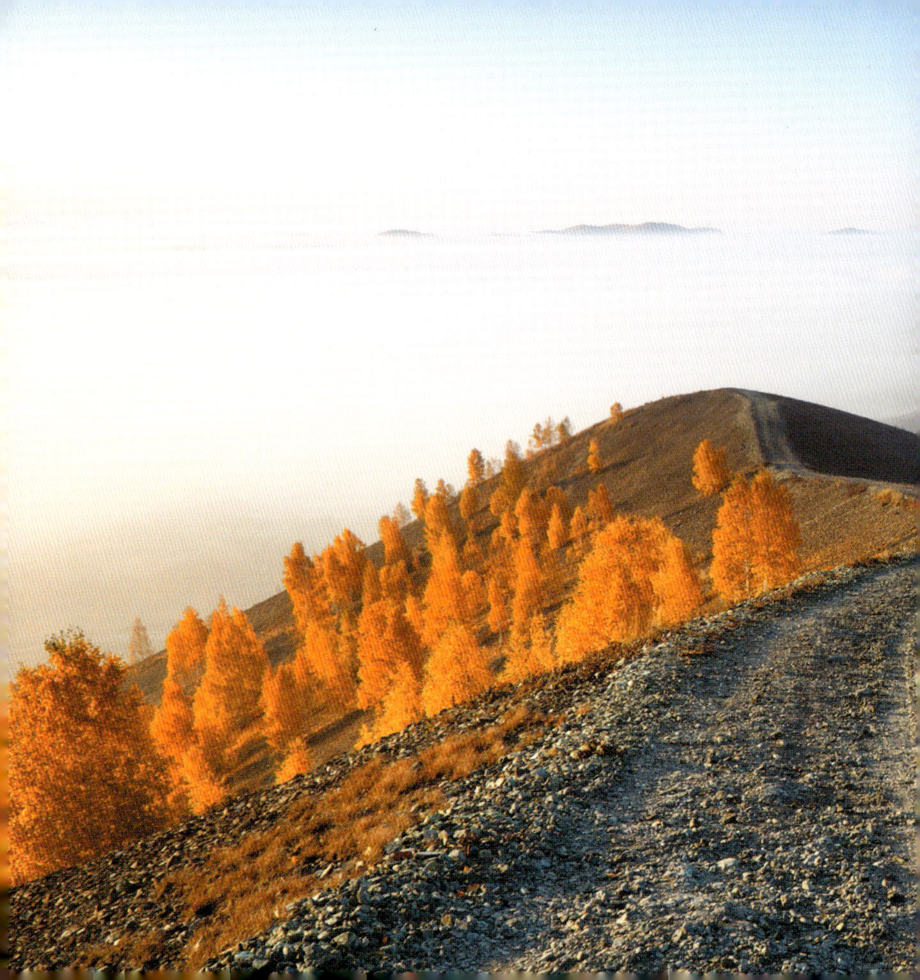

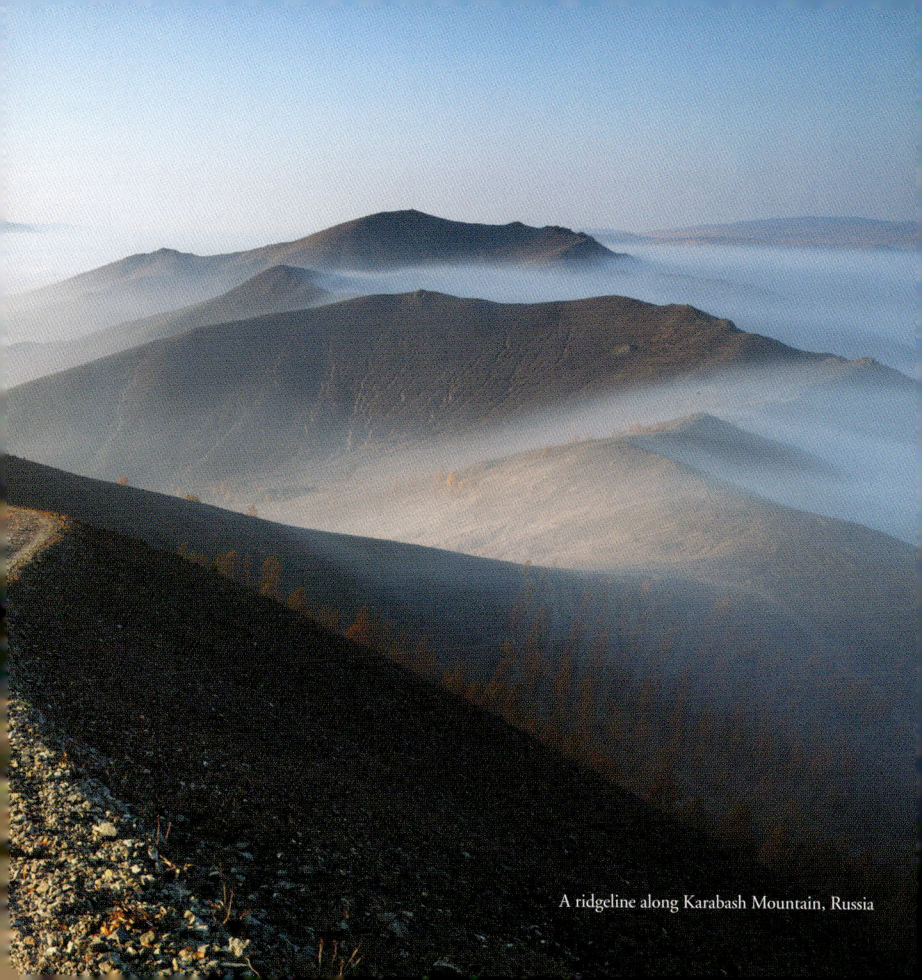

A ridgeline along Karabash Mountain, Russia

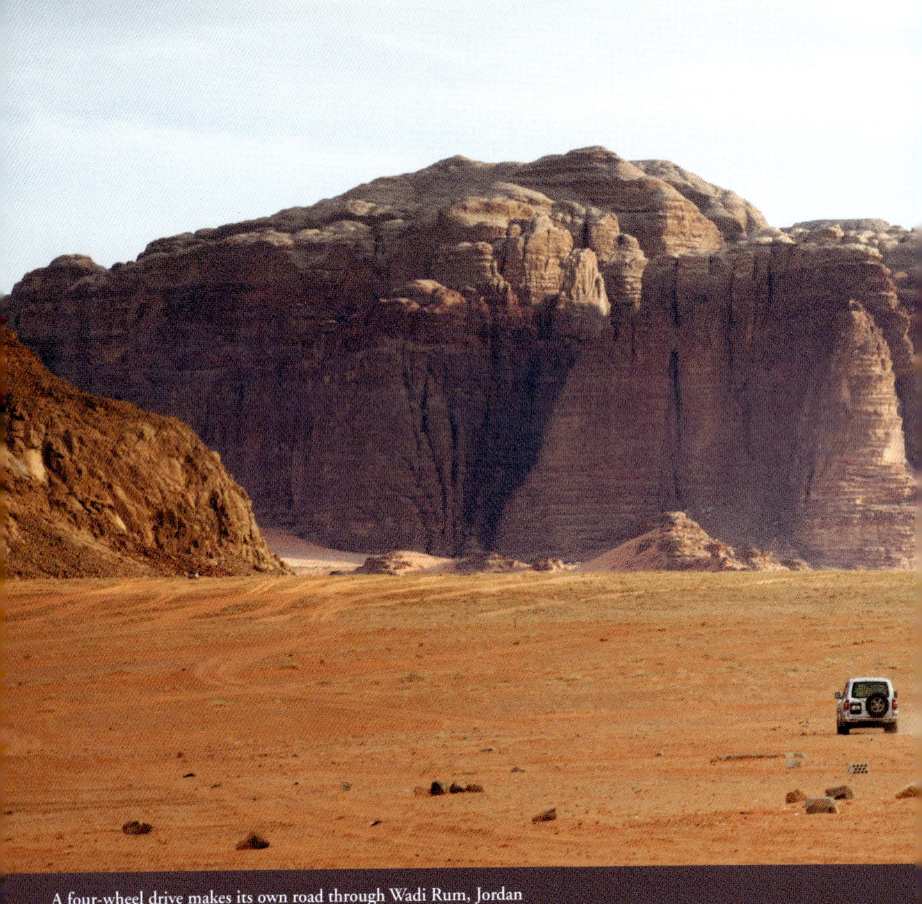

A four-wheel drive makes its own road through Wadi Rum, Jordan

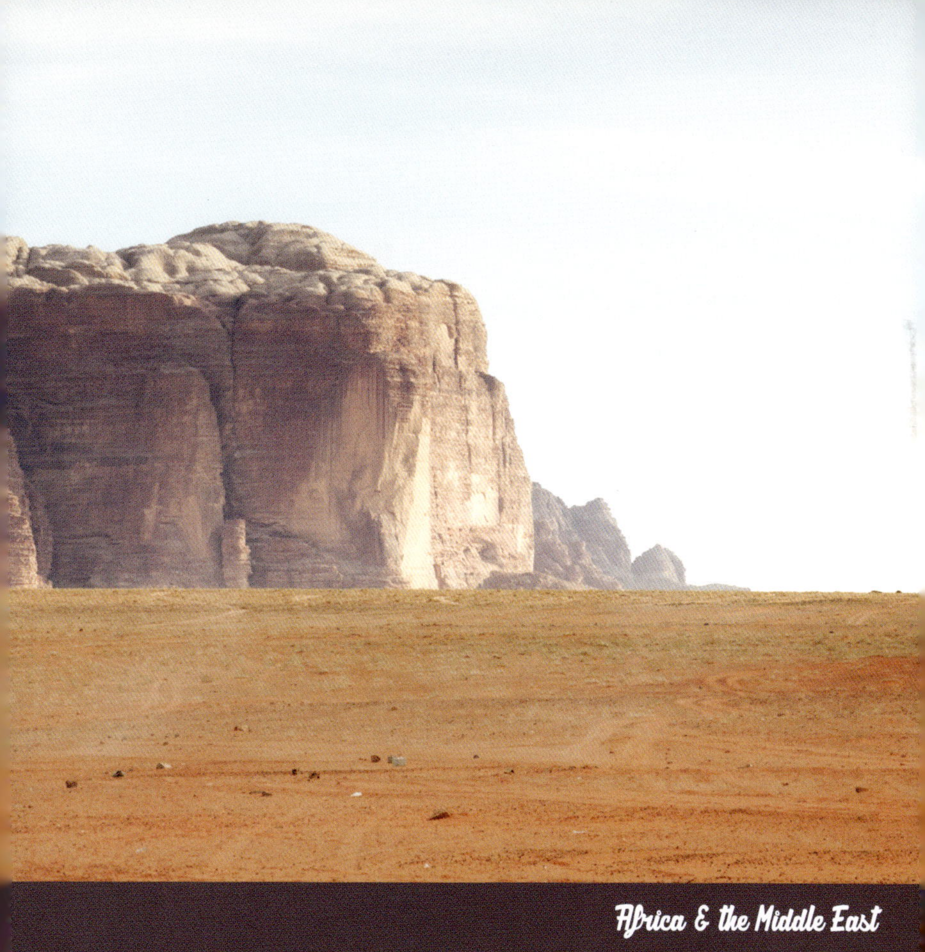
Africa & the Middle East

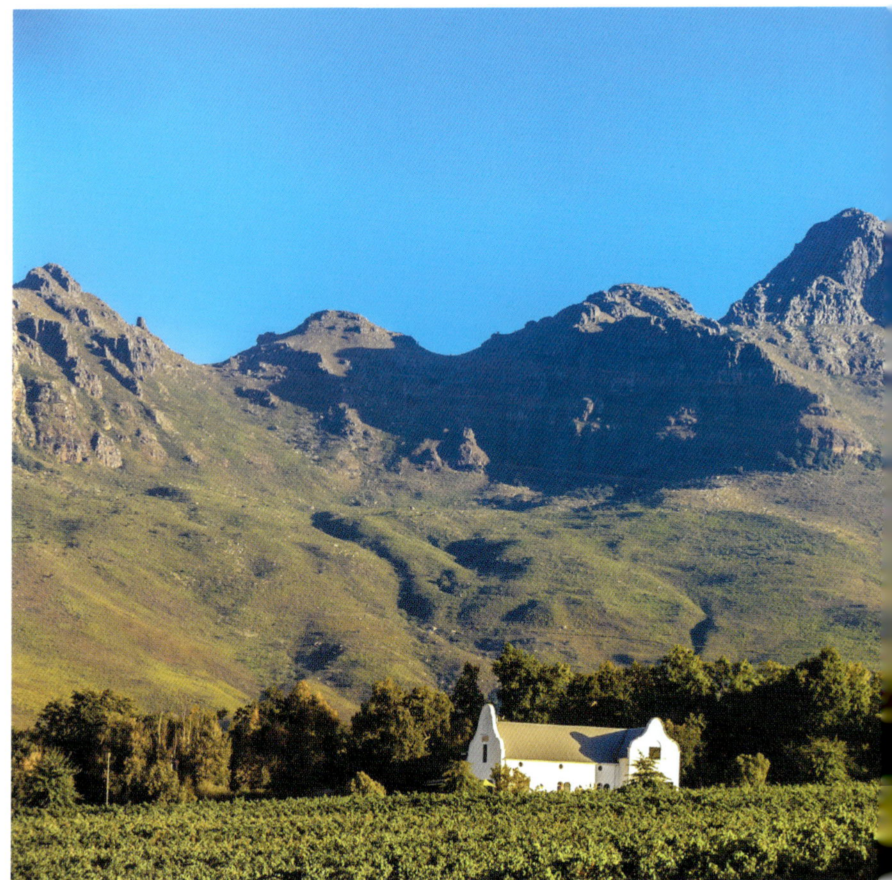

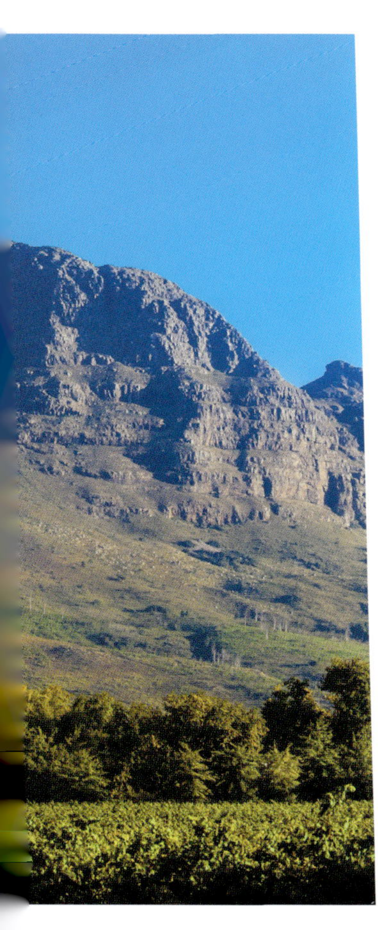

Driving by a winery near Stellenbosch, South Africa

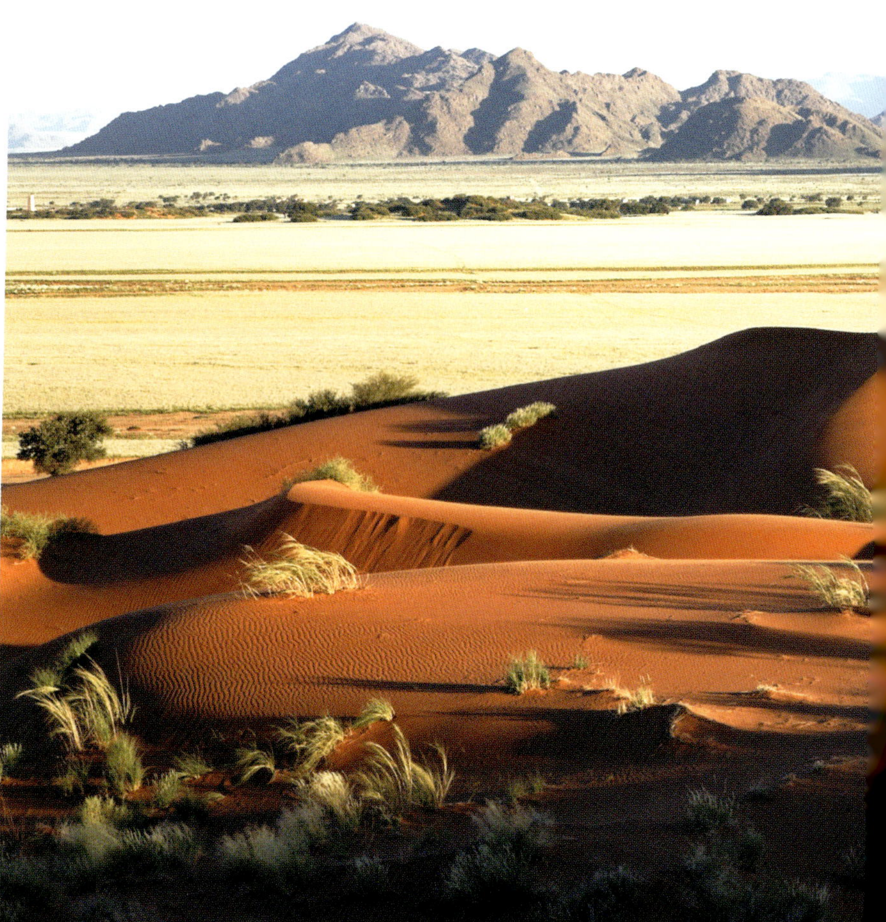

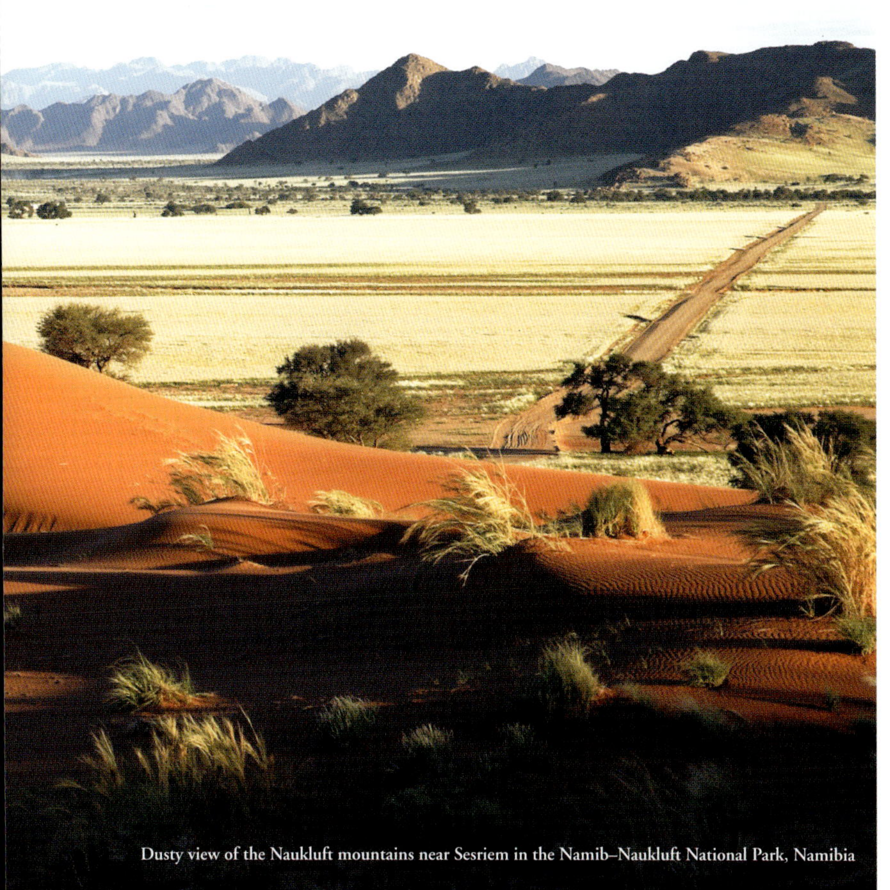

Dusty view of the Naukluft mountains near Sesriem in the Namib–Naukluft National Park, Namibia

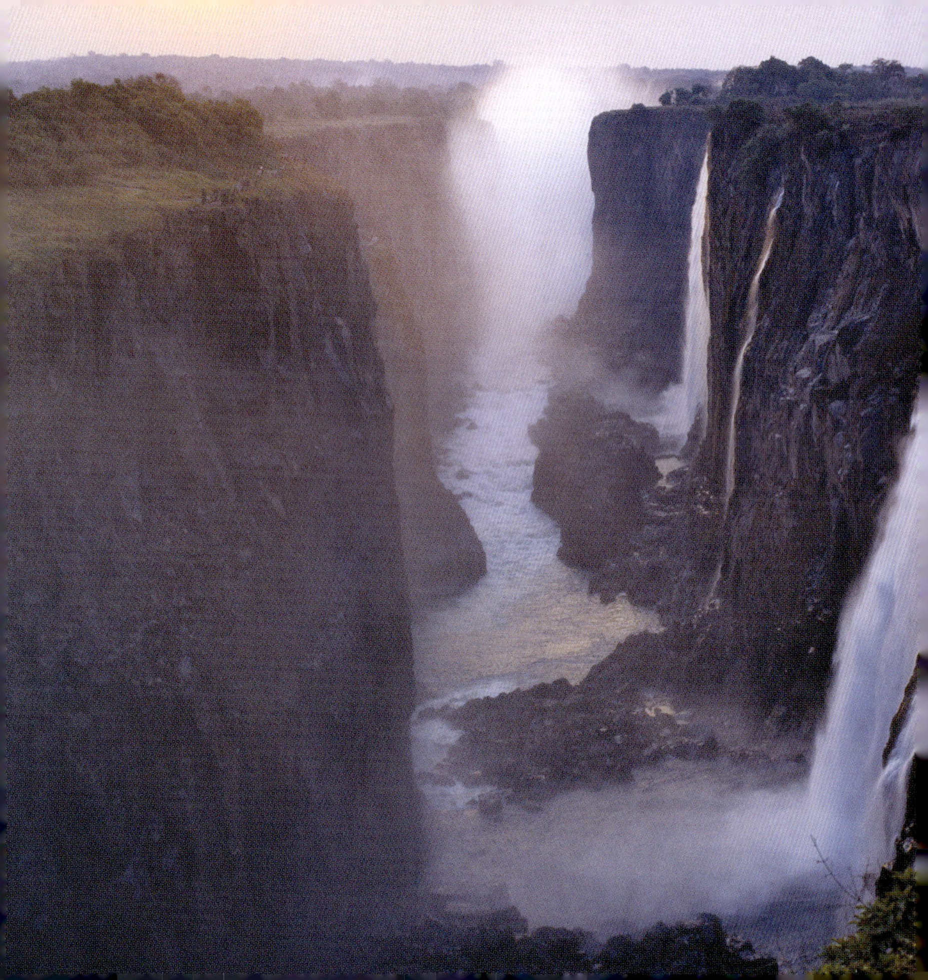

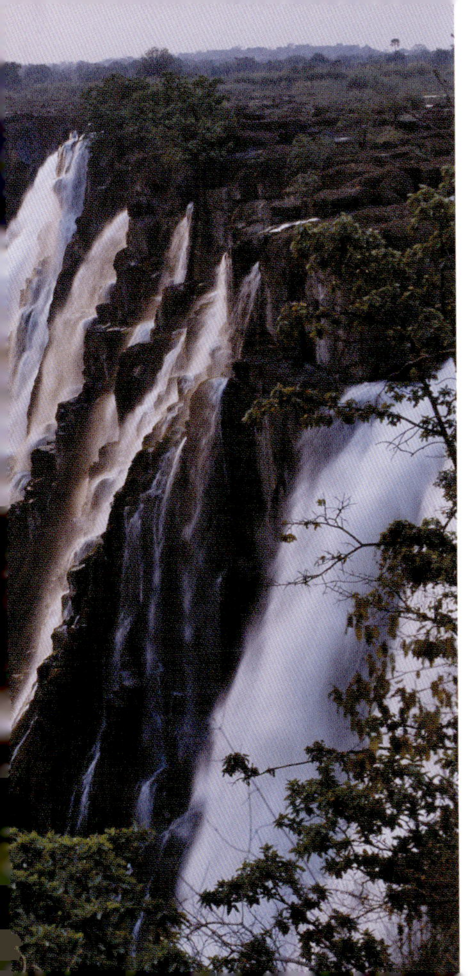

Sunset seen from the Zambia side of Victoria Falls

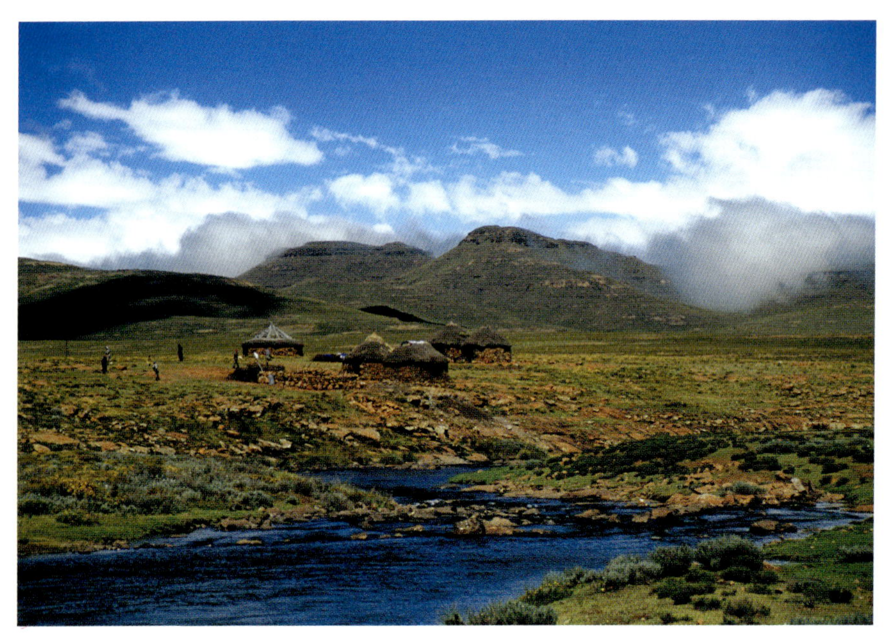

Stone houses at the top of Sani Pass in Lesotho, South Africa

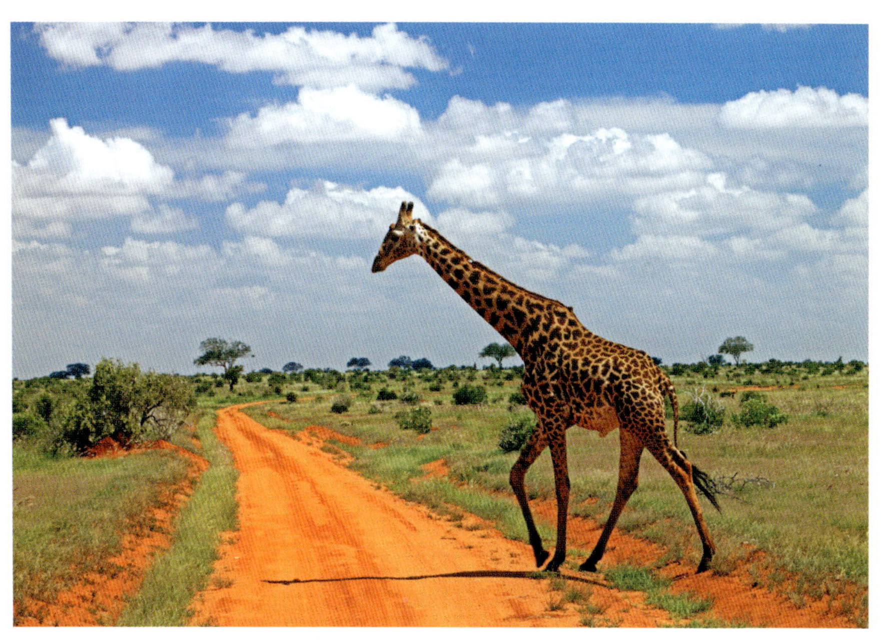

A giraffe crosses the road in Tsavo East, Kenya

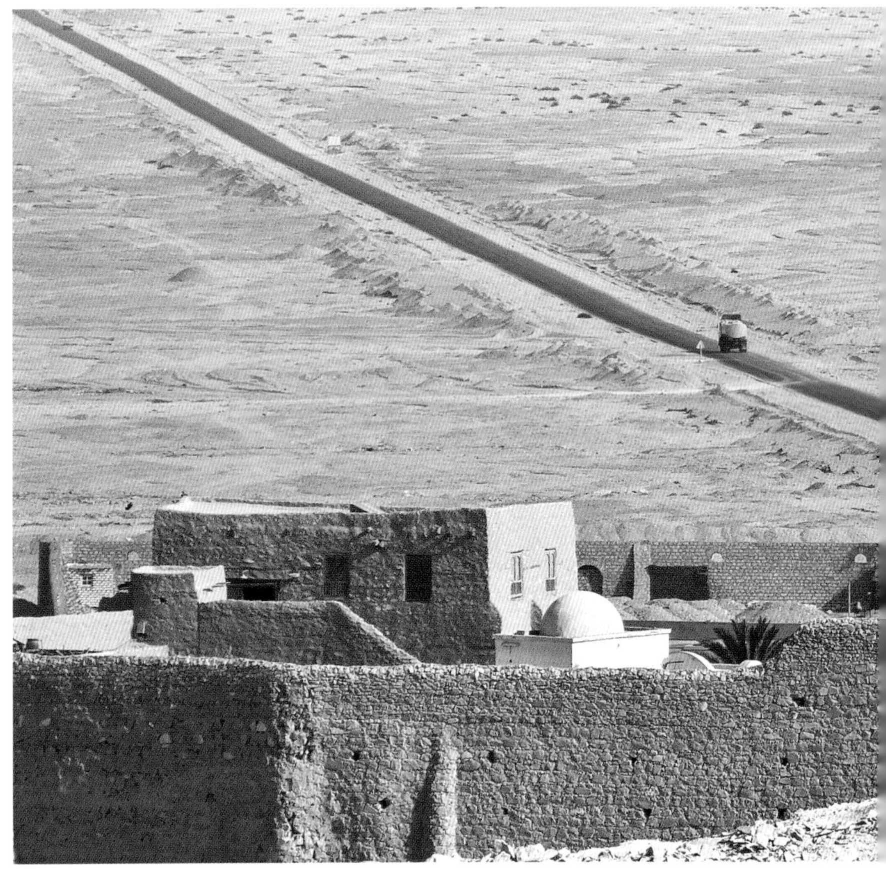

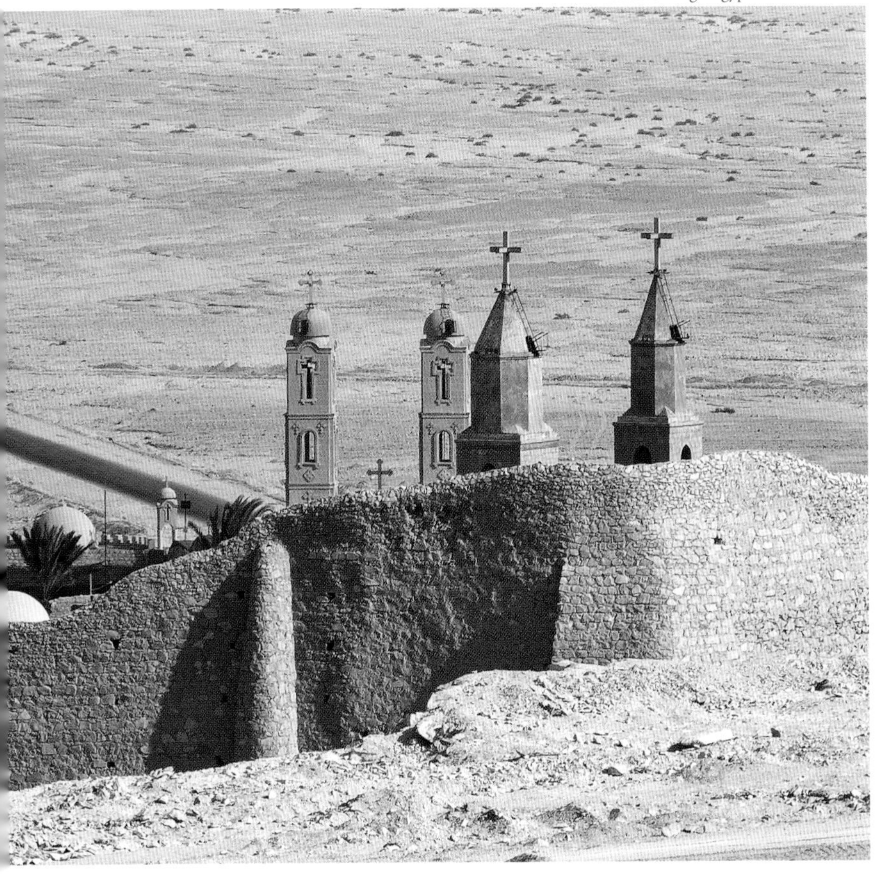

Image acknowledgements

COVER & PRELIMS Van image Underwood Archives/IF; background landscape 500px/IF; rearview mirror landscape Francesco Riccardo Lacomino/IF; ii Zoonar/kavram/IF

OTHER PAGES:
NORTH AMERICA
2-3 Gary Corbett/IF; 4-5 Jeff Chaw/500px/IF; 6-7 (a) Kate J Armstrong, (b) Paul Gablonski; 8-9 (a) Patrick Endres/IF, (b) Lynn Wegener/IF; 10-11 Kate J Armstrong; 12-13 zsolt berend/500px/IF; 14-15 Joe Josephs/500px/IF; 16-17 Tomas Nevesely/IF; 18-19 Alan Copson/IF; 20-21 Bill Bachmann/IF; 22-23 (a) Image Source/IF, (b) Joey Hayes/IF; 24-25 500px/IF; 26-27 Chris Kridler/IF; 28-29 (a & b) Kate J Armstrong; 30-31 Minden Pictures/IF; 32-33 (a) G Rentsch/IF, (b) Dave Walsh/VWPics/IF; 34-35 (a) Kate J Armstrong, (b) James Schwabel/IF; 36-37 Jordan Banks/IF; 38-39 (a) Jared Kay/500px/IF, (b) Kate J Armstrong; 40-41 Neil Farrin/IF; 42-43 (a) Reimar Gaertner/IF, (b) Kate J Armstrong; 44-45 Zoonar/Melanie Viola/IF; 46-47 Michele Falzone/IF

SOUTH & CENTRAL AMERICA
48-49 Zoonar/kavram/IF; 50-51 Zoonar/Galyna Andrus/IF; 52-53 Michele Falzone/IF; 54-55 (a) Cem Canbay/IF, (b) Andy Selinger/IF; 56-57 John Coletti/IF; 58-59 Marla Holden/IF

AUSTRALIA & NEW ZEALAND
60-61 Nick Rains/TNT; 62-63 Misty Norman; 64-65 TNT; 66-67 (a) Akari Hatakeyama/TNT, (b) TNT; 68-69 Auscape/UIG/IF; 70-71 (a) Hamilton Lund/DNSW, (b) James Horan/DNSW; 72-73 Hamilton Lund/DNSW; 74-75 (a & b) Kempsey Shire Council/DNSW; 76-77 Greg Snell/TA; 78-79 Greg Snell/TA; 80-81 (a) SATC, (b) David Wall/IF; 82-83 (a) TEQ, (b) Kate J Armstrong; 84-85 Misty Norman; 86-87 Misty Norman; 88-89 (a) Kate J Armstrong, (b) Aaron Spence/TEQ; 90-91 Peter Lik/TEQ; 92-93 Misty Norman; 94-95 (a) Greg Snell/TWA, (b) Nick Rains/TWA; 96-97 (a) Hamilton Lund/TA, (b) Misty Norman; 98-99 Misty Norman; 100-101 (a & b) Kate J Armstrong; 102-103 Walter Bibikow/IF; 104-105 Ulli Seer/IF; 106-107 One Shot/PNZ/Miz Watanabe/IF; 108-109 One Shot/PNZ/Geoff Mason/IF; 110-111 One Shot/PNZ/Jeff Drewitz/IF

ASIA
112-113 Nicolas Marino/IF; 114-115 Oleksiy Maksymenko/IF; 116-117 CWIS/IF; 118-119 Zoonar/Sergey Pristy/IF; 120-121 500px/IF; 122-123 (a) Zoonar/Andrey Armyag/IF, (b) Blaine Harrington/IF; 124-125 500px/IF; 126-127 Alexander Jikharev/500px/IF; 128-129 JTB Photo/UIG/IF; 130-131 JTB Photo/UIG/IF

THE UK & EUROPE

132-133 Kate J Armstrong; 134-135 (a & b) Kate J Armstrong; 136-137 Cultura/Image Source/IF; 138-139 500px/IF; 140-141 Travel Pix Collection/IF; 142-143 (a) 500px/IF, (b) Graham Lawrence/IF; 144-145 Micah Wright/IF; 146-147 Matteo Colombo/IF; 148-149 Zoonar/N.Sorokin/IF; 150-151 500px/IF; 152-153 ClickAlps/IF; 154-155 Ricardo Ribas/IF; 156-157 (a) Francesco Riccardo Lacomino/IF, (b) 500px/IF; 158-159 ClickAlps/IF; 160-161 Walter Bibikow/IF; 162-163 Shaun Egan/IF; 164-165 Universal Images Group/IF; 166-167 500px/IF; 168-169 Natalia Eriksson/500px/IF; 170-171 (a) K Wothe/IF, (a) McPHOTO/IF; 172-173 (a) 500px/IF, (b) Peter Amend/IF; 174-175 Vadim Balakin/500px/IF

AFRICA & THE MIDDLE EAST

176-177 Walter Bibikow/IF; 178-179 Blaine Harrington/IF; 180-181 Julian Love/IF; 182-183 Nigel Pavitt/IF; 184-185 (a) Adstock,UIG/IF, (b) 500px/IF; 186-187 500px/IF

ABBREVIATIONS

IF – imagefolk.com
DNSW – Destination New South Wales
SATC – South Australia Tourism Commission
TA – Tourism Australia
TEQ – Tourism and Events Queensland
TNT – Tourism Northern Australia
TWA – Tourism Western Australia

Acknowledgements

The publisher would like to acknowledge the following individuals and organisations:

Commissioning Editor
Melissa Kayser

Managing Editor
Marg Bowman

Project Editor
Kate J Armstrong

Research Assistant
Nadja Poljo

Cover and prelims design
Vaughan Mossop

Internal page design and layout
Megan Ellis

Pre-press
Megan Ellis, Splitting Image Colour Studio

Published in 2016 by Hardie Grant Books, an imprint of Hardie Grant Publishing

Hardie Grant Books (Melbourne)
Building 1, 658 Church Street
Richmond, Victoria 3121
hardiegrantbooks.com.au

Hardie Grant Books (London)
5th & 6th Floors
52–54 Southwark Street
London SE1 1UN
hardiegrantbooks.co.uk

A Cataloguing-in-Publication entry is available from the catalogue of the National Library of Australia at www.nla.gov.au

Photos from the Road
ISBN 9781741175271

10 9 8 7 6 5 4 3 2 1

Printed and bound in China by 1010 Printing International